COOK'S

TOURIST'S HANDBOOK

FOR

SWITZERLAND.

LONDON:
THOMAS COOK & SON, Ludgate Circus, E.C.;
SIMPKIN, MARSHALL, & Co.
NEW YORK: THOMAS COOK & SON, 261, BROADWAY.
GENEVA: THOMAS COOK & SON, 90, RUE DU RHÔNE.

1879.

COOK'S

TOURIST'S HANDBOOK

FOR

SWITZERLAND.

CONTENTS.

COOK'S

HANDBOOK FOR SWITZERLAND.

Introductory.

Luggage.—As conveyance of luggage forms an important item in the expenses of a continental tour, this "necessary evil" should be condensed as much as may be. If possible, the tourist should only take a small trunk or valise, that he can carry in his hand. To those who cannot do this, a strong *leather* portmanteau is recommended. It should be of simple construction, and possess a good lock, so that it can be opened in an instant for Customs Examination. In France, as a rule, each passenger is allowed 66lbs. of luggage free, in Holland and many parts of Germany 50lbs., but in some districts of Germany, and in Switzerland, Belgium, and Italy, all luggage must be paid for (except that which the passenger carries in his hand), unless stated otherwise upon the ticket.

Custom House Examinations are generally made at the station nearest the frontier. Thus, between Belgium and Germany luggage is examined at Verviers; but if registered through to Cologne by first-class express train, it is examined at Cologne. Passengers must always be present at the Custom House Examinations, and hand their keys to the examining officer. The Customs Examination is one of the greatest drawbacks to the pleasures of foreign travel, but passengers will do well to remember that civility costs nothing, and may purchase much, and that the custom house officers are merely performing a *duty*, perhaps as disagreeable to themselves as to the traveller. The following is a list of stations at which baggage is generally examined:—

Ala
Avricourt
Arlon
Belfort
Basle
Bellegarde
Bodenbach
Brussels
Camerlata
Como
Cormons
Courtray

Domo d'Ossola	Lille	Salzbergen
Dinan	Lindau	Schaffhausen
Eger	Lugano	Splügen
Elten	Luxemburg	Tilburg
Emmerich	Modane	Tournay
Eydtkuhnen	Mouscron	Thionville
Furth	Oderberg	Udine
Friedrichshafen	Pagny-sur-Moselle	Valenciennes
Goritz	Paris	Verviers
Hazebrouck	Passau	Venlo
Hendaye	Pontarlier	Ventimille
Irun	Roosendaal	Zevenaar
Kufstein	Salzburg	

And the various Sea and Channel Ports.

Passports are not at present really required by British travellers on the Continent (except for visiting Russia, Turkey, Spain, and Portugal), but at the same time a passport is frequently useful, in order to obtain admission to certain Museums, to obtain letters from the *Poste Restante*, and to establish identity whenever required. The cost of a passport is very trifling, and may be obtained, if desired, through Thos. Cook and Son.

Language.—So many thousands flock annually over most of the routes described in this book, that nothing save the mother-tongue is absolutely essential. English is spoken in all the principal hotels, and interpreters may be met with at the principal railway-stations. Of course, a knowledge of French and German will prove of great advantage, and those who explore remote regions will find it indispensable, but no one need hesitate to visit Switzerland on the score of not knowing anything save English. An hour or two spent in learning French and German numerals, and a few phrases, will enable these to combat cab-drivers and others who might be disposed to take them in. "The Tourist's Shilling Conversational Guide," in English, French, German, and Italian, by Dr. J. F. Loth, will be found useful (Cook and Son, Ludgate Circus, or their agents).

Money, if taken in large quantities, should be in circular notes, which may be obtained from many of the London bankers.

Cook's Circular Notes. Messrs. Cook and Son issue Circular Notes of the value of £5 or £10 sterling, which are accepted at all their continental agencies, and by the principal hotel keepers. The chief advantages are safety, as they cannot be cashed without the holder's endorsement, and convenience of exchange, at any hour, in small sums of the currency of each country at the full rates of exchange. Foreign money can also be obtained of Thos. Cook and Son.

English sovereigns are received almost everywhere, and in Switzerland may generally be exchanged without loss. Foreign currency is always puzzling, and it will be well for every tourist to familiarize himself with the following tables :—

France, Belgium, Switzerland, and Italy.

1 franc	(in Italy *Lira*)	= about	9⅗d.
5 franc piece	(„ 5 lire)	= „	4s.
20 franc piece	(„ 20 lire)	= „	16s.
10 centimes	(„ 10 centesime)	= „	1d.

100 centimes = 1 franc; 100 centesime = 1 lira.

Italian paper currency is much depreciated in value

North Germany

12 pfenninge		= 1 silbergroschen.
		2½ silbergroschen = 3d.
		10 silbergroschen = 1s.
1 mark	= 100 pf.	= 1s.
30 silbergroschen	= 1 thaler	= 3s.
6 thalers 20 silbergroschen		= 1 English sovereign.
20 mark piece (gold)		= 1 English sovereign.

South Germany and Austria.

£1	= 11¾ South German florins	=	10 Austrian florins.
16s.	= 9 fl. 20 kreut. S. Germany	=	8 „ „
1 Austrian florin	= 100 kreutzers	=	2s.
10 kreut. pieces	= $\frac{1}{10}$ florin.		
6 kt. ps. S. Ger.	= 9 kt Austria	=	about 2¼d.
1¾ fl. S. Germany	= 1½ fl. Austria	=	3s.
1 fl. „	= 85 kreut.	=	1s 8d.
30 kr. „	= 50 „	=	10d.
1 „ „	= 1½ „	=	⅛d.
3 „ „	= 4 „	=	1d.

The Austrian paper currency is much depreciated, the discount constantly varying.

Holland.

5 cents		=	about 1d.
100 „	= 1 florin or guilder	=	„ 1s. 7d.
	1 gold ducat	=	„ 9s. 4d.
	1 gold 10 florin piece	=	„ 16s. 6d.

Time-Tables.—The official time-tables of the railway companies should be consulted upon every available opportunity, as alterations are constantly taking place; and though such alterations are carefully watched, it is impossible for any general time-table to guarantee complete accuracy. "Cook's Continental Time-Tables and Tourist's Handbook" is published at 1s.; post-free, 1s. 2d.

Postage.—By the recent postal arrangements, letters can be sent to France, Switzerland, Italy, etc., at 2½d. under the half-ounce.

Fees are given by English and Americans with far too lavish a hand, and much annoyance is caused to other travellers, and injury done to the people in the countries visited, by this habit. Porters carrying luggage will generally make extortionate demands. Ask the hotel proprietor to pay what is a fair sum. At churches and galleries half a franc is quite enough for a couple of persons, as a rule, although this may sometimes be increased to a franc. A *sou*, or any small coin, is sufficient for the legions of beggars besetting one's way; and probably one franc put into the box of a local society for relief of the poor would be better spent than two francs distributed amongst them in *sous*. Make a rule of never going out without a supply of small coins, however, but never use them lavishly. Let the traveller make a favour of giving a *sou*, and he will be respected. Never give a *sou* to one beggar in the presence of another.

Hotels abound, and, as a rule, are good. Unfortunately, a system prevails abroad of charging fancy prices, and hotel keepers are not different from their brethren in other branches of business. An agreement should always be made, and even then it is well to have the bill every other day or so, in order to see how things are going. Messrs. Cook and Son supply

Hotel Coupons; and as they are available at Hotels which can be well recommended, every one should provide himself with them. In these pages reference is only made to hotels where these Coupons are accepted. (Full particulars as to Hotels and Hotel Arrangements by Coupons will be found in the Appendix.)

The advantages of taking Hotel Coupons may be briefly summed up as follows:—

I. Time, expense, annoyance in bartering, and ultimate dissatisfaction, are saved by going to a well-recommended Hotel.

II. It is a great drawback to pleasure to arrive in a foreign town beset by porters, commissionaires, and rabble, a perfect stranger, and without any definite idea where to go.

III. Letters from home, or telegrams, may be found upon arrival at the Hotel, thus saving trouble or expense in sending for them to the Post Office.

IV. The charges are all fixed, thus obviating the chance of imposition, and the disagreeable task of having to drive a bargain at each stopping-place.

V. The charges being fixed at the lowest sum to insure good accommodation at one uniform rate, the tourist is enabled to count the cost of his tour before starting.

VI. Travellers with coupons, bespeaking accommodation by letter or telegram, are always provided for, even in the busiest seasons, if they inform the hotel keeper that they have coupons.

Routes should be carefully selected, and plans well digested, before starting; and in order to assist in this matter, a list will be found in the Appendix which will supply all necessary information. It will be sufficient to mention here the principal routes.

VIA PARIS.

London to Paris, via Newhaven, Dieppe, and Rouen
" " via Folkestone, Boulogne, and Amiens
" " via Dover and Calais

There are five principal routes from Paris to Switzerland, namely—
Paris to Strasbourg and Basle, by Epernay, Chalons, and Nancy
" to Basle, by Troyes, Chaumont, and Belfort
" to Neuchatel, or to Lausanne, by Tonnere, Dijon, and Pontarlier
" to Geneva, by Dijon and Macon

VIA HOLLAND, BELGIUM, AND THE RHINE.

London to Harwich,		Boat to Rotterdam
"	Harwich,	" Antwerp
"	Queenboro'	" Flushing (Vlessingen)
"	Dover,	" Ostend

Or by Boat direct from London to Rotterdam
" " Antwerp
" " Ostend

The routes from either Rotterdam, Antwerp, Flushing, or Ostend are various. Those who wish to get quickly into Switzerland should go by the Luxembourg route direct to Basle or Zurich.

For the Rhine journey the steamboat should be taken at Cologne or Bonn, and quitted at Bingen or Mayence.

Travellers who wish to combine a visit to the Black Forest with the Rhine trip should proceed to Heidelberg, thence to Baden, and by the new Baden States Railway to Singen and Schaffhausen; or continue by rail from Baden to Freiburg, and then on foot or by carriage through some of the most charming scenery of the Forest to Waldshut and Basle.

For detailed information as to all these routes see "Cook's Tourist's Handbook to Holland, Belgium, and the Rhine," and "Cook's Tourist's Handbook to the Black Forest."

Time for Visiting Switzerland.—From the beginning of May to the end of October. Mountain climbers will find the end of July and the month of August most suitable for their excursions.

Guides.—Certificated Guides may be found at all the principal centres for excursions on application to the Hotel Proprietors. The fee should not exceed eight francs for a day, but it is necessary to make a bargain. Guides are altogether unnecessary for such well-beaten tracks as the Rigi, Scheideck, *Grimsel*, etc.; but for glacier routes, or difficult passes, &

are invaluable. Twenty pounds' weight of baggage may be given to the guide to carry; but this is the limit, and it is best to give him as little as possible.

Scope of Work.—It is not intended in this work to give precise information as to excursions among the High Alps, nor to mark out minutely the thousand excursions that may be made to obscure and comparatively unknown places. For such there are special works provided. In the present volume such information only is given as it is thought will be found useful to the ordinary Tourist.

Cook's Travelling Coupons are now so well known and universally used, that they need but little description. Suffice it to say, that if there are advantages in knowing of cheap, comfortable, and well recommended Hotels wherein to rest, there are a hundredfold more in having all the difficulties of travel made smooth. The most inexperienced may avail themselves of them without fear of not being able to get on, and the most experienced take them as the simplest, easiest, and cheapest means of travelling.

Churches should be visited in the morning, as they are then open free, and can be viewed with greater pleasure on account of the light. Moreover, it is a great saving in expense, as later in the day a fee is demanded or expected by the sacristan who opens them for visitors. It will not be taken unkindly by the tourist to be reminded that the many attractions in Continental churches sometimes cause him to forget that they are places of *worship*; and if for his own convenience and pleasure he visits them at times when they are frequented by worshippers, he should be careful to abandon the use of opera-glasses, guide-books, and other accessories, if they are likely to prove a hindrance to the devotions of others. Unfortunately, this has been disregarded so much—and notably by English and Americans—that it has been found necessary in some churches to write over the entrance, "Honour is due to God's house." A word to the wise is enough.

English Churches are not mentioned specially in this work, as in every Hotel frequented by the English, notices are abundant in which the time and place of service are recorded. Changes are often made, too, both as regards the place and the time, according to the season of the year, but no difficulty will be found in obtaining accurate information.

Switzerland.

Area, Population.—Switzerland, or Schweiz (Germ), Suisse (Fr.), Svirrera (Ital.), Helvetia (Latin), includes an area of nearly 16,000 square miles, being about 206 miles in length, by 139 at its greatest breadth. Its boundaries are, in most places, grandly defined by river, lake, or mountain. The population in 1877 was 2,776,035.

Surface.—The surface of Switzerland is very varied, rising from 678 feet on the shore of Lago Maggiore, or 800 feet on the banks of the Rhine at Basle, to 15,226 feet at the summit of Monte Rosa. More than half the extent of Switzerland is occupied by the Alps; between these and the Juras to the west is a plain, with a hilly country to the northward.

The Alps are ranged about a central spot west of the St. Gothard Pass, where about a hundred square miles of rocks, etc., lie above the limits of perpetual snow, and the Galenstock, Gletscherhorn, Dichterhorn, and other important peaks, rise to the height of ten or twelve thousand feet. The waters from this elevated region pass by the Rhine to the German Ocean, by the Rhone to the Mediterranean, by the Po to the Adriatic, and by the Danube to the Black Sea.

From this mountain knot a chain extends northward towards the Lake of Lucerne, including the Titlis (11,406 feet), and the Urner Rothstock (10,063 feet). Southward runs a chain of mountains averaging from 6000 to 7000 feet. Westward run the Bernese and Lepontine Alps, whilst the two branches of the Rhætian Alps diverge to the east.

The basin of the Upper Rhone (Canton Valais), and the Valley of the Rhone, 92 miles in length, are important features of the map of Switzerland. As far as Brieg, the Rhone Valley is about half a mile wide. Near Visp it widens, and several very interesting lateral valleys join it. The river finally debouches into Lake Leman, through about eight miles of swampy ground very little higher than the level of the lake.

The Bernese Alps north of the Rhone Valley form one of the grandest features of Switzerland. Six hundred square miles of ice and snow and savage mountain scenery lie between the valley of Hasli and the valley of Kander. The district is intersected by two or three fine valleys, and abounds in numerous lofty peaks, splendid glaciers, mountain passes, torrents, etc., etc., of which attractions the more striking will be found duly noted in subsequent pages of this volume.

The Pennine Alps lie west of the Simplon Pass, stretching southward to Monte Rosa (15,226 feet), and then westward to Mont Blanc. They include Mont Cervin (14,764 feet), and several other peaks of somewhat less altitude. Towards the east and south the ascent is steep, and cultivation creeps up the base of lofty mountains; but towards the north for many miles the elevation is above the line of perpetual snow.

The Lakes of Switzerland are another prominent natural feature. The Lake of Geneva, with its diversified scenery and varied associations, literary, legendary, and historic; the Lake of Lucerne, surrounded by the sacred ground of Swiss history—at one point charming with its tranquil beauty, at another awe-inspiring with its rugged grandeur; the Lakes of Zürich, Thun, and Brienz, so thoroughly characteristic of Switzerland; and the frontier and Italian Lakes of Lugano, Como, etc., which may easily be included in the tour, are amongst the principal.

Geology.—In all the loftiest Alpine chains granite is found mostly in conjunction with gneiss and mica slate. In many parts, especially on the Great and Little St. Bernard, and south of the St. Gothard, granular limestone is abundant; and the celebrated mountain limestone appears on the Diablerets, Dent du Midi, etc.; and Jura limestone has become a term descriptive of a special variety. Particles of gold are found in the sands of several of the Swiss rivers, but not in sufficient quantity to repay the search. In the Grisons are some abandoned lead and copper mines. Iron is widely diffused through the whole country. Rock-salt is found in Vaud; alabaster, marble, sulphur, and gypsum are also named amongst Swiss productions; and the asphalte (from the Val de Travers, etc.) has become of late a prominent object in the streets of London and other great cities. There are many mineral springs, as at Leuk, St. Moritz, etc. Coal of an inferior quality is found in the Cantons of Fribourg, Vaud, Basle, and Thurgau.

Vegetation, Agriculture, etc.—Few countries present a more varied aspect in this respect than Switzerland. Seven distinct regions mark the differing circumstances under which cultivation is carried on—

I. Up to 1700 or 1800 feet the vine flourishes.

II. The hilly or Lower Mountain Region, up to about 2800 feet, contains abundance of walnut-trees and good meadows.

III. The mountain district, up to 4100 feet, is chiefly distinguished by its forest timber. The pastures and fields of barley and oats are good.

IV. The sub-Alpine region, up to 5500 feet, is characterized by pine forests and good grass land; a few kitchen vegetables are grown.

V. The lower Alpine region extends to 6500 feet, and is the region of the celebrated Alpine pastures.

VI. The Alpine region, where, in proximity to glaciers, etc., only a stunted vegetation is found. Summer lasts about five or six weeks.

VII. The region of perpetual snow, above 8000 feet.

Animal Life.—The horned cattle of Switzerland are nearly a million in number, a large proportion of which are milch cows. The chief game are the chamois, hare, marmot, and partridge. Fish, especially trout, abound in the lakes and rivers; the salmon is found in the Aar, the Rhine, and Lake Zürich

Manufactures, etc.—There are manufactures of silks, ribbons, and cotton goods in various parts of Switzerland, the principal being at Zürich and Winterthur. Basle exports silk ribbons to a large extent, also leather, paper, and tobacco. Geneva is famous for its watches and musical boxes. Watches are also largely manufactured in Locle and La Chaux-de-Fonds.

Language.—German dialects are spoken in about three-fourths of Switzerland. In Geneva, Vaud, Neuchâtel, and parts of Berne, Fribourg, and Valais, French is the language (written and spoken) of the educated classes. In Ticino, and some of the southern valleys, Italian is spoken. The dialects known as Romansch and Ladin prevail through about half the Grisons.

Religion.—Calvinistic Protestantism predominates, but there is no State Church, and all religions are tolerated. Since 1847 the Religious Houses have been suppressed.

Special Objects of Interest.—Besides the delightful character of the ever-varying Swiss scenery, the country has many attractions of a special character.

The MOUNTAINS are an unfailing source of enjoyment. General views of mountain scenery can be obtained from two or three points in the city of Berne, from the Dôle near Geneva, the Faulhorn near Grindelwald, Weissenstein, near Soleure, the Rigi near Lucerne, etc., etc. Nearer views of mountain scenery are obtained from various points in the Mont Blanc and Monte Rosa districts, also in the Bernese Oberland, etc. The grand views from the Belle Alp by Brieg; the Brévent by Chamouny; the Eggischorn by Viesch; the Piz Languard by Pontresina; and the Sidelhorn near the Grimsel, and many others, are within the reach of moderate climbers without serious difficulty.

WATERFALLS are very numerous. The Fall of the Rhine at Schaffhausen that of the Aare at Handeck (full, lofty, and grandly situated), the misty Staubbach, Schmadribach, Reichenbach, Giessbach, and many others, will be duly noted at their proper places.

The MOUNTAIN PASSES are of three kinds—1. Carriage Passes, such as the Simplon, St. Gothard, Splügen, etc.; 2. Mule Passes, as the Col de Balme, Grimsel, Scheideck, Gemmi, etc.; 3. Glacier Passes, as the Strahleck, Tschingel, S. Theodule, etc. Surpassingly grand are the ravines by which some of these passes are approached; as, for instance, the Via Mala and the Gasterenthal. The sloping meadows seen at lofty elevations in crossing these lofty elevations are called "ALPS," whence the appropriation of the name to the mountains themselves. Here and there are the rude structures for dairy purposes known as CHALETS, where refreshments can generally be obtained.

The GLACIERS are perhaps the most wonderful of Alpine marvels. Around the loftiest peaks the snow, falling and accumulating in the adjacent ravines, becomes crystallized by ever-increasing pressure into solid ice, and is forced downward by constant accumulation towards the valleys. At Grindelwald, Chamouny

Zermatt, etc., these Glaciers can be inspected at the extremities of the off-shoots thus thrust downwards towards the cultivated districts. But to realize their true wildness and grandeur, the traveller must venture to explore the SEAS OF ICE (*Eismeer, Mers de Glace*) from whence they spring. Of these Ice Seas the most remarkable are those surrounding Mont Blanc, Monte Rosa, and the Finsteraarhorn. The latter is probably the largest ice-field in Europe, covering over 120 square miles, and sending out more than a dozen branches towards the valleys below. By the constant pressure, alternate melting and freezing, and other causes these Glaciers are kept in constant motion, disappearing to feed the rivers at their bases, whilst afresh supplied from the regions of eternal snow at their summits. Down the middle or along the sides of the Glaciers are the huge accumulations of rubbish thrown up by the glacial motion, and known as MORAINES. The deep fissures common in most Glaciers are called CREVASSES. The AVALANCHES, as probably most readers will already be aware, are huge masses of snow and ice, disengaged by the heat of the sun, and rolling down the mountain-side.

The VALLEYS of Switzerland are exceedingly beautiful. The Haslithal, Simmenthal, Vale of Sarnen, and many others, will be found to afford much enjoyment, especially to those who prefer tranquil and yet romantic loveliness, without the fatigue and difficulty of ascending great heights.

Goitre and Cretinism are physical complaints still prevalent in some parts of Switzerland. The former is a remarkable glandular swelling in the neck, the latter a species of idiocy. These complaints are limited to certain low-lying districts, and appear to be owing to deficient sanitary arrangements or local exhalations.

The Swiss People, says Laing, "are the Dutch of the mountains; the same cold, unimaginative, money-seeking, yet vigorous, determined, energetic people." In the parts most frequented by tourists the Swiss are certainly notorious for their efforts to extort money from the travellers; but probably other tourist-haunted spots nearer home might furnish instances of similar rapacity. The Swiss are great lovers of freedom, and at the same time display an unbounded reverence for antiquity; and amongst the upper classes they are exceedingly reserved and exclusive in their social arrangements.

The Government of Switzerland consists of a Federal Assembly, comprising a National Council and a Council of States—the former containing one delegate for every 20,000 inhabitants, the latter having two members for each canton. This Assembly elects a supreme Federal Council of seven. Every adult male in Switzerland has the franchise at the age of twenty, and is bound for military service.

The country consists of 22 political divisions, called Cantons, of which the Grisons, containing 2900 square miles, is the largest, and Zug, containing 85 square miles, the smallest. The Swiss population for the whole country is 165 to the square mile, or 244 to the square mile if Alpine Switzerland be excepted. Geneva is the most densely populated canton, having 847 to the square mile; whilst in the Grisons, the least populous, there are only 33 to the square mile.

WRESTLING MATCHES (*Schwingfeste*) between the men of various Cantons, and the TIR FEDERAL, or general rifle-shooting contest, held once in two years, and similar to our annual Volunteer gathering at Wimbledon, are interesting occasions. The dates of some of the more important will be found in the Travellers' Calendar at the end of this volume.

History.—Not in the pages of the historian, but beneath the surface of her lakes, are found the earliest records of human existence in the country now called Switzerland. As we shall have occasion to show hereafter, the earliest inhabitants seem to have been a mysterious race, who dwelt in houses reared on piles above the waters of the lakes, and who used stone where we should now use metal.

But leaving this primeval race, history shows us the Rhæti, of supposed Etruscan origin, retreating before the advances of the Celtic Helvetii, into the mountainous regions of Eastern Switzerland. Then, in the first century of our era, Rome comes upon the scene, brings Helvetii and Rhæti alike into subjection, founds colonies, constructs roads, and spreads Latin civilization. Save only during the brief rebellion of A.D. 69, promptly suppressed by Cecina, the country remained subject to the Roman power till the downfall of the latter.

And now, as in other outskirts of the Roman Empire, the native population, led to rely on Roman protection, and enervated by Roman luxury, became speedily subjected to the fierce, barbaric tribes that were swarming from the overcrowded regions to which Roman prowess had hitherto confined them. The Burgundians occupied Western Switzerland, and made Geneva their capital, the fierce Alemanni settled on the banks of the Rhine, and Theodoric with his Goths seized mountainous Rhætia.

The Franks next appear under Clovis, driving out the Alemanni in A.D. 496, defeating the Burgundians in A.D. 534, becoming masters of all Helvetia, and, as the Italo-Gothic kingdom declined, conquering Rhætia also. These conquests culminated in the great Empire of Charlemagne, who introduced the feudal system. Meanwhile, Christianity had been disseminated amongst the Burgundians in the fifth century, and amongst the Alemmni by Columbus and his disciples in the seventh century. These monks preached the gospel, destroyed the idols, built the chapels at St. Gall, Dissentis, Zürich, and elsewhere, introduced the cultivation of the vine and corn, and in other ways aided in the culture and enlightenment of the people.

At the dissolution of the Frank Empire, Eastern Switzerland became united to Suabia, and Western Switzerland to the kingdom of Burgundy. Early in the eleventh century the Burgundian power declined, and Rudolph III., in 1016, made over his kingdom to the Emperor Henry II. of Germany: for the German Emperors the Dukes of Zaringia acted as vicegerents; and these latter found it their policy to protect the towns, in order to curb the old Burgundian nobles, who continued troublesome. From this period, Berne, Fribourg, and other important places date their origin.

But the feudal lords of the soil, in course of time, grew more powerful, and less mindful of the imperial rule; and to preserve their liberties, the Swiss free towns were compelled to treat with the nobles. One of the most important of these was Count Rudolph of Hapsburg, with whom Zürich and the three Cantons of Uri, Schwyz, and Unterwalden entered into alliance. He assisted the towns in maintaining their independence, and, after becoming Emperor, continued the same policy.

His son Albert pursued a different line of conduct—attempted to make Switzerland an integral part of the Hapsburg possessions, and sent Austrian bailiffs to oppress the country. The Swiss rose in revolt. The three forest Cantons, led on by Arnold, and Furst, and Stauffacher, confederated to protect their liberties in 1307 (see p. 67). To this period belong the Tell legends.

For more than two hundred years Switzerland maintained a struggle for independence, defeating the Austrians at the memorable fields of Morgarten in 1307, Sempach in 1386, Näfels in 1388, and at the Stoss in 1405. Equally important were the victories over the feudal nobles at Laupen in 1339, and over Charles the Bold and the Burgundian forces at Grandson and Morat in 1476.

In 1499, having refused to aid Maximilian in his war with France, that Emperor struck the final blow at Swiss independence in what is known as the Suabian war. But 6000 Confederates defeated 15,000 Austrians at Dornach, and henceforth the country was only nominally subject to the Emperors, and even this connection was formally relinquished in 1648.

During these long external struggles Switzerland had increased and internally developed. Lucerne joined the confederacy in 1332, Zürich and Glarus in 1351, Zug and Berne in 1352, in which year a Federal Diet was established. In 1422, Valais allied herself as an independent State. Soleure and Fribourg came in in 1481, and Basle and Schaffhausen in 1501. In 1513 Appenzell was received, thus completing the thirteen Cantons which constituted Switzerland till the French Revolution in 1798.

The Reformation of Religion was commenced in Switzerland by the proclamation of the new doctrine at Zürich in 1523; and under the teachings of Zwingli, and subsequently of Calvin and Favel, a large proportion of the population of the country embraced Protestantism, and in 1532 the Helvetic Confession of Faith was put forth. Unfortunately, for a long period, Catholics and Protestants would not agree amicably to differ, and no less than three sanguinary religious wars ensued, viz., in 1531, in 1653, and in 1712, the last being ended by the Peace of Aarau.

It seems that, after the cessation of the wars for independence, the Swiss had become satiated by their conquests. Swiss valour became individual rather than national, and her soldiers were notorious as the mercenary champions of any cause that could afford to pay for their services. Swiss Guards were the last prop of the expiring Bourbon monarchy at the close of the eighteenth century; and by a stroke of bitter irony, the country of those brave hirelings became very shortly the prey of the very people whose rising aspirations for freedom they had been paid to suppress. Vainly at Rothenthurm and Stans did Aloys Reding, and other patriots of the ancient stamp essay to stem the progress of the French Republicans. The country was conquered, and, in reality, annexed, though a so-called Helvetian Republic was established.

In 1802, Buonaparte restored the Cantonal system, under the protection of France. In 1815 the Allied Sovereigns acknowledged the independence of Switzerland. The Cantons, now twenty-two in number, were united under a constitution providing that a Federal Diet should be held alternately at Berne, Zürich, and Lucerne. In 1830, several Cantons introduced important changes in a democratic direction. These changes, especially the suppression of monasteries and ejection of the Jesuits, were opposed by other Cantons, who, in 1841, joined in the league known as the Sonderbund. This organized opposition had to be put down by force in 1847. In the following year a new Constitution, of a more Liberal and Protestant character, was adopted, and Berne was made the permanent seat of Government. Since that time the history of Switzerland has been a record of peaceful and rapid progress, large development of the national resources, and facilities of intercommunication.

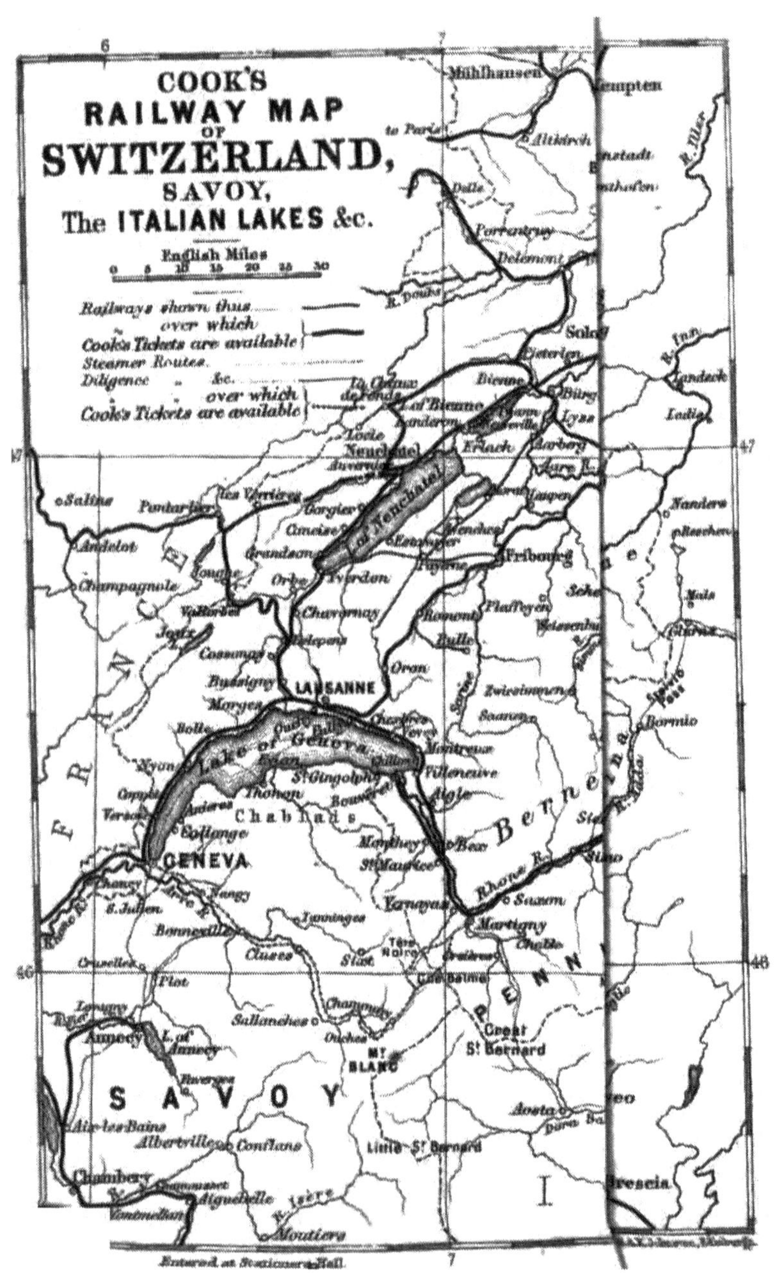
COOK'S
RAILWAY MAP
OF
SWITZERLAND,
SAVOY,
The ITALIAN LAKES &c.
English Miles
0 5 10 15 20 25 30
Railways shown thus
over which
Cook's Tickets are available
Steamer Routes
Diligence &c.
over which
Cook's Tickets are available
Mühlhausen
to Paris
Altkirch
Delle
Porrentruy
Delemont
R. Doubs
Bienne
L. of Bienne
Neuchâtel
Erlach
Aarberg
Lyss
Les Verrières
Pontarlier
Salins
Andelot
Champagnole
Grandson
Orbe
Yverdon
Payerne
Fribourg
Romont
Bulle
Cossonay
Bussigny
LAUSANNE
Morges
Rolle
Nyon
Lake of Geneva
Ouchy
Vevey
Montreux
Villeneuve
St. Gingolph
Thonon
Chablais
Aigle
Bex
St. Maurice
Martigny
GENEVA
St. Julien
Bonneville
Cluses
Sallanches
Chamouny
MT. BLANC
Great St. Bernard
Little St. Bernard
Aosta
Annecy
L. of Annecy
SAVOY
Aix-les-Bains
Albertville
Conflans
Chambery
Moutiers
Rhone R.
Sion
Bormio
Landeck
FRANCE
PENN
Entered at Stationers Hall

BÂLE, BASLE, OR BASEL.

(Hotel Trois Rois.)

(A very fine hotel, beautifully situated, with good view of the Rhine and opposite bank.)

Railway Stations.—There are **two** Railway Stations at Basle, and they are about 40 minutes' walk from each other. Omnibus, 1 franc. Carriage, 1½ franc; 2 francs, if more than two persons.

The **Central Station** is on the S. side of the town, a mile from the Bridge and Hotel Trois Rois. Omnibus to town, ½ franc. Local Railway from one station to the other every 20 minutes.

Trains for the Swiss and Alsace lines start from this station.

The **Baden Station** is in Klein-Basel, nearly a mile from the Bridge and the Hotel Trois Rois. Trains for Baden, Black Forest, etc., start from this station.

Basle (population 45,000) is of Roman origin; its name is derived from Basileia, or Basilis, a "queen"—probably on account of its wealth and importance, and splendid situation on the Rhine. The town is divided by the river into two parts—Great Basle on the left bank, and Little Basle on the right.

The geographical position of Basle is very interesting; until the Franco-German war it was at the junction of Switzerland, France, and Germany. There was a spot near Kleinhuningen where it was said a man might plant his foot on all three countries at once.

The inhabitants of Basle have always had the character of being thrifty traders, and the charge of usury has been laid at their door; they also earned the notoriety, in ancient times, which attaches to the quarrelsome; and as late as the year 1833 the city Basle and the country Basle were engaged in a civil war on so small a scale as would have rendered it ridiculous, but for the bloodshed and death in which it resulted. Since that time the belligerent canton has been divided into two parts, by order of the Swiss Diet. Each half canton has an independent vote, but only one senator is returned to the Ständerath.

Basle has been the scene of several important treaties of

peace; between the Prussians, Spanish, and French, in 1795, and in the same year between Spain and France, when the latter gave up the provinces south of the Pyrenees in exchange for a portion of the Island of St. Domingo, since lost to them. One or two important Councils have been held at Basle, notably that in 1431, convened by Pope Martin V., to suppress the heresies of the Hussites.

Among the celebrated men for whom Basle is famous may be mentioned: *John* and *Charles Bernouilli*, the mathematicians; *Buxtorf*, an eminent professor of Oriental languages; *Œcolampadius* and *Grynæus*. *Holbein* commenced his career in Basle; *Erasmus* resided here in the house *Zur Lust*, near the Münster; and *Euler*, the celebrated mathematician, was born in Basle.

The best starting-point for a tour of the town is the **Three Kings Hotel**, a place of historic interest, if the following statement may be accepted:—

"Basle was founded by the Romans at an early period (perhaps already in the second century). The Alemanni, however, destroyed it about the beginning of the fifth century; but when that savage nation was itself subjugated by Clovis, Basle passed likewise under the sceptre of that prince, and remained under the dominion of the Frank monarchs till 912, when Rodolphus II., sovereign of the newly-established kingdom of Little Burgundy, offered Basle his protection against the ferocious Normans and Hungarians, who infested the German empire at that time. Notwithstanding this promised support, the town was entirely devastated and burnt down by the Hungarians.

"In the year 1004 the rebuilt city was restored to the German empire by Rodolphus III., who bequeathed his kingdom of Little Burgundy to the Emperor Henry II., and gave the town of Basle as a pledge of his promise. In 1024, Henry's successor, Conrad II., and the son of this monarch, Henry III. (already elected as German Emperor) had an interview with Rodolphus III., King of Burgundy, in a field near Muttenz, in the neighbourhood of Basle; after which deliberation the three sovereigns entered the town together, and are said to have alighted and signed their agreement at the old inn, which stood on the spot where this house now stands, and which, from this circumstance, took the name of '*Hotel of the Three Kings.*'"

Maximilian Misson, who visited Basle in 1690, says, in his "Instructions to Travellers,"—"At Basle, lodge at the 'Three Kings,' where you will be well entertained."

Close by the Hotel is the **Wooden Bridge** (280 yards), which connects Gross-Basel with Klein-Basel. This is a very favourite resort is summer evenings; the views up and down the river are good. The tourist will watch with interest the rafts coming down the river, and note the dexterity with which they are shot under the bridge. No boat can force its way against the mighty current here save one, and that is ingeniously contrived to propel itself by the current. It is a curious but simple contrivance, and is worth the price of the fare just to cross and recross.

The **Münster**, one of the finest Protestant churches in the world, is but a short distance from the bridge; its two tall towers (220 feet high) are conspicuous. It was built by the Emperor Henry II. (1010—1019), and has several times since been rebuilt or restored. The west front presents a very striking appearance. On either side are statues of St. George (left) and St. Martin (right). By the doorway, representations of the Emperor Henry, who founded the church, and Helena, his wife. Above, the Virgin and Child.

The northern entrance is graced with a curious representation of the parable of the wise and foolish virgins.

The **interior**, thoroughly restored and re-decorated in 1855, contains some objects of interest. *Open free, Tuesdays and Thursdays, 2 till 4. Other times a small fee.* The **organ** (performance once or twice a week in the summer, between 6 and 7, one franc), was built in 1858, and is a very fine instrument. It is supported by the old rood loft of 1381. Stone **pulpit**, date 1324. **Font**, 1465. **Monument to Erasmus**, the learned editor of the New Testament, and one of the harbingers of the Reformation. **Choir**. Tomb of Empress Anne, wife of Rudolph of Hapsburg. Stained-glass windows by Swiss artists. A stairway leads from the choir to the **Concilium Saal** (Council Hall). It was the scene of the councils held between 1431 and 1445, and remains now exactly as it was then. It contains, among other curiosities, the fragments of the Dance of Death, commemorating the plague. The frescoes were not painted by *Holbein*, as was formerly supposed. Beneath the Council Hall, in the chapel of S. Nicholas, is the **Lällenkönig**, a curious head which formerly stood on the bridge, and every time the clock struck it protruded its tongue, in derision of the inhabitants of Klein-Basel, with whom the people of Gross-Basel were on unfriendly terms. The **cloisters** are extensive, and were used as a burial-

2

place for many centuries. Close by is the **Pfalz**, a pleasant promenade, planted with chestnut trees; it is between 70 and 80 ft. above the Rhine, and commands fine views of the hills of the Black Forest.

Between the bridge and the Münster is the **Museum.** (Open free, Sundays 10—12, Wednesdays 2—4. Other times 1 franc.) Its chief attraction is a collection of paintings and drawings by the younger *Holbein*. There are other works of value and interest. Notice especially in the **Holbein Room**—

13. Portrait of Boniface Amberbach, a friend of the painter, who formed this collection of his works.
14. Erasmus.
20. Holbein's wife and children.
21. Lais Corinthiaca. (Madame von Offenburg).
23. Venus with Cupid. "
26. The Passion of Christ. (Eight compartments.)
34. Froben, the printer.

In the collection of modern Swiss artists, notice—

146. A Mountain Festival . . . . . *Stückelberg.*
150. Watering the Cattle . . . . . *F. Koller.*

In the Birmann collection—

266. Nativity . . . . *Annibale Caracci.*
291. Smoker . . . . *Teniers.*

Modern German school—

351. Macbeth and the Witches . . . . . *J. Koch.*
361. The death of Joseph . . . . . *Overbeck.*

The collection of **drawings** is very good.

In addition to the picture gallery, there is a good collection of **antiquities**, found, for the most part, at Augst, the site of an old Roman colony—*Augusta Rauracorum*, six miles from Basle—and other curiosities.

In the same building is the **Public Library**, with nearly 100,000 volumes, and a collection of MSS., including writings of the Reformers. The **University**, close by, was founded in 1460. Bernouilli and Euler were professors here.

In the market-place is the **Rathhaus** (Town Hall). Built 1508, restored 1826. The arms of the canton Basle adorn the façade, and in front of the inner court is a statue of Munatius Plancus, the supposed founder of Basle and Augst.

Near here, in the Freien-Strasse, is the **Post Office**, a very old building restored, and in the immediate vicinity are several buildings dating from about the sixteenth century.

The **Arsenal** (Zeughaus), contains a collection of armour,

Burgundian cannon, etc. The principal curiosity is a suit of chain armour worn by Charles the Bold at the Battle of Nancy.

A short distance from the Arsenal is a very beautiful **Fountain**, the Spahlenbrunnen, representing a bag-piper, designed, probably, by Albert Dürer. The **Spahlenthor**, or Gate of St. Paul, built in the fourteenth century, is very fine.

The churches of Basle are—

The **Barfüsser Church**, fourteenth century. (Not used now as a place of worship.)

The **Church of S. Elizabeth**, the most magnificent modern building in Basle. It is in the Gothic style, and is the gift of one Christopher Mirian, a merchant of Basle, who left an enormous sum (nearly a quarter of a million) for its erection Good stained-glass windows.

Church of St. Martin, where Œcolampadius preached the doctrines of the Reformation. The English Church Service is performed here.

Basle has long been celebrated for its philanthropists, and there are at the present time, in admirable working order, a number of good institutions for the social, moral, and religious welfare of the people. Among them are the Protestant Missionary and Bible Society, Missionary School, Society for the Promotion of the Public Welfare, besides asylums, and other benevolent institutions.

The **Central Railway Station**, on the S. side of the town, is handsome. On the exterior, reliefs of Newton, Humboldt, Laplace, and Euler. It will be observed that there are also two clocks, which differ by twenty-two minutes. One shows the Paris time, the other the time of Basle. Much interest attaches to the time in Basle, as the following will show:—

"Everybody knows how, until the end of the last century, it was a part of the religion of the people of Basle to keep their clocks an hour in advance of those of the rest of the world. It is somewhat remarkable, however, that the origin of so singular a practice should not be more clearly traced. One theory accounts for it, by the supposition that the people of Basle were an hour lazier than other people, and required this notable device in order to keep them up to the mark. Another, is that the town clock having been struck by lightning, and the hand forced an hour forward, the superstition of the people prevented them from interfering with what they considered to be the act of heaven. A third is, that the attempt of an enemy to surprise the town at a certain appointed hour, was defeated by the town clock, which was to have given the signal, striking an hour in advance, and thus deceiving them into the belief that they were too late; in grateful commemoration of which this tribute of respect was paid to bad clock-making—like that of the Romans to the geese. which saved the Capitol. A fourth theory—and that which finds favour in the eyes of the respectable traveller, Coxe—is, that it is owing to the fact of the choir of the cathedral being built at a little deviation from the due east, which consequently produced a corresponding variation upon the sun-dial which was affixed to it. Whatever the origin of the practice might be, it was considered by the people of Basle as an integral part of their constitution; and every proposition made in the council to alter it, met with a signal defeat." In 1799 they were put right, however, and Basle now keeps "railway time."

Basle is rapidly rising in the estimation of tourists, and a day or two may be spent here with pleasure. There are good Swimming Baths, a Reading Club, and a handsome new Theatre. The Zoological Gardens, which are planned on an extensive scale, will prove a great attraction.

In the **environs of Basle** are some charming walks and drives. About three-quarters of a mile from the town is the

Battle Field of St. Jacob, where, in 1444, 1300 Swiss withstood an army of 40,000 French, under the command of the Dauphin of France, at that time a confederate of the Austrians. The latter army perished, only ten escaping alive, and the battle of St. Jacob is still referred to as the Thermopylæ of Swiss history. The vineyards near here produce a red wine called Schweitzer Blut (Swiss Blood). It was not till 1872 that a **monument** was erected to their memory. It is a very fine one by *F. Schlöth*, and bears the inscription, "Our souls to God, our bodies to the enemy." Well worth seeing.

Augst, six miles. A few Roman remains.

Arlesheim, six miles. Formerly summer residence of Bishops of Basle. Fine English park surrounding the ruined castle of Birseck.

Benedictine Convent of Manastein, six miles. Very picturesque.

Hüningen, three miles. A great establishment for pisciculture.

BASLE TO SCHAFFHAUSEN.

Station of the Baden Railway in Klein-Basel (p. 15). Time, 3 hours.

Grenzach.—A very good wine grown here. *Whylen.*

Rheinfelden, on the left bank of the Rhine, is a little walled town, thoroughly Swiss; it is partly built with the ruins of the old Roman settlement, *Augusta Rauracorum,* founded by Munatius Plancus (p. 18). Basel Augst (p. 18) is about 3 miles from here. Rheinfelden was one of the border forts of the Holy Roman Empire: many battles were fought around it during the Thirty Years' War; it sustained numerous sieges, until, in 1744, it was taken by the French, and all its fortifications levelled. It has formed part of Switzerland since 1801. The Covered Bridge, the Upper Gate, and the Stork's Nest Tower, are curious and interesting. There are some famous salt-works in the vicinity of the town, and baths. The Rhine here narrows, and rushes in a foaming torrent, forming the *Höllenhaken.*

Säckingen (Hotel Schutzen).—A fine old Abbey Church.

Klein-Lauffenburg.—A covered bridge connects it with

Lauffenburg (from *Lauffen,* cataracts).—An ancient Castle here. The Rhine is here very picturesque, passing through a rocky channel, where it forms a series of cataracts, impossible for loaded boats to pass. Good salmon fishing.

Waldshut (Hotel Kühner, near the Station) is a walled town, and a railway junction (pop. 1000). It is on the margin of the Black Forest.

Höchenschwand, the highest village in the Forest, and commanding a magnificent view of the Alps (see Cook's "Handbook to Black Forest"), is about 10 miles from here. Waldshut is an uninteresting town, and has not a vestige of holiday attraction about it. Entering by a gate, there is before the traveller one long street, terminated by another gate, and this is the whole of Waldshut. Some of the houses are old, with large, projecting gables and cranes. The shutters to all the windows throughout the town are green. The church is whitewashed inside, and contains nothing worthy of remark. The walks in the neighbourhood of Waldshut are pretty.

Waldshut to Zürich (p. 34).

Erzingen is the last station in the Baden territory. Wilschingen, the first in the Canton of Schaffhausen.

NEUHAUSEN

(Hotel Schweizerhof, immediately facing the Falls, and with fine view of the Alps.)

This is the best station for alighting to visit the **Falls of the Rhine.**

The Rhine, above the Falls, is about 300 feet wide; the height of the Falls is about 60 feet on one side, 45 feet on the other, and the water rushes in three leaps, with a volume of about 80,000 cubic feet per second, and then falls into a large basin. Descend, through the beautiful grounds belonging to the Schweizerhof Hotel, to the Schlösschen Wörth, where there is a fine **view.** Here also is a camera obscura, a restaurant, and a stall of fancy goods. Then take a boat (3 francs for 1 to 3 persons), and row in the midst of the turbulent waters to the middle rock in the Falls. The boat will rock violently, and the spray may fall heavily, but there is no danger—in fact, an accident has never been known. You will alight just at the foot of the great volume of water, and will find it hard to make yourself heard in conversation without an effort. Ascend to a pavilion ("the Umbrella," as it is called in the neighbourhood), and a view of unspeakable grandeur will be witnessed.

If the traveller is nervous, and does not care to visit the rock, go by ferry direct to **Schloss Laufen** (30c).

Schloss Laufen is beautifully situated immediately above the Falls. Admission to the grounds, 1 franc. Although the general effect of the Falls is grand from any point of view, it is impossible to fully realize their true beauty and grandeur except from the Schloss Laufen.

Passing through the rooms, in which will be found a good collection of Swiss carvings, photographs, water-colour drawings, and curiosities, the traveller enters the enclosed grounds, and sees first a pavilion from which a good general view is obtained (with or without stained glasses). Descending by a pleasant path, he then enters a small tunnel in the rock, against which the waters are booming, and it seems as if the rocks shook. This leads to the **Känzli**, a wooden platform beside the Falls. There descend again, and enter through a doorway to the **Fischetz**, an iron platform, overhanging the troubled sea of waters. (Here waterproofs are kept, and are often needed, as the spray continually dashes over.) The most imposing view and the finest effects are to be seen here.

A description by John Ruskin will be read here with pleasure:—

"Stand for an hour beside the Falls of Schaffhausen, on the north side, where the rapids are long, and watch how the vault of water first bends unbroken in pure polished velocity over the arching rocks at the brow of the cataract, covering them with a dome of crystal twenty feet thick, so swift that its motion is unseen except when a foam-globe from above darts over it like a falling star; and how the trees are lighted above it under all their leaves at the instant that it breaks into foam; and how all the hollows of that foam burn with green fire, like so much shattering chrysoprasi; and how, ever and anon startling you with its white flash, a jet of spray leaps hissing out of the fall, like a rocket bursting in the wind and driven away in dust, filling the air with light; and how, through the curdling wreaths of the restless, crashing abyss below, the blue of the water, paled by the foam in its body, shows purer than the sky through white rain cloud; while the shuddering iris stoops in tremulous stillness over all, fading and flushing alternately through the choking spray and shattered sunshine, hiding itself at last among the thick golden leaves which toss to and fro in sympathy with the wild waters, their dripping masses lifted at intervals, like sheaves of loaded corn, by some stronger gush from the cataract, and bowed again upon the mossy rocks as its roar dies away."

The tourist should now return to the Castle, and after passing out into the road, turn to the left, and descend by a path to the **Railway Bridge.** This he will cross by a footway, and will notice the river bed, the gathering waters rushing to the Fall, and the unequal arches of the bridge. Then through vineyards on the left, and back, past the village, to the hotel. The Falls should be seen in the early morning, when the rainbows are around them; by the light of the sunset; and, if fancy so dictates, illuminated with magnesium and Bengal lights. The best time in the year for witnessing a mighty rush of waters is in June or July, when the snow of the Alps is melting, but the Falls are always grand. On a moonlight night the effects are exquisite.

Dr. Forbes thus describes the scene:—"We walked out on the terrace in front of the hotel to enjoy the view of the Falls by moonlight. The evening was as lovely as the day had been —warm, cloudless, and without a breath of wind. The huge white mass of tumbling foam lay straight before us, the only bright spot in the dimly-lighted landscape, and attracting and fixing the eye exclusively on itself. No sound was heard but the one continuous roar of the water, softened by the distance, and seeming to fill the whole air like the moonshine itself. There was something both wild and delightful in the hour and its accompaniments. The mind yielded passively to the impressions made on the senses. A host of half-formed, vague, and visionary thoughts crowded into it at the same time, giving rise to feelings at once tender and melancholy, accompanied with a sort of objectless sympathy or yearning after something unknown. The ideas and emotions most definite and constant were those of power and perpetuity, wonder and awe. What was now impressing the senses and the mind seemed a part of something infinite, which they could neither comprehend nor shake off; the same mass, the same roar, the same rush day and night, year after year, age after age, now and for ever!"

Schaffhausen is the capital of the same named Canton. The name Schaffhausen is derived from the "skiff-houses," which were once ranged here along the river bank when it was a mere landing-place for goods, and was principally peopled by boatmen. It is a remarkably picturesque town, and retains some good specimens of the Suabian style of the sixteenth century. Notice the frescoes on some of the houses, especially the House Zum Ritter, opposite the Krone Hotel. **The Cathedral**, founded 1052, was once an Abbey Church; the style is Romanesque, very massive. The inscription on the great bell (cast in 1468) gave the suggestion to Schiller for his exquisite "Lied von der Glocke." It runs as follows:—"Vivos voco, mortuos plango, fulgura frango." The **Castle** of Munoth, with a thick, bomb-proof wall and a round tower, was built 1564; visitors may inspect it, enjoy the view, and enter the subterranean passages for a trifling fee. The **Library** is only celebrated for the works of Johann von Müller, the Swiss historian. On the **Promenade** (Vesenstaub) is Müller's monument. A good swimming-bath in the river. The **Imthurneum** (named after its founder, M. Imthurn, a native, who presented it to the town) contains a good Theatre, Concert and Ball Room, etc.

FROM SCHAFFHAUSEN TO ZURICH

(Time, 2 hours.)

A long tunnel is entered, then the great bridge over the Rhine is crossed, and another tunnel, passing under the Castle of Laufen, on emerging from which a glance at the Falls may be obtained. The scenery is very beautiful in the neighbourhood of Dachsen, after which there is little to call for special attention until Winterthur (p. 53) is reached. The stations after Dachsen are *Marthalen, Andelfingen, Henggart, Hetlingen, Winterthur.*

Winterthur to Zürich, p. 53.

SCHAFFHAUSEN TO CONSTANCE, BY RAIL.

(Time 1¼ hours.) The first station of any importance is **Singen**, a junction for Donaueschingen. Near Singen is the fortress of **Höhentwiel**, celebrated in the history of the Thirty Years' War, partly destroyed by the French in 1800. Magnificent view from the tower.

Radolphszell, a walled town, with a fine Gothic Church (1436). A good view of the Lower Lake is obtained here, in the centre of which is the Island of Reichenau. (See below.)

The journey from this point is on the margin of the Lake, past stations *Markelfingen, Allensbach, Reichenau.* The Rhine is then crossed by a handsome bridge thrown across that part of the lake, which is here contracted to a river.

Schaffhausen to Constance. By boat (Time, 4 to 5 hours; reverse journey Constance to Schaffhausen, 3 hours). **Paradies**, formerly a nunnery. The Austrian army, under the Archduke Charles, crossed the Rhine here 1799. **Diessenhofen**, where the French army in 1800 effected a passage before the Battle of Hohenlinden. **Stein**, a fine old town. Abbey of St. George. Ruined Castle of Hohenklingen, with a good view.

Soon after leaving Stein the river widens, and the **Untersee** (Lower Lake) is entered. The Castle of Freudenfels is seen on the right, and below it the village of *Eschenz.* To the left, *Oberstaad,* near which are the Quarries of Oehningen, remarkable for fossils; on the right, *Steckborn* and *Feldbach,* nunnery. At *Berlingen* the **Island of Reichenau** is seen to advantage. It is 3 miles long, and 1½ miles broad. In the Church of the Benedictine Abbey, Charles the Fat, great-grandson of Charlemagne, is buried. To the right of Berlingen is the Castle of Eugensberg, built by Eugene Beauharnais; the Castle of Salenstein; *Arenenberg,* where Queen Hortense died, and now the occasional residence of the Ex-Empress of the French. Soon after leaving *Ermatingen,* the narrow passage connecting the Untersee with the Lake of Constance is entered.

On the right is the castellated Monastery of **Gottlieben**, where John Huss and Jerome of Prague were imprisoned by order of the Emperor Sigismund and Pope John XXII. It was a curious coincidence that Pope John XXII. should have himself been confined in this very castle a few years later, by order of the Council of Constance (p. 27). The remainder of the journey is somewhat uninteresting.

CONSTANCE (BADEN).

(Hotel Hecht.)

The population of Constance was once over 40,000; it is now about 11,000. The town is on the Swiss bank of the Rhine, but was, by the Treaty of Pressburg (1805) ceded to Baden.

There is not much in Constance for the mere sightseer; it is rich, however, in historical associations. As Geneva is the city of Calvin, and Zürich the city of Zwingli, so Constance is the city of Huss.

The **House of Huss**, in the St. Paulsstrasse, is adorned with his effigy. The **Dominican Monastery** of Gottlieben, where he was imprisoned, is on an island near the town (see above). The place where he stood to receive the sentence of death is pointed out in the **Münster**. The **Kaufhaus**, in which the Council met who condemned him, may be visited; and the **field** at Brühl, where the last act in the tragedy was performed, is still to be seen; and here the visitor, as he stands on the very spot where the stake was planted, will be asked to buy an image of the Reformer, made from clay taken from the place above which the flames crackled.

It is not necessary here to tell the story of Huss again; but as the visitor looks at his prison at Gottlieben, it may not be uninteresting to recall one of his dreams, as related by D'Aubigné in his "History of the Reformation":—

"One night the holy martyr saw in imagination, from the depths of his dungeon, the pictures of Christ that he had had painted on the walls of his oratory, effaced by the Pope and his bishops. This vision distressed him; but on the next day he saw many painters occupied in restoring these figures in greater number and in brighter colours. As soon as their task was ended, the painters, who were surrounded by an immense crowd, exclaimed, 'Now let the popes and bishops come! They shall never efface them more!' 'And many people rejoiced in

Bethlehem, and I with them,' adds John Huss. 'Busy yourself with your defence rather than with your dreams,' said his faithful friend, the Knight of Chlum, to whom he had communicated this vision. 'I am no dreamer,' replied Huss; 'but I maintain this for certain, that the image of Christ will never be effaced. They have wished to deface it, but it shall be painted afresh in all hearts by much better preachers than myself. The nation that loves Christ will rejoice at this; and I, awaking from among the dead, and rising, so to speak, from my grave, shall leap with great joy."

Nor can the visitor walk out to the suburb of Bruhl, on the Zürich road, where he was burnt at the stake, without thinking of the remarkable pun and prophecy he made as he was entering the flames in allusion to his own name, which signified in the Bohemian tongue a goose. He said, "Are you going to burn a goose? In one century you will have a swan you can neither roast nor boil." And in one century came forth Luther, who had a swan for his arms.

The **Münster**, or Cathedral, was founded 1052, but did not assume its present form till the beginning of the sixteenth century. The Gothic tower at the west end was erected during the years 1850-57. From the platforms round the open-work spire a magnificent **view** is obtained of the town, the lake, the valley of the Rhine, and the mountains of the Tyrol. The **oak doors** of the chief entrance are decorated with reliefs by *Simon Haider* (1470), in twenty sections, representing scenes in the life of our Lord.

In the **interior** observe the sixteen monolith pillars which support the nave; the **choir-stalls**, with old carvings; the **Tomb of Robert Hallam**, Bishop of Salisbury, made of English brass. In the nave is a light-coloured stone, marking the spot **where John Huss stood** when the cruel sentence of death was delivered, July 6, 1415, and where he knelt before his accusers, and cried, "Lord Jesus, forgive my enemies!" It is affirmed that this stone always remains dry when those surrounding it are damp. The **sacristy** contains some curious missals, miniatures, plate, and other relics. A good collection of stained glass, by *Vincent*, may be seen in the **Chapter-room**. The **Crypt** below the church is very old, and contains a representation in stone of the Holy Sepulchre. The **Cloisters**, though now much dilapidated, exhibit some excellent workmanship.

The **Hall of the Kaufhaus** is where the Council of

Constance held its sittings, and condemned Huss and Jerome of Prague. Many memorials of the former are preserved here in a kind of museum, admission one franc.

In the **Wessenberg-Haus** may be seen a good collection of engravings and pictures. On the **Town Hall,** *Stadt-Kanzlei,* are frescoes illustrating passages in the history of Constance.

The walks in the neighbourhood of Constance, and the **promenades** surrounding the town, are pretty. The **pier** is attractive, on account of the good views it commands. There is also a good **Swimming Bath.**

In the **environs** of Constance are several very interesting places; among them the **Abbey of Kreuzlingen**—or, rather, the building which once bore that name, for it is now an agricultural school. The present structure has been erected since the Thirty Years' War, as the former one was destroyed during that time. In one of the chapels is a marvellous piece of wood-carving, adorned with many hundreds of miniature figures, the work of a Tyrolese; also an embroidery, adorned with pearls, presented by Pope John XXII. on his journeying to Constance in 1414.

Mainau, the beautiful seat of the Grand Duke of Baden, is situated on a small island, about four miles from Constance. The island is connected with the mainland by a bridge. No pleasanter day's excursion than this can be undertaken in the vicinity of Constance.

The **Field of Brühl** is outside the town, on the road to Zürich, and possesses the melancholy interest of being the place where Huss was burnt in 1415, and Jerome of Prague a year after. The spot is marked by a rough monument of stones, upon which is an inscription.

THE LAKE OF CONSTANCE.

(Latin, *Lacus Brigantinus.* German, *Boden See.*)

This spacious reservoir of the Rhine is over forty miles in length, and eight in width; it is a glorious sheet of water in fine weather, but rather turbulent in storm, being elevated about 1,300 feet, and not protected by lofty mountain embankments; it is by no means an uncommon thing for tourists to suffer from sea-sickness when being rocked on its bosom. There are some fine views from it, especially of the Appenzell Alps, including the snow-clad Sentis and the Vorarlberg Alps. Lake Constance would probably be considered very beautiful, were it not in Switzerland; but being there, it suffers from odious comparisons with its fairer neighbours.

The position held by the lake is curious, as it forms the boundary of five different states, *viz.*, Baden, Württemberg, Bavaria, Austria, and Switzerland, to each of which states a portion of the coast belongs.

For **steamers** to all parts of the lake, see local time-tables.

Friedrichshafen, nearly opposite Constance, is the principal bathing place on the lake, and the views from here are among the finest in the neighbourhood. It is a pleasant town, with about 3000 inhabitants. The **Schloss** is the summer residence of the King of Wurtemberg. Friedrichshafen is the terminus of the Stuttgart Railway.

Lindau, a pretty town at the E. end of the lake, is the terminus of the Bavarian Railway.

Bregenz, in the Vorarlberg, is a good starting-point for the Tyrol. It is thus sketched by Adelaide Proctor:—

"Girt round with rugged mountains,
The fair Lake Constance lies;
In her blue heart reflected,
Shine back the starry skies;
And, watching each white cloudlet
Float silently and slow,
You think a piece of heaven
Lies on our earth below!

Midnight is there; and silence,
Enthroned in heaven, looks down
Upon her own calm mirror,
Upon a sleeping town;
For Bregenz, that quaint city
Upon the Tyrol shore,
Has stood above Lake Constance
A thousand years and more.

Her battlements and towers,
From off their rocky steep,
Have cast their trembling shadows
For ages on the deep;
Mountain, and lake, and valley,
A sacred legend know,
Of how the town was saved one night,
Three hundred years ago."—etc., etc.

CONSTANCE TO COIRE (CHUR).

The journey may be made by boat to Rorschach, and thence by rail, or the whole route by rail, the line skirting the bank of the Lake as far as to Rorschach. In either case the principal places passed will be *Kreuzlingen* (p. 28), *Münsterlingen*, (with a large lunatic asylum, formerly a monastery), ***Altnau***, *Güttingen*, *Kessweil*, *Uttweil*, Romanshorn (a steamboat-station, eight miles from Friedrichshafen, and a junction with line to Winterthur), *Egnach*, *Arbon* (once the Roman Arbor Felix), *Horn* (with its good bath), and then *Rorschach*.

RORSCHACH.

(Hotel Seehof.)

Behind the town, which has a population of 3492, is a hill called the Rorschacher Berg, commanding a view of the entire length of Constance and the Alps of the Grisons. There are some old castles dotted about on hills, some good baths not far off from the town, and very pretty walks and drives, and the air is said to be very beneficial to invalids. It is not, however, a place to choose for a lengthened stay.

A large traffic passes through here or by the coast steamers from Romanshorn, across the lake to Lindau, where it is transhipped from steamer to railway for Bavaria, Austria, etc.

It was a busy place during the late war, as it was the route selected for traffic from the eastern line from France.

The trip to Bregenz can be made from this town by steamer (p. 29).

Leaving Rorschach, the lake is skirted and the valley of the Rhine is entered. Rheineck is a pleasant village, situated in a bend in the river, and surrounded with vineyards; travellers who are seeking the Molken-kur, or Whey-cure (made of goat's milk) alight here for Heiden, said to be one of the cleanest and healthiest towns in Switzerland. Diligence twice daily, 1½ hour. From Heiden a diligence runs to St. Gallen (p. 54).

Altstätten has a population of nearly 8000. Beautiful neighbourhood. Good roads from here to Appenzell, St. Gall, and a pleasant footpath to Heiden. The manufacture in this neighbourhood is a muslin fabric known as St. Gallen muslin, the handiwork of all the women of the villages round about. From Altstätten to Coire the scenery is extremely picturesque.

Oberried, a ruined castle (Blatten) is seen to the right, and below it is a defile known as the *Hirschsprung* (stag's leap.)

Rüthi. A pathway from here leads to Weissbad, by the Kamor Pass, the views from which are magnificent. Sennwald, at the foot of the Kanzel, or pulpit, is near here.

Haag. Railway from here to Feldkirch, for the Tyrol. At **Buchs** is a castle, once the residence of the Counts of Werdenberg.

At **Sevelen** is the ruined castle of Wartau, and on the opposite bank of the Rhine, Vaduz, to which place a coach runs from Trübbach.

Sargans. Inquire here if a change of carriage must be made. Sargans is the junction with the railways from Wallenstadt and Zürich. In this neighbourhood are the mountains Falknis and Scesaplana.

RAGATZ

(Hotels Quellenhof and Hof Ragatz.)

On the Tamina, is annually crowded with thousands of visitors, sometimes as many as 50,000 in a season, on account of the Baths, the mineral water which supplies them being conveyed from Pfäffers by tubes or wooden pipes made of hollow pine trees, and reaching a distance of 12,500 ft. Ragatz has some fine hotels, a Cursaal, and charming environs. **Bad-Pfäffers,** up the gorge of the Tamina, should on no account be missed. It is an easy walk of 2½ miles from Ragatz. The old Baths are between frowning rocks above the torrent of the Tamina. The **Gorge** is traversed by a wooden pathway above the torrent, and with gloomy walls of rock overhanging. In many respects it resembles the Gorge du Trient (p. 121), although, probably, that remarkable spot is more than equalled by the savage grandeur of Pfäffers. In one part of the Gorge (the *Schlucht* or abyss) the rocks are not more than 20 feet apart. The journey from Ragatz may be made with perfect safety either by carriage or on foot, and, although a very timid person might fear to walk upon a mere shelf of planks, with a brawling river below and threatening rocks above, it is nevertheless perfectly safe. A charge of one franc is made to each person for admittance, and a guide invariably accompanies the visitors. The journey may be made in from two to three hours, but those who have time at their disposal will do well to visit also the **Village of Pfäffers,** which has a fine Benedictine Abbey, now used as a Lunatic Asylum. The road from the village to

Ragatz is exceedingly picturesque, and passes the ruined castle of Wartenstein. Innumerable pleasant excursions may be made in this neighbourhood.

Resuming the railway, the Rhine is crossed, and the traveller, leaving the Canton of St. Gall, passes into the Grisons.

Mayenfeld.—Fine views. An old Tower of the fourth century, built, it is said, by the Emperor Constantius, is seen here; and also the Convent of Pfäffers.

Landquart.—Diligences run from here to the Engadine (p. 185).

COIRE.

(German, *Chur;* Romansch, *Cuera.*)

(Hotel Steinbock.)

Coire (pop. 8000) is the chief city of the Canton of the Grisons (*Graubünden*), whose history is quite as eventful as that of the Forest cantons, and equally as interesting. Some of the principal inhabitants of the country called Canton Grisons met together in a forest near the village of Trons, to form a league and concert measures by which they might throw off the oppressive tyranny of the petty lords and barons who had so long held them in subjection. In May, 1424, they met at the village of Trons, and there established "The Grey League" (*Graubund*), so called from their being dressed in grey. Two similar leagues were formed: one called "The League of God's House," and the other "The League of the Ten Jurisdictions." These three leagues, known as the Grison Confederacy, warred against the barons to such good purpose, that, had not the Episcopal lords directed their movements, it is likely that their oppressors would have been forced to flee the land. As it was, however, they contented themselves with forming their country into a number of small republics, each with a perfectly independent government and machinery. The result of this was an endless storm of petty feuds and quarrels between the citizens, which did not really end until, in 1814, they became a canton of the Swiss Confederation. Since then a new set of laws concerning the administration of the canton has been put in operation, by which all the old landmarks connected with the earlier form of government have been obliterated, and it is now settled down to the ordinary peace and prosperity of the rest of the Swiss cantons.

The language of the Grisons is Romansch, divided into three different dialects; the inhabitants, however, can nearly always supplement their own tongue with German or Italian. The tourist will be interested in perusing a newspaper published in Coire, in the Romansch, entitled "Amity del Pievel," the "Friend of the People."

The canton is very large, occupying about one-sixth of the whole of the Swiss territory, and has a population which, in 1870, numbered 91,782. The scenery is very beautiful throughout the canton, consisting of barren mountains and fertile valleys, and every charm that variety can give.

There are several places of interest for the fleeting tourist to note as he passes by, although the town of Coire does not hold out sufficient inducement for any lengthened stay. The situation of the town is extremely picturesque; the streets are narrow and irregular, but abounding with good views. The Plessur, a river flowing into the Rhine, passes through it. Part of the town is surrounded with walls. The **Cathedral**, or Church of St. Lucius, is the most remarkable building in Coire; it dates from the eighth century, and is a good specimen of the early pointed Gothic. St. Lucius is of doubtful origin; but the legends say he was a King of Scotland, who came as an evangelist to Switzerland, and suffered martyrdom. Observe the portal of the entrance court, representing Christ as the Lion of the tribe of Judah. In the **interior** are many objects of interest—

Tomb of Bishop Ortlieb de Brandis.
Madonna . . . . . . *Stumm (pupil of Rubens).*
High Altar, with fine carved work . . *Jacob Roesch.*
Christ bearing the Cross . . . . *Albert Dürer.*

In the **Treasury** are many valuable curiosities, including a miniature on lapis lazuli, by *Carlo Dolce.*

The **Episcopal Palace**, not far from the church, is also very ancient; and it is said that the chapel is one of the earliest Christian edifices extant. It is in an old Roman tower, called **Marsöl**, in which tower, says tradition, St. Lucius was murdered in the year 176. Above the Cathedral is a very fine walk, commanding extensive views of the Viâ Mala and the Splügen.

The **Chapel of St. Lucius**, beautifully situated at the foot of the Mittenberg, commands a fine view, as also does the Rosenhügel, a promenade a short distance from the town, on the Julier Road. The tourist may, perchance, hear the watchman perambulating the town at night, and if so, he may catch a couplet of the following ancient chant:—

"Hear, ye Christians, let me tell you
Our clock has struck eight,
Our clock has struck nine, etc.
Eight—only eight in Noah's time
Were saved from punishment. *Eight!*
Nine digests no thanking:
Man, think of thy duty! *Nine!*
Ten commandments God enjoined:
Let us be to Him obedient. *Ten!*
Only *Eleven* disciples were faithful:
Grant, Lord, that there be no falling off. *Eleven!*
Twelve is the hour that limits time:
Man, think upon eternity! *Twelve!*
One,—O man, only one thing is needful:
Man, think upon thy death! *One!*

From Coire over the Splügen Pass (p. 177).
„ Coire to St. Moritz (p. 184).
„ Coire to Andermatt by the Oberalp (p. 182).

A diligence runs between Coire and Andermatt, from whence another diligence runs to Brieg and Leuk; and hence the railway may be taken to Geneva (p. 124).

BASLE TO ZÜRICH.

There are three ways by which the journey may be made. 1. Waldshut and Turgi. 2. By Olten and Turgi. 3. By Rheinfelden, Stein, and Brugg.

(1) From Basle to Waldshut (see p. 21). At **Waldshut** the Swiss Junction Railway crosses the Rhine a short distance from Coblenz, and traverses the right bank of the river **Aare** (which joins the Rhine at Coblenz — Confluentia) to **Turgi**. A short but interesting journey brings the traveller to **Turgi**, from which place the journey to Zürich is continued, as in Route 3. (See below.)

(2) Basle to Olten, Turgi, and Zürich. Soon after leaving the station, the battle-field of St. Jacob (p. 20) is passed, where 1600 Swiss withstood for ten hours a French army ten times more numerous, commanded by the Dauphin. The whole of the journey from Basle to Olten is through very charming country. As soon as the Rhine valley is left, the valley of the Ergolz, in the Jura, is entered. **Liestal**, the capital of the half-canton. Basle-Champagne (p. 15), reminds the traveller of the animosity existing between it and Basle-ville. It is a poor town, possessing nothing of great in-

terest except the cup of Charles the Bold found at Nancy. Stations, *Lausen, Sissach, Sommerau*, and *Läufelfingen*.

Soon after passing the latter station, the great Hauenstein Tunnel is entered. It is one and a half miles long. A terrible accident occurred here in May, 1857, when fifty-two workmen perished by a fall of the earth. The Hauenstein commands a magnificent view of the Alps, which is not seen from the railway. Many tourists, therefore, leave the train at Läufelfingen, ascend the mountain (time, one and a half hours), and descend to Olten, where the journey can be continued.

Olten, junction for Lucerne, Berne, Geneva, etc. Inquire if carriages have to be changed here. The town is pleasantly situated on the Aare, in a valley of the Jura. There is nothing in Olten except its situation to interest the traveller.

Leaving Olten, the journey continues still through pleasant scenery, with the Aare and the Jura mountains in sight. Stations, *Dänikon, Schönenwerth*, with a ruined castle.

Aarau (Hotel de la Cigogne), the capital of the Canton Aargau, is on the Aare, and under the Jura. Henry Zschokke, the historian, lived here. The Baths of Schinznach can be reached from here by way of the Gyslifluh, 2539 feet. A pleasant excursion, commanding good views.

Stations: *Rupperswell, Wildegg*, near to the Baths of Brestenberg; *Schinznach*, celebrated for its baths; visited chiefly by the French. The Castle of Habsburg is close by here, once the seat of the Imperial house of Austria, but now a ruin.

Brugg, a pleasant and pretty place, once belonging to the House of Habsburg; its old towers are very quaint and curious. Near here the Aare, the Reuss, and the Limmat, three of the principal rivers of the country, join and travel in company under the name of the Aare, until they reach *Coblenz*, near Waldshut. A mile to the south-east of Brugg stands the **Abbey of Königsfelden**, "founded by the Empress Elizabeth and Agnes of Hungary, on the spot where the Emperor Albert, husband of the one and father of the other, was assassinated two years before. How much religion went in those days to the building of an abbey we may judge by the ferocious revenge which Agnes, unable to lay hands on the conspirators themselves, took upon their families and friends, when, on occasion of the butchery of sixty-three guiltless victims before her at one time, she exclaimed, 'Now I bathe in May-dew!' The actual murderers succeeded in making their escape, with the exception of Wart, who was undoubtedly present, though his share in the deed is disputed. He was sentenced to be broken alive upon the wheel; but the usual 'stroke of mercy' was denied, and he lingered for two days and two nights before death relieved him from his sufferings. I know few stories more affecting than that of the devotion of Wart's wife in the hours of his long agony. During the day she concealed herself in the neighbourhood, and as soon as it was dark, eluding the guards, she contrived to climb up to the scaffold, and kneeling by his side through the slow and terrible night, wiped away the sweat of anguish from his brow, and whispered into his ear the consolation of faith and love. Before the morning broke she hastened away to hide herself near the spot, and to pray that when she came back again she might find him dead. There came in the morning a gay troop of knights to see the sight, and bitterly spoke one when he looked upon the unmutilated face. 'Are there no crows in your country?' was his stern demand. It was the cruel Agnes in disguise. Strange indeed it is that two such passions should have a common origin of woman's affection—that the same source should send forth such sweet waters and such bitter!"

Brugg was the birthplace of Zimmerman, the author of the well-known book on "Solitude."

Turgi, junction, with branch line to Waldshut.

Baden (Hotel Hinterhof) is the oldest of the watering-places of Switzerland; its ancient name was *Aquæ Helvetiæ*. It was visited by fashionable Romans, and now fashionable cosmopolitans visit it to the number of 15,000 annually. Its springs are good for rheumatism, catarrhs, and almost everything else. A curious fact connected with this place is, that it was an ancestor of Baden-Baden; that is to say, it was once a "hell" of the Romans, if all accounts be true; for it is said the *Wurfel Wiese*, or Dice Meadow, is so named on account of the dice found in it.

The season at Baden is May to September, and the principal frequenters are Swiss and French.

Stations, *Killwangen, Dietikon, Schlieren, Altstetten* junction with branch line to Lucerne (p. 54). As the traveller draws near to Zürich, he will be struck with the picturesque nature of the scenery in its immediate neighbourhood, and with the view of the great range of Alps seen on the right hand.

Crossing the river Sihl, the train arrives at **Zürich** (p. 37).

(3) By Rheinfelden, Stein, and Brugg. This is the most direct route from Basle to Zürich, and is not less interesting

than either of the other two. There is a good service of trains, namely, from seven to ten daily each way. The railway passes through Rheinfelden (p. 21), and the picturesque surroundings of this quaint and interesting town are therefore much better seen than from the railway—Basle to Waldshut and Turgi—where the line is on the other side of the river. Before reaching Stein, the next station of any importance on the route, the line turns southward, thus—as may be seen in the map—saving the long distance to Waldshut on the one hand, or to Olten on the other. Then comes Brugg (p. 35), and the remainder of the journey is the same as in the other routes.

ZÜRICH.

(Hotel Belle Vue, on the shore of the Lake; commands the best view of the Alps and the Lake.)

Population, 60,000, chiefly Protestant.

Zürich is the centre of Swiss intelligence and industry; its staple trade is the manufacture of silk and cotton. Its University is noted for the proficient medical men it sends forth, for its liberality in the matter of lady students, and for the advanced thought and ultra-democratic views entertained there. Every new idea is grasped with ardour and agitated with vigour. While the University is the nucleus of enlightened views, ethical, religious, and political, the town preserves the severely Calvinistic character that made it a stronghold of the Reformation. Police regulations exist with regard to keeping Sunday, that sound strangely arbitrary and somewhat incongruous to English ears. The spirit of clique largely animates its society; the merchant does not visit with the learned bodies, nor the students with the *bourgeoisie*. The people are brusque in manner and speech. "*Grossier comme un Zurichois*" has become a proverb.

Zürich's history is ancient, rough, and not always honourable. Long before the ubiquitous Romans founded the colony of Turicum, it was a Keltic community, as remains amply prove. Excavations in the neighbourhood have furnished rich yields of antiquities, Keltic, Etruscan, and Roman. Zürich early ruled itself, and knew the horrors of civil war, dissension, and treachery. The Zürichers appear fond of fighting; their records abound in narratives of attacks and quarrels. Nor were they good Swiss; oftentimes they made secret alliances with the Austrians against their neighbouring countrymen, afterwards they wearied of the Austrian yoke, and joined the forest cantons in their revolt against the Habsburgs. When, early in the fourteenth century, Duke Albert besieged Zürich, the women donned armour, and aided the men in routing the enemy. They drove him across the frontier to his ancestral castle of Habsburg; and near here, while he was halting to admire the exquisite view the valley of the Reuss presents, he was treacherously murdered by his own nephew. From this date Zürich grew in importance, acquiring much land by conquest and by purchase. It was in the van of the Reformation; the Protestants banished under Queen Mary found a sure asylum here; the first English Bible printed issued from its press. It was in Zürich Cathedral that Zwingli thundered forth the new doctrines he had recently embraced. His eloquence converted the whole congregation, and the church has ever since been Protestant.

Zürich boasts of many distinguished names. Conrad Gessner, the celebrated naturalist, was born here, March 26, 1516. Among his multifarious labours, he designed and painted over 1500 plants, and left five volumes consisting entirely of figures. He was buried in the cloister of the great Church in Zürich, 1565. Solomon Gessner, the poet and painter, was born here in 1730. He was the author of "The Death of Abel." He died in Zürich, and his monument may still be seen. And Lavater, the thoughtful, amiable Lavater, was born and lived here. Zimmerman dwelt for some time near here on the lake, and wrote in one of his letters: "I can never recall these sublime and tranquil scenes which I have enjoyed in the company of Lavater without the most intense emotion." Lavater met his death in Zürich when the town was entered by the French army in 1799. There are several versions of the story of his death, but the most credible is that which says he was shot by a French soldier while dressing the wounds of his dying comrade. The perpetrator of the crime had but a few hours before received the hospitality of the man he thus cruelly slew. Although Lavater knew who it was that had shot him, he refused to divulge the information, notwithstanding a large reward had been offered by the French commander, Massena, for the discovery of the murderer. Lavater lingered for more than a year, much of which time was spent in extreme bodily torture consequent upon his wound.

It would take long even to name the famous men of Zürich. *Pestalozzi*, the children's friend, Orelli, Bodmer, Horner, Meyer, the friend of Goethe, not to speak of exiles innumerable, past and present—for the gates of Zürich have always been open to the politically oppressed.

Zürich is divided, by the rapid river Limmat, into two parts; the Grosse-stadt (right) and the Kleine-stadt (left). **The Lake**, at the north end of which the town lies, is 26 miles long and 3 wide, and is one of the chief glories of Zürich, and the greatest attraction to strangers. Steamers traverse its length and breadth, stopping at the various villages, remarkable for little but their industry. An excursion round the lake is an afternoon well spent; but halting at each station to explore the neighbourhood repays the longer time it demands (For Lake of Zürich, see p. 43.)

The principal things to be seen in Zürich will not detain the visitor long.

The **Gross-Münster**, built in the Romanesque style of the eleventh century. It was in this church that Zwingli uttered his protests against the sins of his day. It is a massive pile, that rises precipitously above the town, approached by a steep flight of steps; an object that would have been imposing, had the eighteenth century not crowned it with towers modelled after the fashion of bridecake erections. Below them, on one side, is niched an ancient equestrian figure of Charlemagne, in his time a benefactor to the foundation. Here he sits, grey, impassive, wooden, clutching his sword and sceptre, while pigeons nestle at his feet, and swallows build in his golden crown. He has witnessed a good slice of history from his elevated post. Full in view spreads the lovely lake, closed in by the snowy peaks of the Sentis, Tödi, and Glärnisch; close to the shore lies a tiny islet, one green mass of chestnuts, amid which a solitary poplar rears its slender head. This is the sole remains of the fortifications, that once defended the city; they are now levelled, and turned into pleasure gardens. A **bridge** spans the Limmat, closed in on either side by two churches. Half of the one actually rose from the water, whence it gained its name of Wasserkirche (Water Church). The cloisters, dating from the thirteenth century, deserve careful attention; the fantastic ornamentation of their fan-shaped capitals, and the grotesque heads peering between the vaulting of their arches, present architectural beauties such as the cathedral cannot boast. It is a tall, Romanesque, white-washed building, Protestant *au bout des ongles*.

The Town **Library** (admission 1 franc), at the corner of

the Münster Bridge, is in the building which was formerly the Wasserkirche, or Water Church, founded, it is said, by Charlemagne. It was much enlarged in 1860, and contains about 50,000 works. Among the MSS. are valuable autograph letters of the early Reformers, and Zwingli's Greek Bible, with his own annotations in Hebrew; letters of Lady Jane Grey, Frederick the Great, etc. There is also a very fine **Model, in relief,** of Switzerland, well worthy of careful attention. A **Collection of Antiquities** will be viewed with much interest by those who are acquainted with Professor Keller's work, as they are relics of the Swiss lake dwellings and dwellers, those

> "Unknown. mysterious dead!
> Whose relics Science from the shelly marl
> Has gathered, and with vague conjecture based
> On fact, essays to read, like some weird scroll,
> Or dark enigma by Cadmean Sphinx
> Propounded." *

"The objects which have been recovered reveal the habits, arts, conditions of life, and much of the internal history of those who formed and used them. About the events of their external history, though much of this can be pretty well imagined, of course they are silent. Nor have they anything to tell us in reply to the questions of who the people were, whence they came, or what became of them? The information they give us begins with the time when men in Central Europe had not attained to a knowledge of metals, and were using implements of bone and stone for war, hunting, and domestic purposes. Abundance of their stone tools have been found, and also of specimens of the work done with them. For instance, some of the series of piles upon which the dwellings were placed—and these piles are found by the hundred—we see were hacked to the point, which was to fit them for driving, with stone chisels and hatchets. And then, in other series of piles, we pass on to the era when stone had been superseded by bronze and iron tools. It is very interesting to have thus before us the actual tools and the actual work done with them, together with ocular demonstration of the way in which, by the superiority of their work, the first metal tools superseded their perfected predecessors of stone."—*Zincke.*

The **Hohe Promenade,** under a fine avenue of trees, commands a beautiful view of the Lake. Lavater is buried in

* "The Lake Dwellings of Switzerland." By Rev. F. H. Wood, B.A.

the churchyard of St. Ann, close at hand. The **Arsenal** (*Zeughaus*) contains the battle-axe used by Zwingli at the fatal engagement at Cappel, together with his sword and helmet. There is also a display of ancient armour, and the crossbow with which it is alleged William Tell shot the apple from his son's head.

In the **Augustine Church** there are two good pictures by *Deschwanden*. The **Botanical Gardens** contain some fine specimens of Alpine plants, and a high mound, called the Katz, from which there is a splendid view.

The **Polytechnic** is a handsome building, and was founded for the purpose of a large national school. It embraces in its curriculum all branches of national industry. It has an endowment of 25,000 fr. per annum from the State. It is built upon a commanding terrace-like piece of ground, from which a very fine view may be enjoyed. In this same building is the **University**, which has been so deservedly noted for the home which it afforded to many eminent men who were obliged to fly their fatherland for either political or religious opinions.

In the **Environs of Zürich** the most interesting excursion is to the

UETLIBERG,

one of the Albis range. It is only 2864 feet, but commands a magnificent view. A **railway** with sharp gradient, similar to the Rigi line, pulls the idle up to its summit in less than an hour (see p. 42). The wise Romans erected a specula on this site, whose plateau commands the entire lake which lies outstretched below, a blue, narrow crescent, encircled by its fruitful hills. In the far distance, the Stockhorn, the Jungfrau, Rigi, and Pilatus uprear their splendid heads; on clear days the Vosges and the Black Forest are also plainly distinguishable. The Uetliberg is a favourite afternoon excursion, and no wonder; for to see the sun cast its last loving evening rays upon these beauties is a sight not soon forgotten. It is customary for the school-children of the neighbourhood to make an excursion up the Uetliberg on Ascension day, and many of the masters let their flocks plant nurseries of pines on these occasions. Little forests of various ages thus mark the flight of time, for the youth of Zürich link their lives with the mountain that overshadows their city. It becomes identified with their home, their childhood, and youth; and in old age they can seek the shelter of self-planted trees. It is a poetical fancy, and deserves imitation. In this manner, the past and present are joined hand to hand; the Keltic tumulus, Roman watch-tower, and modern forest all forming portions of one chain of human brotherhood, while the lake flows calmly on, beautiful then, now, and for ever.

The Uetliberg Railway.—Early in 1872 a committee of the inhabitants of Zürich was appointed to take steps to form a line up the Uetliberg. Messrs. Culmann and Pestalozzi, and Mr. J. Tobles, chief engineer, were consulted on the subject.

A special difficulty presented itself in the formation of the ground. The incline from the town to the foot of the mountain itself was so slight as to need only the ordinary adhesion principle. But a special system was indispensable for the ascent of the steep mountain. Thus it would be necessary either to proceed to the foot of the mountain with an ordinary locomotive and continue the journey up with one adapted to incline travelling, or to continue the journey from the incline to the town with an incline locomotive. It was finally decided to use the ordinary locomotive under special precautions.

The incline is at its steepest in the last 810 metres before the station of Uetliberg.

In order that in the descent journey the driver may have full control over the speed, the locomotive is provided with an air break, such as is used on the Rigi line, and which can be made available instantaneously. Additional breaks are used for stopping the train at stations. The break machine is always at the lowest part of the train, to prevent accidents by breaking of couplings, etc.

The trial journeys were from Wiedikon to Uetliberg, a distance of eight kilometres. In the first journey, which was accomplished in 21 minutes 26 seconds, the total weight of train (consisting of one passenger-carriage, containing 30 persons at 70 kilog. each, and one truck containing 28 rails of 175 kilog. each) amounted to over 17 tons. The second journey, with an additional weight of eight tons (nearly), performed the journey in 22 minutes 31 seconds.

It was concluded, from these attempts, that the locomotives would amply fulfil the appointed conditions, which has proved to be the case.

In good weather—in bad the line is less frequented—three passenger-carriages, containing forty persons, can be forwarded without any danger. These would weigh, together with the breaks, driver, and stoker, 26 tons, a weight reached in the second descent journey It is hoped that as a lighter model of passenger-carriages is contemplated, the weight of the train will be reduced and risk lessened. Later trials which the company have sanctioned, promise important results, in connection with this railway, to scientific knowledge. These at present show that the theory (of using ordinary locomotives) has asserted its right against cavillings of all sorts. The ascent of the steepest railway inclines is practicable with the ordinary adhesive locomotives without any danger.

(For fares and times of starting, see local time-tables.)

ZÜRICH TO COIRE.

The whole journey may be made (1) by railway; but the pleasantest route is (2) by steamer to Rapperschwyl, and thence by rail to Coire.

1. Crossing the Sihl, the road curves, and then crosses the rapid Limmat by an iron bridge. After passing *Oerlikon*, and crossing the Glatt, *Wallisellen* (p. 53) is reached. The traveller is now in the Lancashire of Switzerland; cotton-mills are continually met with, especially in the neighbourhood of *Uster*. The church in this town has an elegant pointed spire, and the picturesque Castle, utilized as a Court of Justice, Gaol, and Inn, is a conspicuous feature in the landscape. Four stations, *Aathal*, **Wetzikon** (see below), *Bubikon*, the highest part of the line near the **Bachtel**, with an inn on the summit; fine views. *Rüti*; diligence from here to the foot of the Bachtel.

Rapperschwyl, at the extremity of the Lake of Zürich (p. 45).

2. By steamboat on

THE LAKE OF ZÜRICH.

The Lake is twenty-six miles long, and three miles wide. It is the Windermere of Switzerland, beautiful and picturesque, but not grand. There are many pretty villages on the banks, and the background formed by the Alps of Glarus and Uri is remarkably fine.

The steamboat journey to Rapperschwyl is very interesting, and should not be omitted, unless the traveller has an important object in view in taking the train.

On the left bank the first station of interest is **Meilen.** Here, in the winter of 1853, when the water was unusually low, were first discovered those remarkable lacustrine buildings that puzzle ethnologists? Who were these lake-dwellers? Whence came they? For what purpose did they isolate themselves from the mainland? Arrows, beads, hammers, spindles, grain, bones of tame animals, bread, plaited straw, seeds, and many other evidences of civilization, were exhumed on this spot, and can now be seen in the Zürich Museum (p. 40). For the water once more covers the piles at Meilen—they are, indeed, 132 feet from the shore—and to see remains of such pile-buildings it is needful to go farther inland to Wetzikon, where a former lake has become a peat-moor. Imbedded herein are the remains of such dwellings. It certainly needs some imagination to reconstruct them; but the owner, an enthusiastic ethnologist, has assisted fancy by a little model, that shows a structure built somewhat after the manner of a Swiss châlet, standing on an elevated platform, and connected with the shore by a rude bridge. It was in one of these lake communities that Sir Arthur Helps laid the scene of "Realmah."

Meilen produces a fairly good wine; indeed, most of the low hills round the Lake of Zürich are planted with vineyards, but the wine produced is only average.

Nearly opposite Meilen is Horgen, a good place for striking off for Zug and the Rigi.

The next station of interest is Männedorf, known for an establishment where maniacs may be healed by prayer. The house is always full, and cures are said to be effected—chiefly, however, it appears, upon hysterical and hypochondriacal patients. The Swiss are in the minority of those who seek its founder's aid, while Germans predominate. Lately the Government has taken the place under its jurisdiction, the villagers, who are not favourable to the establishment, having complained of the abuses practised.

Stäfa is the richest and one of the largest of the lake villages. It was here that Goethe lived for a while, and wrote his little play, "Jery and Baetely," inspired by Swiss scenery. Nearly opposite lies the islet of Ufenau, amid whose greenery a ruined church uprears its walls. In this retired spot, the property of the Convent of Einsiedeln, Ulrich von Hutten found an asylum and a grave. When striving to regain health at the Baths of Pfäffers, he was pursued, and would have fallen into the hands of his enemies, had not Zwingli shielded him, and, commending him to the care of the Ufenau pastor, directed him thither. He died in his protector's arms, who laid the restless spirit to rest at the early age of thirty-six. No stone marks the clod that covers the remains of Luther's friend, as trusty a champion of truth as ever enlisted in her service. His pen, some letters, and an edition of his minor works, with MS. notes, were his sole possession on his death. They are preserved at Zürich. Ufenau, it appears, was a favourite burial-place long before Christian times; its earth has yielded some curious relics—skeletons, ornaments, and pottery, dating from the very earliest times.

Wädenschwyl is quite a considerable place, owning a castle, elegant villas, crape and silk manufactories, tanneries, and dye-houses; indeed, it is the chief industrial town on the lake. From here a diligence starts daily for Einsiedeln, reaching the village in less than two hours (p. 48).

Richterschwyl, built round a sheltering bay, is another favourite starting-point for Einsiedeln pilgrims. Its green slopes are remarkable for the scarlet pocket-handkerchiefs, printed with Black Madonnas, or views of Einsiedeln, that appear to grow on them perennially. They are spread out to dry, and a pretty bright touch they give to the landscape. Zimmermann lived here for many years; he lauds the attractions of Richterschwyl as a home for philosophers in his famous book on "Solitude."

The thriving, picturesque town of **Rapperschwyl** closes the extreme eastern point of the lake, a conspicuous object long before the steamer touches below the knoll on which stand its dark old houses, snugly grouped together, overtopped by a monastery, and a venerable castle, built for a Crusader lord on his return from Palestine. The paved terrace commands a fine vista of the lake, a very gentle view of water and cultivated slopes; the hills fall back here, while the Alps are behind the spectator. Rapperschwyl **Rathhaus** (Town-hall) deserves a visit, if only on account of its carved Gothic portal and sculptured wooden roof, not to mention a stove of colossal height, decorated with allegorical, scenic, and architectural bas-reliefs, executed in a manner that stamps them contemporary with *Holbein*, and not unworthy that master. The artistic beauty of its ancient stoves is a characteristic of Switzerland. They are generally made of porcelain tiles; this, and another preserved in the barracks at Zürich, are the only known specimens in iron.

Rapperschwyl has played a large part in Swiss history; its site made it important, and it has had to endure several sieges. It was here the conspirators met in 1350, before the massacre at Zürich; while as for Zürich, their feuds with that town appear to have been chronic.

Opposite Rapperschwyl, on a narrow tongue of land jutting far out into the lake, lies **Hurden.** **A wooden bridge** of the most primitive kind connects the two spots. While three-quarters of a mile in length, its breadth is restricted to twelve feet, and consists from end to end of loose planks, laid (*not nailed*) on wooden piers. It boasts no railing, so that in a strong gale it is difficult, sometimes impossible, to traverse; the meeting of two waggons is never without danger. Only invalids (but never very nervous ones) or very lazy people will care to drive across; it is quite sufficiently unpleasant to meet horses walking, lest they turn shy. Fortunately the traffic is not considerable. The bridge dates from 1358, and has always been repaired after the primitive style of its first construction. It is held to be an indubitable testimony for a man's sobriety if he can cross safely after a convivial evening. On the great pilgrimage days to Einsiedeln this bridge is one mass of pedestrians; and a strange sight they present, men, women, and children, all clad in their best, clasping a rosary, and muttering Aves and Litanies as they walk. On these festival days the stream has been known to extend in one unbroken line from Rapperschwyl to Einsiedeln itself.

This bridge ends the Lake of Zürich proper; the sheet of water beyond is called the **Ober See.** It is a shallower basin, dotted with some pretty villages, little visited except by fishermen, and in the winter, when it regularly freezes over, and becomes the skating rink of the whole neighbourhood. The larger lake rarely freezes entirely; it did so last in 1830, when practised skaters flew from Zürich to Rapperschwyl in less than two hours, a distance of twenty-four miles. At the end of the Ober See the Linth Canal flows into the Lake of Zürich (see below).

Resuming the journey to Coire, the r ilway passes along the edge of the lake as far as *Schmerikon*. From **Uznach** diligences run to Brunnen, Lachen, Einsiedeln, Schwyz. Numerous towns and villages noted for their manufacturing industry are passed.

Near *Schänis*, where the French and Austrians met in arms in 1799, the **Linth Canal** is approached. This canal owes its existence to a noble-hearted Swiss, Conrad Escher. Before its formation, the wide plain that extends from Rapperschwyl to Wallenstadt was a pestilential morass; the water meandered over the fields, carrying ague in its train; the track became depopulated year by year. To obviate this, Escher proposed to lead the water into a navigable canal, that should connect the lakes usefully. He gave a large sum of money towards the undertaking, demanding help in return from the Cantons. In 1822, thanks to his resistless energy, the canal was completed, the land redeemed, and rendered wholesome. Since that time, the Escher family are permitted to bear the name "Von der Linth," the nearest approach to a title possible in the Swiss Republic.

At **Wesen** passengers for Glarus (p. 52) change carriages. A fine excursion is made from Wesen to the Speer, 4600 feet above the lake, commanding a magnificent view. Wesen is situated at the western extremity of

THE LAKE OF WALLENSTADT,

next to Lucerne, probably the grandest lake in Switzerland; it is only twelve miles long, and three broad. The northern shore, with precipitous cliffs, crags, and precipices, is rugged and almost savage in its character, while on the southern shore the scenery is fertile and pretty. On the top of the northern precipices is the village of Amden, with 3000 inhabitants.

Leaving Wesen, the train passes along the southern side of the lake, through a series of tunnels, two of which are pierced with apertures on the side nearest the lake. The views on emerging from the tunnels are magnificent, especially after the first two—the Bayerbach Waterfall, the village of Amden, the Falls of the Serenbach. At **Mühlehorn** excursions may be made to Mollis, in the valley of Glarus, or boat journeys to the waterfalls, or to Wesen. At **Murg** the traveller may be tempted to lose a train, in order to enjoy the wonderful combination of mountain, lake, and valley, which here forms a grand and imposing spectacle. Near **Wallenstadt**, which is an uninteresting place in itself, a view may be obtained of the entire length of the lake.

Sargans (p. 31), the junction of the railway to Rorschach, Romanshorn, and Constance; the valley of the Rhine is reached, and from this point the route to Coire is the same as that described on pp. 31, 32.

FROM ZURICH TO EINSIEDELN, SCHWYZ, AND BRUNNEN.

From Zürich to Waedenschweil by boat or by rail (p. 45). Or to Richterswyl by the new railway recently opened from Zürich to Glarus. From thence by railway to Einsiedeln in 1 hour.

The carriage road winds uphill all the way. It leads for some time past rich meadow-lands bordered by fruit-trees, until ascending higher, the vegetation grows scantier; blue-eyed gentians and other mountain flowers peep out from the grass, while alongside the road rushes the Sihl, its cold grey colour betraying its recent glacier origin. The scenery loses its softer character, and grows Alpine and desolate; and by the time Biberbruck, the half-way station, is reached, the grand dark chains of the Glarner Alps, with their glacier-crowned summits, come full in view. The road still winds upwards, till the destination is reached.

Stretched before the wanderer's eye lies a wide green table-land enclosed by an amphitheatre of pine-clad hills, dotted with patches of snow; beyond which three isolated peaks, almost dolomitic in their quaint outline, uprear their majestic heads. In the midst is **Einsiedeln** (Hotel du Paon), a clump of barrack-like houses, of which there are over seven hundred, five hundred being inns. No wonder they thrive; even out of the pilgrimage season the place is full of devout worshippers, and at these periods people are glad to sleep under the shade of an awning in their carts and carriages. On a single elevation, so as to be in full view, stands the **Monastery-Church** of Einsiedeln, the *raison d'etre* of the place, so strangely placed in a wide, desolate, barren moorland, distant from civilization and communication. No doubt, it is to these causes it owes its continued popularity; and it depends on the idiosyncrasy of the casual visitor whether his first thought on arriving is, this is the home of the miraculous Madonna, or, this is the birth-place of Paracelsus. A keener air blows here than by the lake, that is very healthful for a late autumn linger or an early spring outing.

Einsiedeln's fame rests upon the miracles worked by its Black Madonna. The foundation of the monastery dates back to Charlemagne. Meinrad, a count of Hohenzollern, and also a Benedictine monk, feeling a great craving for solitude, retired to a spot near Biberbruck to pursue his devotions unmolested. Thither he brought his image of the Virgin, presented to him by the Abbess of Zürich, and here, by the help of another pious lady, he built a chapel to contain it. In vain did Meinrad try to live alone; people flocked from far and near to seek his advice. In despair, he retreated still farther into the wilds, pitching his tent in the present village of Einsiedeln, as the most inaccessible and unfrequented spot he could find. Food being scanty, two ravens daily supplied him with the necessaries of life; and so he lived for some time in lonely peace, till robbers, finally, foully attacked and murdered him, fancying he owned hidden treasures. The murder was discovered by means of the ravens, who followed the men to Zürich, shrieking around their heads, and, by their strange demeanour, attracting attention. A chapel was built over Meinrad's grave: pious men loved to dwell in its precincts; thus, by degrees, a stately monastery and church sprang into being. In the year 946 the whole stood ready for consecration; and the Bishop of Constance was invited to perform the act. Rising at midnight to say his orisons, he fancied he heard sweet sounds of music proceeding from the church, accompanied by all the offices customary at consecration. Next day, when about to begin the ceremony himself, a voice cried three times through the church, "Brother, desist, God himself has consecrated this building." This was on September 14th, and since that date the festival of the Angelic Consecration has been the grand ferial of Einsiedeln. A papal bull acknowledged the miracle, and promised special indulgences to pilgrims. Einsiedeln rose in importance, until it became the richest and most influential monastery in Switzerland; its abbots were held by the Habsburgs as peers of the realm, and to this day they are known in the Catholic cantons as Princes of Einsiedeln. Their arrogance grew so great that, even in the twelfth century, some of the neighbouring communities revolted against their pretensions. Arnold of Brescia, then preaching at Zürich against the abuses of the clergy, found willing listeners. But the priests, backed by royalty, obtained the upper hand, and the leaders of revolt had to sue for pardon on their knees. From 1515 to 1519 Zwingli was an inmate of Einsiedeln, and it was on the feast of the Angelic Consecration that he denounced the Romish errors with such vigour that all the monks left their cells, and the monastery stood empty for some time. The French revolutionists plundered the church, and thought to rob the sacred image, but that had been carried over into Tyrol for safety before their approach. The year after its return 260,000 pilgrims came to visit it. The church has many filials as well as landed possessions, vineyards, orchards, and farms, and the brothers have considerable property in America.

The present pile of buildings is the sixth or seventh erected since the foundation. Fire has been busy in its attempts at destruction, but it has always spared the sacred image. The present monastery flanks the church on either side, forming a square, around it, which contains all the conventual requisites. The **church** is in very bad taste, a roccoco aberration of the very worst type conceivable, gaudy with colour, overladen with gold, jewels, and marble; an eyesore to a cultivated eye, a very vision of paradise to the ignorant peasant. It is a large building, consisting of nave and aisles in which side-chapels are niched; each of these is sacred to a local saint, whose skeleton lies beneath the altar. Near the chief entrance is the **Madonna's Chapel**, a structure of black marble standing quite isolated in the nave, a church within a church. The priests performing the offices enter it by gilt doors, and are enclosed like sheep in a fold, while without kneel the worshippers. Waxen *ex votos*, arms, legs, cows, bulls, horses, dogs, etc., are hung on its railings; votive candles, varying from little tapers to sturdy candles, are affixed to its spikes, injuring the marble by their constant drippings.

It is not possible to see the Madonna closely, since none but priests may enter the railed enclosure of this chapel; but seen at a distance, the colour is a rich bronze, not black, and there is something quaint and benign about the figure that lends it a curious grace. Of course it, too, is overladen with jewels and fine clothing; but the faces of the Virgin and Child are far from unattractive, despite their gaudy envelopments.

Outside the church, a little below the broad flight of steps that leads to it, is erected a semicircle of booths, entirely devoted to the sale of rosaries, images, trinkets, devotional prints, and prayer-books. These rosaries are strung along the walls by the hundred, and one wonders how the dealers can sell enough to render the trade lucrative. Rosaries bought at Einsiedeln are, however, in great demand, and no pilgrim leaves without buying at least one for himself and every member of his family and friends as a memento. They are of every colour, shape, size, and variety, and a booth hung round with them from ceiling to floor presents quite a kaleidoscopic scene.

All Einsiedeln is devoted to the manufactory and sale of articles of this kind, and to the printing of devotional works.

A little below the booths stands a handsome **Marble Fountain**, shaped like an open-worked crown, which shelters a statue of the Virgin. The water trickles from fourteen spouts. Tradition says the Saviour drank from *one* on an occasion not further particularized, and left his blessing on the waters evermore. It is the custom for pilgrims to put their mouths to each of these openings, so as to be certain that their lips have touched the right one. It is a most strange spectacle to see them, men and women, going from one to the other spout, and drinking a little of the water from each.

From Einsiedeln a diligence runs twice daily **to Schwyz**, or the journey may be made on foot by the Hacken, a pass commanding fine views from the summit. On the diligence road the village of *Rothenthurm*—so named from a red tower of defence there standing—is passed. Between two and three miles from here, on the W., is the Lake of Egeri, and on the borders of the lake is **Morgarten**, where, in 1315, a fierce encounter took place between the Swiss and Austrians, under Duke Leopold. The Swiss only mustered 1300, while the Austrians had a force of 20,000. The battle did not last two hours, but the Austrians were cut to pieces.

"It was on a clear winter morning that Duke Leopold and his army rode through this mountain pass towards the lake. The sun glinted on the bright spears and helmets of the men, who rode along jauntily, apprehending no danger, when suddenly the rocks seemed to become alive and precipitate themselves down in massive blocks upon their heads; it literally rained stones and rude missiles. The Swiss had got wind of the Austrian intentions, and hearing the Duke's boast that he would 'tread these peasants under foot,' determined to be beforehand with him, and hiding themselves in their rocky fastnesses, thus surprised and utterly routed their enemies, for escape was impossible. Many gallant knights met their death in this ignominious manner, or were drowned in the lake into which their frightened horses dashed full speed. Thus was won the famous day of Morgarten, of great importance in Swiss annals, as from that time forward the power of the Austrian was broken. A chapel on the southern shore of the lake marks the burial place of the fallen, to whose memory an annual service is still held every 16th of November. The altar-piece is a picture of the battle."

Schwyz (Hotel Rössli), with a population of 6,000, is the capital of the canton. It is pleasantly situated at the foot of the two-horned Mythen. Switzerland takes its name from this little out-of-the-way town (p. 66).

Three miles from Schwyz is **Brunnen** (p. 66), on the Lake of Lucerne.

Diligence from Schwyz to Zürich, Lucerne, Arth, or the Muottathal.

FROM ZÜRICH TO GLARUS.

A new line of railway has been opened from Zürich to Glarus. It continues by the Lake of Zürich to Richterswyl (pp. 43—47). Then past stations *Pfaffikon, Lachen, Siebnen.* The Linth Canal (p. 46) is then approached. After station *Bilten*, the line turns abruptly southward, omitting Wesen, and joins the Wesen and Glarus line at Näfels (see below).

Glarus (see below).

FROM WESEN TO GLARUS.

The journey occupies only half-an-hour. The only Roman Catholic town in the Canton of Glarus is Näfels, which is passed in the railway. **Glarus**, the capital of the canton, is in the midst of innumerable manufactories, the canton being famous for its various industries. It is situated at the foot of the Glärnisch, Wiggis, and Schilt. In 1861 it was almost entirely destroyed by fire. A fine view of the town and neighbourhood is obtained from the Burghügel. Zwingli officiated at the church from 1506 to 1546. Curiously enough, this church is used by Roman Catholics and Protestants in common.

Glarus is celebrated for the number of pleasant places for excursions within an easy distance. Among them, 1. the **Baths of Stachelberg**, unrivalled for the beauty of their situation, and held in great repute for a strong sulphurous alkaline water which dribbles from a spring about two miles off. 2. The *Pragel Pass*, by the Muottathal to Schwyz. 3. To Linththal, where the scenery is magnificent, the valley being enclosed with snow mountains, the finest of which is the Tödi.

GLARUS TO DISSENTIS OR TRONS.

This route passes Mitlödi in a picturesque valley, and *Schwanden*, where the Sernf Thal and Linth Thal diverge.

Proceeding up the Linth Thal, Leukelbach, with its waterfall, Luchsingen, Häzingen, Diesbach (with fine waterfalls), are successively passed.

Near Rüti are the **Baths of Stachelberg**, with a powerful mineral spring, but of very limited supply. The views in the vicinity of the Selbsanft, Kammerstock, and other peaks, are very good. Excursions to the Tödi mountain can be arranged from here.

Linththal has numerous factories in the neighbourhood. Hence to Dissentis, in the Vorder Rhein Valley, is an arduous twelve hours' journey by the Sand Grat Pass (9138 feet). Magnificent views are obtained of the Piz Russein (11,887 feet), and other summits of the Tödi group. The path joins the high road near the wonderful bridge over the Russeiner Tobel from which either Dissentis or Trons is readily reached.

GLARUS TO ILANZ OR FLIMS, FOR COIRE.

Glarus to Elm by the Sernf Thal. (See p. 52.)

From Elm to Ilanz is by the Panixer Pass (7907 feet). A guide is necessary, and the expedition requires thirteen hours' fatiguing toil. By this route the Russians retreated in 1799.

From Elm to Flims is by the Segnes Pass (8612 feet), under the Tschingel Spitz (10,230 feet). The path crosses the glacier, and passes the Martinsloch, the hole through which the sun shines twice in the year. A guide is needed. This route is shorter but more difficult than the Panixer.

FROM ZURICH TO ROMANSHORN.

Time, 3 hours. Stations, *Oerlikon*, **Wallisellen**, where the line to Coire, diverges (p. 43), *Dietlikon*, *Effretikon*, *Kempthal*.

Winterthur. Junction with line to Schaffhausen, St. Gallen, and Rorschach. Population 7000. This town was once free, but gave up its freedom and became subject to Austria. For the last 400 years it has belonged to Zürich. Stations, *Wiesendangen*, *Islikon*. **Frauenfeld**, a large manufacturing town on the Murg. The capital of the Canton of Thurgau. Stations, *Felwen*, *Mülheim*, *Märstetten*, *Weinfelden*, *Bürglen*, *Sulgen*, *Erlen*, *Amriswyl*. **Romanshorn**, p. 30.

Romanshorn to Friedrichshafen (p. 29), to Schaffhausen and Basle (p. 21), to Rorschach and Coire (p. 30).

FROM ZÜRICH TO RORSCHACH (BY ST. GALLEN).

Zurich to Winterthur, (p. 53). Stations, *Räterschen*, *Elgg*, *Aadorf*, *Eschlikon*, *Sirnach*. **Wyl**, where a view of the Sentis is obtained. A long lattice bridge over the Thur, then *Schwarzenbach*, *Utzwyl*, **Flawyl**, a large manufacturing village. After crossing the river Glatt, stations, *Gossau*, *Winkeln*, and **Bruggen**, where there is a remarkable bridge over the valley of the Setter.

St. Gall (Hotel de St. Gall). This town, situated at a great height, is the capital of the Canton St. Gallen. It has considerable cotton manufactories, and is sometimes called the Manchester of Switzerland. The **Abbey**, founded by St. Gallus, an Irish monk, early in the 7th century, was at one time (8th century) the most celebrated seat of learning in Europe. The **church**, rebuilt 1760, possesses some very ancient relics. In the town are a Museum, Town Library, and Reading Room. The favourite excursion from St. Gall is to **Appenzell** and **Weissbad**, by way of Trogen and Gais by diligence. Whey cure establishments abound in all this neighbourhood. Innumerable excursions can be made from Weissbad, notably the **Wildkirchli**, a hermitage dedicated to St. Michael, where Mass is held on St. Michael's Day. Close by here is a stalactite cavern. The ascent of the Sentis, the highest mountain in Appenzell, can be made from Weissbad in about four hours.

From St. Gallen to Rorschach, a distance of 9 miles. Stations *St. Fiden*, *Mörschwyl*, are passed, frequent views of the Lake of Constance are obtained; and soon after the train has passed the stone bridge over the Goldach, a very fertile region is entered, and continues to **Rorschach** (p. 30).

ZÜRICH TO LUCERNE BY RAIL.

[For Zürich to Lucerne by way of Lake of Zürich, Horgen, and Zug, p. 57.]

By railway the journey occupies about two hours. Stations, *Altstetten* (views of the Uetilberg), *Urdorf*, *Birmensdorf*, *Bonstetten*, *Hedingen*, *Affoltern*, *Metmenstetten*, *Knonau*, *Zug*. **Zug**, population between 4000 and 4500, of whom only a few are Protestants. The town, which is the capital of Zug, the smallest canton of the Confederation, contains various objects of interest.

Among them, is the **Arsenal**, wherein is to be found the ancient standard, stained by the blood of its gallant but unfortunate bearer, Pierre Collin, who perished at the battle of Arbedo, in 1422, when 3000 Swiss valiantly, but fruitlessly, strove to maintain the field against 24,000 Milanese.

In the church of the Capuchins is an Entombment by *Fiamingo*. In St. Michael's church is a bone-house, where hundreds of skulls, labelled and inscribed with the name, age, and place of residence of the deceased, are piled up.

THE LAKE OF ZUG

is 9 miles long and 3 broad, and is 1370 feet above the level of the sea.

The lake is most beautiful, and possesses many points of interest. The adjacent country is highly picturesque; the richly wooded banks, with the distant hills, and to the south, the stately Rigi, forming a very picturesque background. Small steamers are continually plying in various directions across the lake, affording tourists every facility for visiting the more interesting portions of the surrounding shores. See local time tables.

A short distance from Zug, on the steamboat journey, Pilatus, the Ross-Stock, and the Frohnalp are seen. **Immensee** is a charming little place, and those who have left the railway and intend to ascend the Rigi on foot, had better do so from this place. **Arth**, at the Southern extremity of the lake, is between the Rigi and the Rossberg. Train or omnibus from here to Goldau, where, in 1806, a large portion of the Rossberg, penetrated by the heavy rains, was precipitated from a height of 3000 feet into the valley below, swallowing up four villages, with upwards of five hundred of their inhabitants, together with several visitors. The traces of the disaster are still to be seen at **Goldau** and **Lowerz.**

Railway from Arth to the summit of the Rigi (see p. 71).

A diligence runs twice a day from Arth to Brunnen, (p. 66).

Omnibus from Immensee to Küssnacht (p. 64).

Zug to Lucerne by rail. The bank of the Lake of Zug is skirted. Stations, *Cham* (look out for a charming view of Zug here), *Rothkreuz,* where the valley of the Reuss is entered, *Gisikon, Ebikon.* Then the line unites with the Swiss Central Railway, and Lucerne is reached.

Lucerne (p. 58).

ZÜRICH TO ZUG, BY THE ALBIS.

The Albis road skirts the west bank of the Lake of Zurich as far as to Wollishofen; then in a southerly direction to Adlischwyl, where a wooden bridge crosses the Sihl. The ascent then commences to **Ober Albis**, the highest part of the road. Near here is the **Hochwacht**, and the traveller is recommended to ascend to the pavilion on the summit, where a magnificent view is to be obtained. Then descend past the Türler See, a miniature lake, to Hausen, a pleasant village, with villas and a homœopathic establishment. Then continue to **Kappel**, a place memorable in the history of the Reformation. When the Roman Catholic Cantons of Lucerne, Zug, Schwyz, Uri, and Unterwalden had declared war against Zürich and Berne, their troops advanced to Kappel, where a battle was fought, October 11, 1531. And here Zwingli fell. "When the first ranks had fallen and the rest fled, Zwingli, with a halbert in his hand, which he stretched across their course, in vain attempted to restrain their flight, calling out to them 'not to fear, for that they were in a good cause; to commend themselves to God, and stand their ground.' He appears to have been first beaten to the ground by a stone, and afterwards, on rising, or attempting to rise, to have been repeatedly thrown down, and trodden upon by the crowd. At length he received a wound in the throat from a spear, which he supposed to be mortal; when, sinking down on his knees, he exclaimed, 'Is this to be esteemed a calamity? They can kill the body, but the soul they cannot touch.' When the soldiers came to strip the slain, he was found yet alive, lying on his back, with his hands clasped together, and his eyes lifted up to heaven. He was asked if he wished a confessor to be sent for; then if he would invoke the Virgin; and on his declining both, he was immediately despatched. When the body was discovered to be that of Zwingli, it was condemned by a military tribunal to be cut in quarters, and then burned to ashes; which barbarous but impotent sentence, with other indignities, was accordingly carried into execution."

The spot where the body of Zwingli was found is indicated by a metal plate in the rock, with a Latin and German inscription.

In the old Gothic Church at Kappel may be seen some good stained glass. Continuing from Kappel, the traveller will next reach Baar (p. 57), where the road from Horgen to Zug is joined.

Baar to Zug, two miles.

ZURICH TO THE RIGI AND LUCERNE, BY HORGEN AND THE LAKE OF ZUG.

There is not a pleasanter journey from Zürich to Lucerne than by this route, although it takes a much longer time than by rail.

The traveller will take steamboat from Zürich to Horgen (p. 44), and then proceed on foot, by carriage, or by omnibus to Zug. The road ascends as far as to Hirzel, and then descends to the valley of the Sihl. From the covered Sihl Bridge to Baar the views are very beautiful. **Baar** (p. 56) is celebrated for its charnel-house, where may be seen the skulls of many generations of the inhabitants piled up in a pyramid. Zug is a little more than two miles from Baar.

For the Rigi the traveller will proceed as far as to Arth (p. 55) by steamboat on the Lake of Zug, where he will disembark, and ascend the mountain either on foot or by rail (p. 71).

For Lucerne, take the steamboat to Immensee, where omnibus can be taken to Küssnacht (p. 64), and from Küssnacht by steamboat to Lucerne (p. 58).

For this trip, as it is most desirable to arrange it so that steamboats and omnibuses may be found in correspondence, the traveller is recommended to start from Zürich by the first boat in the morning, and consult local time-tables for the rest.

FROM BASLE TO LUCERNE.

From Basle to Olten (p. 34).

The short journey from Olten to Lucerne (thirty-three miles) is through delightful country; and as many travellers approach Switzerland by this route, it is a memorable one with them, as they get their first glimpses of the glories of the Bernese Oberland. Take a seat on the left of the carriage.

Aarburg is the first station after leaving Olten. The old castle (1660) was once the residence of the governors, then a State prison, and it is now a gaol and arsenal. Aarburg was destroyed by fire in 1840. **Zofingen,** celebrated, amongst other things, for two good ball-rooms, built on the branches of some old trees, close by the Schützenhaus, and for remains of a Roman bath, and other ancient relics. **Reiden;** the large house on the hill near the station was once a Lodge of the Knights of Malta. Stations, *Dagmersellan*, *Nebikon*, *Wauwyl* (here the first view of the Mönch, Eiger, Jungfrau, and other mountains, is obtained). **Sursee**, a pleasant old town, with some quaint architecture. The double eagle of the House of Habsburg is still upon its gates. A little beyond *Nottwyl* the Lake of Sempach is skirted. The lake is small—six and a half miles by two and a half, and not beautiful. The neighbourhood all around **Sempach** is, however, very interesting, on account of its being the scene of one of the most thrilling chapters in Swiss history. The Austrians for the third time invaded Switzerland. Only 1400 Swiss met their overwhelming army, under the command of Duke Leopold. The battle would have been fatal to the Swiss, but for the heroism of Arnold von Winkelried, who threw himself upon the Austrian spears.

> "Still on the serried files he pressed,
> He broke their ranks and died."

Inspired with a new courage, the Swiss, rushing over Winkelried's dead body, slew 2600 of the enemy, and signally defeated the Austrians. The battle took place July 9, 1386; four stone crosses mark the site of the engagement.

Between Sempach and *Rothenburg*, good views of the Rigi and Pilatus. *Emmenbrücke*, by the side of the Reuss (left), then through a tunnel, and Lucerne is reached.

LUCERNE (GERM., LUZERN).

[Hotel du Cygne (Swan), conducted by Mr. H. Haefeli. This Hotel is delightfully situated (reconstructed in Renaissance style in 1878) close to the steamboat stations on the lake, and commands magnificent views. Circular Tickets and Hotel Coupons of Messrs. Thos. Cook and Son may be obtained here.]

The **Railway Station** is on the left bank of the lake. The New Bridge crosses the Reuss between the station and the town.

The **Post Office** is also on the left bank, near the Church of the Jesuits. There is a branch office on the Schwanenplatz.

Steamboats (which touch at the Railway Station) run at intervals throughout the day to Flüelen and back (p. 65). See local time bills.

Rowing Boats (not recommended). See fixed tariff.

Diligence Office, at the Branch Post-office, Schwanenplatz.

Lucerne, one of the most populous towns in Switzerland (16,000 inhabitants) is situate on the western extremity of its lake, by the River Reuss. Its walls and watch-towers date from the 14th century, and in ancient days the town of Lucerne occupied a far more important position among Swiss towns than now. It has always been a residence of the Papal Nuncios, and at the present day nine-tenths of its inhabitants are Roman Catholics.

Lucerne contains numerous old buildings. Its lake is the finest in Switzerland, and in its immediate neighbourhood are two of the most celebrated Swiss mountains, Rigi and Pilatus—famous, not for their height, but because from them most can be seen.

As the traveller leaves the **Railway Station**, he will be charmed with his first view. In front is the lake, which, in other parts rugged and sublime, wears at this point a fair and smiling aspect. To the right is Pilatus; far away in the distance, seeming to rise from lake to sky, are the mountains of the Bernese Oberland; opposite is the Rigi, with the villages nestling at its feet; and to the left is the town, with its churches, its towers, its queer old streets, and its four bridges. Of these bridges, two are modern, but the other two number with the special sights of Lucerne. They are not thrown straight across the river, and are roofed over.

The oldest is the **Kappelbrücke** (Chapelbridge), dating from the beginning of the 14th century. It is decorated with 154 curious paintings, so suspended, that anyone crossing from the north side beholds in succession seventy-seven scenes from the lives of the joint patron saints of the town, SS. Maurice and Leger; but coming in the opposite direction, the pictures seen are commemorative of events in the history of the Swiss Confederation. This structure, however, is likely to be replaced by one that will be passable for vehicles; and then, at the behest of modern convenience, will a truly historical landmark disappear. Near the north end of the bridge is a **Chapel**, dedicated to St. Peter, and containing four good paintings by *Deschwanden*. Hard by stands the **Wasserthurm**, rising from the middle of the river. It is now used as a depository for the archives of the town. It was originally a Roman lighthouse (*Lucerna*), from which the town probably derived its name.

The other covered bridge, near the Basle Gate, is called the **Mühlenbrücke** (Mill-bridge). It was erected early in the

15th century. It is decorated with thirty-four "strange pictures, with strange inscriptions," representing "The Dance of Death." Our readers may remember the conversation between Prince Henry and Elsie in Longfellow's "Golden Legend"—

"The dance of Death.
All that go to and fro must look upon it,
Mindful of what they shall be; while beneath,
Among the wooden piles, the turbulent river
Rushes impetuous as the river of Life."

The **Stiftskirche**, or Hofkirche, dedicated to S. Leger, stands at the eastern end of the town. The body of the church is in the Italian 17th century style; the two slender towers are older, and date from the beginning of the 16th century. It has two side-altars, with carved wood reliefs, and finely-carved stalls and painted glass windows; also an excellent organ, upon which there are daily performances, for the benefit of those willing to invest one franc for the privilege of hearing it. The peal of bells is fine, and the ancient mode of ringing is still adhered to. On the largest bell is the inscription, "Vivos voco, mortuos plango, fulgura frango" ("I call the living, bewail the dead, disperse the storms"). Round three sides of the churchyard are arcades; the southern one affords beautiful views of the lake and the mountains. In these cloisters are some fine frescoes (two by *Deschwanden*), and numerous monuments in good preservation. The old tombstones are very curious; on some of them are carved the insignia of the guild or trade to which the deceased belonged in his lifetime; as, for instance, a hammer and tongs for a blacksmith, a fish for a fishmonger, etc.

The **Church of the Jesuits**, with its handsome interior, is a good example of the characteristic style of that order. Notice the altar-piece and relics in the second chapel on the right.

The **Schweizerhof Quai**, with its fine avenue of trees, which is the promenade of Lucerne, stands on ground reclaimed from the lake, over which there was at this part formerly a very long bridge, stretching as far as the Stiftskirche. On the parapet will be seen an **index** to the chain of the **Alps**. The view from hence comprises a fine semicircle of mountains, from the Rigi to Pilatus. The Rigi Kulm, the Rossberg, Vitznauer Stock, Ross Stock, Bürgenstock, Buochser Horn, the Titlis, Stanserhorn, etc., etc., will be readily distinguished by means of the indicator referred to.

In the **Town Hall** are some fine carvings, done in 1605,

by a native of Breslau. There is also an old fresco, representing the death of Gundolfingen, who led the men of Lucerne at the battle of Sempach.

The **Arsenal** (fee demanded) is full of objects of interest to the antiquary. The reputed sword of Tell is shown here; also a number of halberds, battle-axes, and suits of armour from native battle-fields, especially from that of Sempach. Two flags captured at sea in the memorable battle of Lepanto, when the maritime power of the Turks in Europe was finally broken. These were presented by a Knight of Malta, who was a native of Lucerne.

The famous **Lion of Lucerne**, near the Stiftskirche, is the greatest curiosity of the place. It is a large lion hewn out of the solid sandstone rock, in memory of the Swiss Guards who died in defending the royal family of France, in August and September, 1792. It is truly a magnificent work of art, "admirable in conception and execution, and touching forcibly both the imagination and the feelings." This colossal piece of sculpture, 28½ feet long and 18 feet high, represents a dying lion, with his side transfixed by a broken spear, and protecting the shield of the Bourbons even in the agonies of death. It is surrounded with ivy and other creeping plants, and from the rock beside it a mountain stream leaps down to a pool below in which the lion is reflected. This exquisite monument was originally suggested by General Pfyffer, one of the surviving Swiss. The model (still to be seen in a building hard by) was finished by Thorwaldsen, and from this design (with some slight alterations) the actual monument was sculptured by Ahorn, of Constance. Near the lion is a chapel where, on August 10th, a special solemn mass is celebrated in memory of the slain. The altar-cloth is the work of the Duchess d'Angoulême, daughter of Louis XVI., the last survivor of the terrible scene annually commemorated.

Close at hand is **Stauffer's Alpine Museum**, which is well worthy the attention of any tourist with a taste for natural history. There are numerous groups of Alpine animals and birds, and extensive collections of butterflies and botanical specimens. All the specimens in the Museum are the work of Stauffer, the proprietor, an intelligent man, who is always ready to give information as to the natural history of the Alps. Duplicates of his specimens are on sale. He is proposing to establish a collection of living specimens of Alpine birds and animals.

In the same immediate neighbourhood is the celebrated **Glacier Garden** (*Gletscher-garten*). Here, in the so-called "Giants' Pots," and other phenomena, the student of nature may see the still existent results of the mighty forces that were at work in that marvellous undated epoch, when enormous glaciers, to which any now known are mere bagatelles, covered the whole of Europe. Besides the sixteen excavations illustrative of glacial action, there are other attractions for visitors to this garden, especially a collection of objects found in the "lake dwellings" discovered at Baldegg, 12 miles from Lucerne, in 1871. These objects are of great interest; they consist of 66 instruments made of bone, 6 of wood, and 140 of stone; besides about 100 fragments of pottery, various specimens of fruit and leather, and a number of teeth, bones, antlers, and horns of animals. Amongst the bone implements we may specially note a drinking-vessel, very elegantly wrought; a spade of stag's horn; a stag's horn with two stone chisels; a weaving or knitting instrument; various pointed and cutting instruments; a knitting-needle made of a boar's tooth; a well-preserved bone knife in shape of a dagger. Amongst the wooden instruments, a little oval plate, with a small hole in each focal point, is the most noticeable. Amongst the stone implements are many hatchets—one made of flinty slate, very well wrought; another of greenstone, with an edge as sharp as a knife; also many chisels, hammers, knives, spear-heads, and grinding-stones. The pottery includes conical weights for fishing-nets, and fragments of various clay vessels, some prettily ornamented. On one is *the crust of something cooked, and partly burnt!* The vegetable collection consists of hazel-nuts, an acorn, some carbonized wheat, carbonized pieces of apple, etc. The animal specimens are two small pieces of untanned thick leather, and the teeth, horns, claws, bones, of the boar, stag, roebuck, bear, badger, beaver, ox, sheep, goat, horse, and dog.

It is not so much for any special attractions in the town itself, as for its beautiful **situation and surroundings**, that Lucerne is justly celebrated. From the windows of the Swan Hotel you may gaze upon the lovely lake, and count upwards of a score of mountain peaks in the encircling prospect; or you may stroll through groves of trees, and along pleasant promenades close at hand, and enjoy magnificent scenery with but little exertion. Short walks to the Drei Linden, Allenwinden, or Little Rigi, in the vicinity, will afford varied and more extensive prospects.

Of somewhat longer expeditions in the neighbourhood there are plenty for which visitors can arrange to walk or ride, as suits their strength or convenience. There is the fine view from the chapel in Herrgottswald (God's Wood), reached by following the carriage road for 4½ miles, and then tracking the forest paths for an hour, and finally by ascending a prodigious number of wooden steps. This jaunt may be extended to the beautiful valley known as the Eigenthal.

The pretty village of Adligenschwyl (4½ miles) is a favourite drive; the route can be varied, and pedestrians can take a pleasant footpath from the Küssnacht road.

Lovers of the rod and line will find good sport at Rothsee, 1½ mile along the Zürich road.

For the view from the Gütsch, at the back of the Hospital Church, in the Basle road, it is well worth taking the trouble of the ascent.

An interesting drive of about 10 miles is to take the Berne road for nearly 4 miles, then turning off by the Gorge of the Renkloch, at the foot of Pilatus, and returning by Kriens to Lucerne.

But these short trips are all on *terra firma*, whereas it is by crossing the bosom of the lovely lake that the places of chief interest are reached, and the fairest charms of the district disclosed.

THE LAKE OF LUCERNE.

There is not to be found in Europe a lake more complete and perfect in the grandeur of its mountain scenery, the quiet beauty of its banks, the poetry of its legendary associations, and the endless variety of its charms, than the Lake of Lucerne, otherwise known as the Vierwaldstätter See, or Lake of the Four Forest Cantons. It is between twenty-five and twenty-six miles long, and varies from one to four miles in breadth. In shape it is nearly cruciform. A thousand objects will interest the traveller on every hand. "So clear is the lake, that you can in some deep places see to the bottom; it does not look like water, but a sheet of blue glass spread over deep caverns; and the fish look as if they were floating in air, and the weeds like uncultivated gardens.........Enchantment gilds the scene; now a castle on a hill, now a shrine with a richly decorated image of the Virgin reared upon some isolated piece of rock; now an arm of the lake, disclosing a world of wonders that we never dreamt were there." These are some of the things for which the eyes must be kept open.

The **steamers** for the Lake Tour start from the station immediately facing the Swan Hotel. There are six or eight boats a day, some of which are express. Tickets are issued for the tour of the lake, in which case the journey may only be broken at Flüelen. It must be noted that different steamers stop at different places, and proper inquiries must therefore be made before embarking. Tourists who have not much time at their disposal will probably be content with the trip to Flüelen and back (which will give them a general survey of the lake), and *of course* an ascent of the Rigi (see p. 70).

Soon after leaving Lucerne by the steamer, a splendid view of the town and its environs is obtained. After passing the bold promontory of the Meggenhorn, and the little island of **Altstad**, the Bernese Alps lift their snowy summits into view. So far, the adjacent shores have been low hills, sprinkled with villas; we now see the two bays of Alpnach and Küssnacht stretching away to west and east respectively.

The former bay affords a picturesque trip to **Alpnach** (Hotel Pilatus) by steamer in 1¼ hour, or by rowing boat in 3 hours. The landing-places are **Hergiswyl** (for the ascent of Pilatus, p. 69); **Stanzstad**, with its bridge across the lake to Acheregg, its old fourteenth century tower by the waterside; and the majestic Titlis, rising to the height of 11,000 feet, in the background. The Castle of Rotzberg, on the east side of the lake, has its romantic legend, telling how, when Switzerland was expelling the Austrians in 1308, Jagelli, a young Swiss soldier, was admitted to the castle by Annelli, a damsel within it, and then managed to introduce a band of his companions, who speedily made themselves masters of the stronghold.

The next stopping-place is Rotzloch, and at the extremity of the lake is Alpnach-Gestad. Here was situated the noted "slide," an immense wooden trough down the slopes and across the ravines, down which timber hewn on Mount Pilatus rushed eight miles in six minutes, for transmission by the Reuss and Rhine to Holland. Napoleon I. was the chief customer for his dockyards, till his retirement to Elba. The church is built of wood that came down by this slide.

The western bay (that of Küssnacht) has on its northern bank the ruins of an Austrian fort, New Habsburg, destroyed in 1352 by the Swiss. The town of Küssnacht stands at the extremity of the bay.

A capital and very enjoyable excursion can be made by leaving the steamer at Küssnacht, and taking the omnibus to Immensee (p. 55), thence proceeding by steamer to Arth, and on by diligence to Schwyz and Brunnen (p. 66). From thence Lucerne is reached by steamer. The whole round would occupy between nine or ten hours, exclusive of stoppages.

We will now pursue the central route across the lake to Flüelen, first pausing to notice the two giant forms that tower so conspicuously on either hand—Pilate on the right, grim and formidable, frowning in rugged grandeur; the Rigi on the left, beautifully clothed with forest, and field, and orchard, smiling as if storm and tempest were things undreamt of.

Passing the promontory of Tanzenberg, and the ruined Castle of Hertenstein, we reach **Weggis**, the best landing-place for those who mean to walk up the Rigi. It is a tranquil little village, whose inhabitants subsist chiefly by selling fruit to the people of Lucerne; and if any traveller wishes to linger by the lake, free from anything like town distractions, he cannot do better than seek the calm stillness of Weggis. **Vitznau** is the next place reached, wearing more of an air of bustling importance as it is the terminus of the Rigi railway (p. 71). Behind the village is the high, precipitous Rothenfluh, containing the stalactite grotto, 400 yards long, known as the Waldisbalm, little visited, however, as it is difficult of access. At Vitznau it appears as if the end of the lake was reached; for a promontory from the Rigi on the left, and another from the Bürgenstock on the right, somewhat overlap each other. But between these two points, called the Nasen (Noses), the steamer pursues its course, and a new scene bursts upon us in the broad and beautiful gulf of Buochs, with the Stanzer Horn (6000 feet), and the Buochser Horn (5600 feet), watching over it. Near the foot of the latter mountain stands Buochs, sacked by the French in 1798. A little farther on, on the same shore is **Bekenried**, a picturesque little village, and a justly popular watering-place, with ample facilities for excursions to Stanz, Meiringen, Seelisberg, etc.

On the opposite side of the lake is the pretty little village of **Gersau**, well sheltered from wind and storm and with a climate so mild, that it affords a capital resting-place for invalids in the colder months of the year. Gersau has a notable history. In the year 1390 it bought its freedom from the Lords of Moos, and remained a well-administered, independent republic till its conquest by the French in 1798. It was annexed to the Canton of Schwyz in 1817. East of Gersau is the Kindlimord Chapel, which derives its name from the tragic act of a poor fiddler, who returning from a marriage festival, murdered his starving child, at the place indicated by the black cross on the rocks. Excursions may be made from Gersau to the Rigi-Scheideck and the Hochfluh.

Proceeding from Gersau, we see the Mythen, or Mitre Peaks (5900 feet), and at their base Schwyz, the capital of the Canton of the same name. From Treib, at which the steamer next calls, Seelisberg is visited, and also the picturesque and well-sheltered retreats for invalids near the chapel of Maria-Sonnenberg.

Opposite Treib is Brunnen (Hotel Adler), once a town of considerable commercial importance. There are some good hotels and pensions. The air is pure and cool, even in the summer months, and the surrounding scenery very fine On the Sust are two legendary paintings, one representing a contest for the baptism of the land between two of the old Swedish invaders, on which occasion, as the inscription testifies, "Swyter besiegt Swen und gründet Schwyz" (Swyter conquered Swen, and founded Schwyz); the other picture represents the three confederates of Grütli. It was at Brunnen that Aloys Reding roused his compatriots to resist the French in 1798.

From Brunnen a number of pleasant trips may be readily undertaken. To ascend the Stoss (4000 feet) will take two and a half hours; the Frohnalp will require two hours longer.

Schwyz can be reached in half an hour's drive. It is a town of nearly 6000 inhabitants, and of some historical importance. The Canton gave its name to Switzerland, as its sons were the most distinguished in the celebrated defeat of the Austrians at Morgarten in 1315. At Schwyz may be seen an historical model of the Muotta and the retreat of the Russians before the French in 1799, when, in a fearful struggle, lasting for eighteen days and nights, Suwarrow was beaten from point to point, losing 6000 men, and most of his horses and artillery, and only returning to Russia himself to die within sixteen days. Of other places easily reached from Brunnen, we may just mention the much-frequented Curhaus Axenstein, on the Brändli (three miles), to which an omnibus runs twice daily; Morschach; the Frohnalpstock; Lake of Lowerz; Fall of the Gestubtach; the Gross Mythen, etc.

Brunnen to Schwyz, Einsiedeln, and Zurich, p. 48.

Brunnen by Arth to Zug, p. 55.

On leaving Brunnen, we enter that portion of the lake of which the shores are sacred ground in the legendary lore of Switzerland. This is the Bay of Uri. The scenery is here much bolder than in other parts of the lake; in many places bare, perpendicular cliffs rising in romantic ruggedness. At the entrance to the bay, close to Treib, is the Mytenstein, with its inscription in huge gilt letters, executed in 1859. It commemorates the gratitude of Uri, Schwyz, and Unterwalden to the German poet Schiller, for the drama in which he has embodied the legend of Tell. At Grütli, which is simply a green plain, 650 feet above the water, with a few unpretending dwellings spread on its fertile surface, was held the meeting of the Swiss confederates (one of whom was the father-in-law of the celebrated William Tell), who determined to maintain their independence against the tyranny of Austria. It was on November 8, 1307, that Arnold of Unterwalden, Fürst of Uri, and Stauffacher of Schwyz, and thirty others, bound themselves together, "for the good of their brethren, and the evil of no man," and solemnly swore to drive out the Austrians, without taking revenge for their oppression. So well did they carry out their resolution, that, after a series of wars, lasting one hundred and fifty years, their descendants succeeded in establishing their independence, which they have ever since retained. At Grütli are still pointed out the three springs which are said to have made their miraculous appearance when the confederates joined hand in hand in solemn covenant.

> "For the father-soil which they trod,
> For freedom and hearth, they stood,
> While they vowed to the mightiest God
> To cast out the tyrant brood.
> Thus our hearts, with thy spirit still glowing,
> O Grutli, thy name shall retain,
> So long as our Rhine shall be flowing,
> So long as our Alps shall remain."

The Swiss Practical Guide states that "the owner of the Grütli was about to build an hotel there in 1858. The children of Switzerland undertook a subscription to prevent this desecration; they limited each offering to ten cents (one penny), and the result was double the amount required."

Tell's Platte is a small rocky shelf, on which it is said that the Swiss patriot leaped from the boat of Gessler. Above the ledge of rock is a little chapel called "Tell's Chapel," which was erected about thirty years after the death of Tell;

it contains some pictures and rough frescoes illustrating the hero's history. On the Friday after Ascension Day, this little chapel is the scene of a national demonstration, mass being performed, and a patriotic sermon delivered, in presence of large numbers of people assembled for the occasion from all parts of the Swiss Republic.

Above Tell's Chapel is the fine new **Axenstrasse**, with its tunnel a little further on through the cliffs of the Axenberg, from the openings in which exquisite panoramic views are obtained. This wonderful road, from Gersau and Brunnen to Flüelen, is a fine specimen of engineering. Till 1865 the east shore of the Bay of Uri was impassable, except by a very difficult mountain path, leading by Morschach and Sisikon.

The terminus of the lake journey is at **Fluelen** (Hotel Croix Blanche et Poste). At a distance of two miles (omnibus, half-franc) is **Altdorf**, at an elevation of 1500 ft. Here are a colossal plaster statue of Tell, and a fountain—the former marking the position of the father, and the latter that of the child, in the celebrated trial of skill directed by the tyrant Gessler. The tall tower is of earlier date, the frescoes having been added since. It will be remembered that, according to the legend (now generally received as mythic), Gessler had elevated his hat in the market-place, and ordered all passers-by to make obeisance. For refusing, Tell was ordered to show his famed skill in archery by shooting an apple off his son's head. He was successful, but Gessler saw a second arrow, which Tell had secreted. On being questioned, the bold archer said it was for Gessler's heart, had the child been harmed. Tell was then, for his audacity, taken prisoner, and hurried away in Gessler's boat towards his castle at Küssnacht. A tempest arose; none but Tell could steer; he seized the opportunity, sprang ashore at what is now known as Tell's Platte, intercepted Gessler at Küssnacht, and killed him. At Bürglen (one and a half miles from Altdorf), a chapel marking Tell's birthplace, and a bridge where Tell died in trying to save a drowning child, are shown.

Of late years the William Tell legends have been gradually passing from the domain of history into that of fiction. The first book which dared to broach so startling a heresy was publicly burnt at Altdorf by the hangman. But in spite of this spirited protest, the idea has gained ground. Contemporary chroniclers make no allusion to the alleged events of his career and not for a century or two do we find any trace of the tradi tions in their present form. The establishment of the chapels, and the widespread belief in the legends are almost the only arguments in their favour. Those most qualified to judge, whilst conceding that there probably was a William Tell amongst the confederates, assert that the events linked with his name by imaginative patriots rest upon no more solid basis of fact than do the stories of Sir Lancelot of the Lake, or the Lily Maid of Ashtolat, in the fascinating pages of the Laureate.

For route over the St. Gothard Pass, see p. 172.

PILATUS

may be ascended either from *Hergiswyl* (p. 64), or *Alpnach* (p. 64), to which places steamers ply three times daily, the journey to *Hergiswyl* occupying thirty-five minutes, and to *Alpnach* one hour and a quarter. On either side there is a good hotel—that of the Klimsenhorn on the *Hergiswyl* side and Bellevue on the *Alpnach* side. The route which gives the greatest variety of scenery is to ascend by way of *Hergiswyl* and descend to *Alpnach*. The ascent occupies three and the descent four hours. In ascending this mountain we shall be treading in the footsteps of royalty, inasmuch as Her Majesty Queen Victoria, with the Princess Louise and Prince Arthur, ascended it from *Alpnach*, on August 31, 1868.

It is one of the most interesting mountains in these parts; being easy of access from Lucerne, and not difficult of ascent, except just toward the summit. The name of the mountain has been the subject of much dispute, some alleging that it is merely a corruption of the Latin "*pileatus*," capped, in allusion to the clouds which generally surround its summit. It has been, and is to this day, the weather guide to all this part, and the popular saying runs thus:—

> "If Pilatus wears his cap, serene will be the day;
> If his collar he puts on, then mount the rugged way;
> But if his sword he wields, then stay at home, I say."

Others aver that the name is derived from Pontius Pilate, the governor of Judea, who, when he had committed the terrible sin which makes his name a reproach, filled with remorse, fled from Judea, and took refuge in the fastnesses of this melancholy mountain; there the wild crags and dark precipices were his lonely resorts; upon these gloomy scenes his mind dwelt for many years, until at last, unable to bear his remorse, and filled with despair, he committed suicide in a lake near the summit of the mountain. But his spirit continued to haunt the place, and when travellers have gone up those dismal heights, they have seen him come up from the waters, and slowly and solemnly go through the ceremony of washing his hands. Then the tempest howled, the lake heaved, dark clouds and heavy mists gathered round the mountain's head, and a storm or a hurricane always followed. And so, as the spirit showed such evident dislike to being disturbed, severe penalties were inflicted by the magistrates of Lucerne upon any one who might dare to visit the haunted place.

For an interesting account of the mountain and its traditions, see Sir W. Scott's "Anne of Geierstein."

The original name of the mountain was Fracmont, from *mons fractus*—broken mountain. Many other traditions appear to have sprung up as occasion required; such as its being the abode of other evil spirits—the Türst and the Bergmannlein; of dragons, of a colossal statue carved without hands in the black rock of a cavern, and so on. But these tales of horror and wonder have died out, and the tourist of weakest nerves need not fear an encounter with infernal spirits, as he wanders over the green pastures or the rugged wastes of the mountain, and beholds a glorious panorama, superior, say some, to that from the Rigi.

The path to the summit of the mountain leads from Hergiswyl past *Brunni*, the *Gschwänd Alp*, the *Frakmünd* Châlets, and other resting-places, to the Hotel *Klimsenhorn*, whence the journey must be made on foot. From the hotel the path leads to the *Krisiloch*, which is a hole cut upwards through the rock, where a ladder is placed for the convenience of travellers. On emerging from the funnel-shaped cutting, the whole of the Bernese Alps lie disclosed to view. From here to the Hotel Bellevue is the next stage, and hence to the Esel. The path then leads down to Alpnach.

It may be mentioned that carriages may be taken to Hergiswyl, at the east base of Pilatus; and the remainder of the journey performed, except the last steep ascent, by mule.

THE RIGI.

Rigi-Kulm—Hotel du Rigi-Kulm, Hotel Schreiber.
Rigi-Staffel—Hotel Rigi-Staffel.

Whether the ascent of Pilatus be made or not, the traveller *should not* omit to ascend the Rigi. It would be like going to

Rome and not seeing the Coliseum, or going to Naples and not seeing Pompeii.

It is so easy to ascend, that the poorest mountain climber need not fear his abilities; or if he does, there are half-a-dozen ways by which he may avoid the toil. It can be walked from Weggis in three hours and a half. There is now a railway from Vitznau (both Weggis and Vitznau are a short and pleasant steamboat journey from Lucerne), or from Arth (p. 55); or, if this is not desired, there are horses, or chaises (sedan chairs).

The Rigi Railway (3½ miles in length) first demands consideration, as it is one of the most novel features in mountain climbing. It was completed in July, 1873. After passing through a tunnel 230 feet long, it crosses a bridge 262 feet in length. On one side are fine views of the lake, on the other is a precipice a thousand feet in height. The stations are *Freiberger, Kaltbad, Staffelhöhe, Romiti, Staffel,* and *Rigi-Kulm.* The trains run in correspondence with the steamers from Lucerne; and as a limited number only can be taken, each passenger has a "numbered and reserved seat." The carriages are two stories high, carrying eighty persons each trip. The rate of travelling is slow, not exceeding three miles an hour, and it is well it is so, as the gradient "over about one-third of the line is one in four, *i.e.*, for every four feet of length, the line rises one foot." The tourist should notice the toothed wheel working between the rails by which the train ascends, the breaks by which each carriage can be held fast to the rack-rail, and the various other appliances for insuring safety. The engine "has little resemblance to an ordinary locomotive, the boiler being upright; and, with a view to give it a vertical position when on the steep gradient, it slopes considerably when standing at the station, which has a very odd appearance." No one should miss inspecting the railway, and making a journey, either ascending or descending by it. At Staffel there is a junction with a still newer railway, which starts from Arth, and passes through the village of Goldau, and then near the convent of Maria zum Schnee, to join the line from Vitznau.

But it is a delightful walk if time permits, and the points of interest to note on the way are worth seeing. Starting from Weggis by a path which it is impossible to mistake, we pass a spot where, in 1795, a thick bed of mud descended like a stream of lava, and swept away everything before it; but as it took fourteen days to slide down, the inhabitants were able to save themselves and much of their property. Then we reach a curious little chapel, the Heiligkreuz (Chapel of the Holy Cross), where the shepherds come to pray, and where travellers can obtain refreshments. Soon after we pass through the Hochstein, or Felsenthor, a natural archway of rocks fallen from the heights. Then on to

Kaltbad, where there is a very beneficial mineral spring, and a spacious hotel, etc. A festival is held here on Aug. 10.

From Kaltbad there is a railway to the Rigi Scheideck.

From Kaltbad to Staffel there are two paths. The less direct leads by the Schwesterborn (Fountain of the Sisters), so named from three maidens, said to have been protected by angels from Austrian license, "in the time of Tell." Thence proceed to the plateau known as the Känzli, and observe the charming view of Lucerne, etc., and then on to Staffel.

At **Staffel** all the different routes meet; and then the summit is soon reached. All along the way the views are interesting and beautiful. The ascent to this point can also be made from Küssnacht, past Tell's chapel (commemorating the death of Gessler), and the Seeboden Alp and Châlet.

On account of the great number of visitors to the Rigi Kulm, it is necessary for those wishing for accommodation for the night, to send a telegram to the proprietor, notifying their wish, or it may not infrequently happen that it will be impossible for them to remain at the Kulm.

If it is determined not to stay the night at the Rigi, there is ample time to get down the mountain in the twilight.

The **Rigi Kulm** is 5,905 feet high. It is the highest and most northerly point of the range, and is grass-grown to the top. The name is said by some to be derived from *Regina Montium*, the Queen of Mountains; and by others from *Mons Rigidus*, the firm or compact mountain, in opposition to *Mons Fractus* (Pilatus), the broken mountain. The **view** from the summit is absolutely indescribable. We will just enumerate the chief features.

Standing on the Belvedere at the hotel, we see on the left the Rossberg close at hand, sloping down towards the Lowerz See. Traces of the terrible fall in 1806 are plainly visible. Beyond this, in the background, is the Sentis, in the Canton of Appenzell. Almost due east rise the white summits of the Glärnischer Alps. Then, following the sky line, the Tödi group are conspicuous. Just facing us are the Windgelle and the Bristenstock. The Blackenstock and Urizothstock are nearly due south; and then the precipitous, rugged Titlis comes into view. The mountains of the Bernese Oberland stand next in order, presenting a magnificent appearance, with their mantles of eternal snow. The conspicuous summits of this group are the Finsteraarhorn, the Shreckhorn, the Wetterhorn, the Mönch, the Eiger, and the Jungfrau. The chain ends with the crags of Pilatus on the extreme right. We have mentioned the prominent objects bounding the scene. In this area are included a vast number of nearer and lower summits—as the Englestock, the Fluhbrig, the double-headed Mythen, with the town of Schwyz at its base. Then the mountains encircling the Muotta Thal, the Hohfluh, Scheideck, and Dossen, in the immediate foreground; the Axenberg, just beyond the Scheideck; with the Buochserhorn, Stanzerhorn, and Burgenstock, more to the right. Ten lakes can also be counted from the Lowerz See, under Rossberg, to the Bay of Alpnach, under Pilatus.

On the other side of the Rigi Kulm, the view comprises the whole of Lake Zug, the town of Lucerne, and most of the canton, with the rivers Emme and Reuss, the bay of Küssnacht, part of Lake Egeri (on the banks of which Morgarten was fought), part of the town of Zürich, Lake Sempach, the Jura mountains, and the Black Forest.

The Rigi is more than a thousand feet higher than Ben Nevis, but the ascent has become almost a matter of course with Swiss tourists. Many others deem the whole affair so hackneyed as to be beneath their notice. In fine weather the roads up and down are alive with visitors, and the various hotels thronged. The evening view is very fine, and by some preferred to that in the morning. It is, however, the **sunrise** that constitutes the great attraction of the Rigi. Half an hour before that time a horn is blown to arouse the visitors from their slumbers, and all turn out, in every variety of greatcoats, rugs, and wrappers, to witness the scene. Note that there is a penalty for using the hotel blankets. Soon the stars begin to fade; a streak of dawn gradually brightens to a golden line on the horizon's verge, the mountain peaks blush rosy red, the shadows melt away, and the varied charms of the landscape gradually reveal themselves, till the sun bursts forth in all his glory, and the full splendour of the vast panorama is displayed.

In certain atmospheric conditions, a phenomenon called the **spectre of the Rigi** is witnessed, which is also observable on other lofty mountains. The figures of persons standing on the Rigi are occasionally reflected, and surrounded by a prismatic halo, on a bank of mist rising from the valley below, without enveloping the mountain itself.

Besides the two hotels at the Rigi Kulm (summit), there are other hotels and numerous pensions on the lower slopes of the mountains, where, amidst delightful scenery, and amongst pleasant society, travellers from all parts of the world sojourn for longer or shorter periods; some to recruit exhausted nature with the now fashionable Swiss air-cure.

The neighbouring height of the Rigi Scheideck (5000 feet) is reached by railway from Kaltbad, or by a two hours' walk from Gersau.

LUCERNE TO BRIEG OR SIERRE (FOR GENEVA) BY THE FURCA PASS.

Lucerne to Flüelen by steamer (p. 64)
Flüelen to Hospenthal (St. Gothard route, p. 172).

There is a daily communication by diligence between Andermatt or Hospenthal and Brieg, along the new Furca road. The entire journey occupies about 12 hours; a stoppage for dinner being made at the Rhone Glacier Hotel.

Leaving the St. Gothard route at Hospenthal, we proceed by a level road along the Urseren Thal—a valley of rich pasture land, through which flows the Reuss—and arrive at **Realp.** This is a poor little village, celebrated for its pancakes, where Father Hugo, a Capuchin monk, entertains travellers.

From Realp, an ascent of about 9 miles, through somewhat monotonous scenery, treeless and barren, brings us to the summit of the Furca.

The **Furca,** or Fork, so named from its two peaks, between which the Pass lies, is 8150 feet above the sea, and the road descends on each side so abruptly, that no one can fail to be conscious of being on the summit of the Pass. It is a rare thing to find the Furca entirely free from snow.

There is a very good inn here, at which Queen Victoria stayed three days in August, 1868. The views are very fine; giant peaks are visible in abundance. The Furca-horn may be reached in an hour, and is worth visiting for the fine panorama. The higher Furcahorn (9,934 feet) will take 2½ hours, and a guide is advisable. The Galenstock (11,900 feet) is recommended to those accustomed to mountain expeditions. From the Furca (with a guide) a path may be taken across the Rhone Glacier to the Grimsel in about 4 hours.

The descent from the Furca is by a series of zigzags, very abrupt, and giving the unnecessarily nervous traveller the impression that he is going to the bottom with a bound. There are seven zigzags, which are marvels of engineering skill. This road, costing £20,000, only dates from 1867. The views obtained in the descent more than compensate for the poverty of those in the ascent. Nowhere can finer views be had of those grim giants of the Oberland, the Schreckhorn, and the Finsteraarhorn, or of the glorious Alpine chain from Monte Leone to the Weisshorn. Beside all this, the marvels of the

Rhone Glacier are seen; one of the finest sights in Switzerland. Every minute during the descent some fresh impression of the magnitude of its frozen billows and its yawning crevasses is obtained.

At the foot of the glacier the traveller will be struck with its wonderful appearance, which now assumes a fresh form. Above it stand the Gelmerhorn and the Galenstock, and from between them is the great sea of ice, "resembling a gigantic frozen waterfall," extending for 15 miles. This is the source of the river Rhone, which flows onward to the sea at Marseilles, 500 miles away. It has been said to issue "from the Gates of Eternal Night, at the foot of the Pillar of the Sun;" and really any poetry is excusable in sight of a scene of such unparalleled grandeur. The Hotel du Glacier du Rhone is a good place to dine. The Ice Cavern should be inspected before the journey is resumed.

The diligence takes about 5 hours to perform the journey from the Rhone Glacier to Brieg (31 miles). Walking will not be found worth while.

The road, after crossing the deep ravine along which the Rhone rushes, winds down to **Oberwald**, the highest village of the Upper Valais (4,316 feet), surrounded by far-reaching pastures.

The next town is **Obergestelen**, burnt down in September, 1868. It is an important depot for the exportation of cheese. In the graveyard will be seen the large grave of eighty-four victims of an avalanche in 1720.

Ulrichen, Münster, Reckingen, Niederwald, are successively passed, and numerous other places sighted in this populous district. Upper Valais is German in speech and manners, and was never conquered by the legions of Rome.

Soon after passing Niederwald, the route rapidly descends

to a lower level of the great Rhone valley, and arrives at Viesch.

Viesch is a flourishing little place, splendidly situated under the Viescher Hörner, whose highest peak (Grosse Wannehorn) rises to the altitude of over 12,000 feet. From Viesch a glorious excursion can be made to the **Eggischorn** (9649 feet). The ascent will require four and a half hours, the return about an hour less. A horse can be ridden nearly to the summit. At the height of 7153 feet is the Hotel Jungfrau. The student of botany will be delighted with the flora of the vicinity. At the hotel a guide should be hired, and then, proceeding to the termination of the bridle-path, an arduous climb over rocks and stones brings the traveller to the wooden cross marking the summit.

The view is superb. The most prominent object is the great **Aletsch Glacier**, nearly twenty miles in length, and varying in breadth from one to four miles. This glacier, the largest of the great ice-streams of Switzerland, has its source at the foot of the Jungfrau, Mönch, etc. Its course is direct and uniform for about a dozen miles, till the Eggischhorn turns it aside, when it becomes steeper and narrower, and it is seen disappearing, a few miles to the south-west, into the gorge of the Massa. The Viescher Glacier, which, compared with the broad, smooth expanse of the Aletsch, more nearly resembles a torrent of ice, is also in front. Just below him, the visitor sees the Märjelen See, a mountain lake, hemmed in on one side by the ice-cliffs of the Aletsch. From these ice-cliffs huge portions break off. The encircling panorama comprises a great number of mountain peaks. The Olmenhorn and Dreieckhorn are seen to the north-west, encircled by the two principal arms of the Aletsch Glacier; whilst beyond these rise the Aletschhorn (left), and the Jungfrau (right). More to the right are the Mönch, Eiger, and companion peaks. Due north rise the Viescherhörner, and then the Finsteraarhorn, Rothhorn, Oberaarhorn, Wasenhorn, and Galenstock, Mutthorn, etc., bring us to the east. Due east is the Blinnenhorn, and due south Monte Leone. Between these two latter, amongst others, we see the Ofenhorn, Mittelberg, Kelsenhorn, etc. Continuing the circle from Monte Leone, the Weissmies, Fletschhorn, Monte Rosa, Mischabelhörner, Matterhorn, Weisshorn, Mont Blanc, Sparenhorn, Sattelhorn, complete the panorama.

Numerous mountain and glacier expeditions may be made *from the* Eggischorn. A grand but easy mountain and glacier walk leads to the splendidly situated **Belle Alp** hotel, built on a cliff, around which curves the great Aletsch Glacier. The views are magnificent.

Resuming the route from Viesch, we pass on to **Lax**, still tracking the downward course of the Rhone along its romantic and rugged ravine. By devious windings we reach, at the *Bridge of Grengiols*, a lower level of the Rhone Valley. *Mörel* is next passed. Hard by notice the Hochfluhkirche, on a prominent rock; also the junction of the Massa, bringing the watery tribute of the Aletsch Glacier to swell the Rhone. No other Alpine glacier stream equals the Massa in magnitude.

Passing orchard-encircled **Naters**, with its two ruined Castles of Weingarten and Auf der Flüh, we next arrive at Brieg.

BRIEG, OR BRIGUE,

(Hotel de la Poste.)

is a small town at the junction of the Rhone and Saltine, and the terminus of the Simplon railway. Notice the Stockalper Chateau, with its tin-capped turrets. The Hotel Belle Alp (see above) can be reached by bridle-path in about five hours; the summit of the Sparrenhorn in less than three more. At Blatten, on the way to Belle Alp, a footpath leads to the source of the Massa, amongst the ice-grottoes of the Aletsch Glacier.

Brieg to Domo d'Ossola, by the Simplon Pass (see p. 171).

The next station is **Visp**, or **Vispach**, at the mouth of the Visper Thal, once containing so many noble families, that the lower of the two churches was appropriated solely to their use. The nobles have disappeared, and the town is peopled by poverty-stricken inhabitants, in continual danger of destruction from floods, which are only kept off by constantly renewed dykes. All the houses but seven were made uninhabitable by an earthquake in 1855. In 1868 a flood occasioned great destruction.

Visp to Zermatt (see p. 160).

From Visp the road conducts us to **Tourtemagne**, from whence a beautiful excursion can be made to the Tourtemagne Valley, with its waterfall, glacier, etc. The next station of any importance is **Susten**, on the left bank of the Rhone. **Leuk** is on the opposite side of the river, at the confluence of the Rhone and Dala.

To the Baths of Leuk and Gemmi Pass (see p. 97).

Between Susten and Sierre, Pfyn is passed, marking the boundary between the French and German-speaking districts. The route lies amongst pine-clad hills, once the resort of brigands, and then reaches **Sierre.**

Sierre, p. 170.

FROM LUCERNE TO BRIENZ AND MEIRINGEN

(Over the Brünig Pass).

Take the steamer to Alpnach (p. 64), from which place the diligence, or one of the (preferable) supplementary carriages, will convey the tourist to Brienz. Places must be booked at Lucerne, or on board the steamer. If the tourist cares to ride only to Lungern, and then walk the remaining distance, it is well worth the extra exertion.

The road from Alpnach leads along the bank of the river Aa, through park-like scenery, with a background of glorious mountains, to the Lake of Sarnen.

SARNEN

(Brünig Hotel and Hotel de l'Oberwald)

is the chief town of Obwalden, in the Canton of Unterwalden, and is the seat of government. 4000 inhabitants. There is a monastery, a nunnery, and a conspicuous church on a hill. The green hill called the Landenberg, with the Arsenal upon it, was once crowned by the castle of the cruel bailiff, Beringar, who put out the eyes of the aged father of Arnold von Melchthal, for resisting his tyranny. The castle was destroyed by the Swiss a few weeks after the Vow at Grütli. Since 1646, the terrace where the castle once stood has been the place of assembly, whereon the citizens of the canton have met for consultation, the choice of magistrates, etc. In the Rathhaus are portraits of the Obwalden magistrates for nearly five centuries, and also a painting representing the celebrated St. Nikolaus von der Flüe. The visitor to Sarnen will scarcely fail to notice the peculiar head-dress of the Unterwalden peasant women—the plaited hair, interlaced with white ribbon, and fastened up with a spoon-shaped buckle of silver. East of Sarnen lies the romantic mountain-girdled valley of the Melchthal, fifteen miles long. Here dwelt Arnold von Melchthal and his aged father (see above); and here also lived the venerated St. Nikolaus von der Flüe, who, with timely words of *peace*, prevented the break-up of the Swiss Confederacy in 1481.

At the Lake of Sarnen pedestrians will save a good step by taking a boat for a couple of francs to the other end, four and a half miles.

On the east of the lake stands Sachseln. In the church are the bones of St. Nikolaus (locally known as Bruder Klaus), with a jewelled cross under the ribs where the heart throbbed in life. Numerous relics and votive tablets are to be seen.

The next village is Giswyl, which in 1629 was partially destroyed by an inundation of the Lanibach. The ascent of the Kaiserstuhl now begins, and at Bürglen, at an altitude of 2283 feet, the Lake of Lungern is reached. This was once one of the loveliest spots in Switzerland; but the draining of half its waters into the Sarner See by a subterranean canal, in 1836, has much detracted from its beauty. Still, the surrounding scenery is very fine, and we must solace our regrets for the lake's departed charms by remembering that five hundred acres of good land have been redeemed and brought under cultivation. Passing along the steep cliffs east of the lake, we see the three peaks of the Wetterhorn to the south. The lake is two miles in length; and near its south end, as it were in a basin of the mountains, stands the wood-built village of Lungern, at the foot of the Brünig.

From Lungern (Hotels Lion d'Or, Brünig, and Oberwald), a well-constructed and costly zigzag road winds through the woods up to the summit of the Brünig Pass. The occasional views looking back through the trees are very fine. At the culminating point (3648 feet) the northern view shows the Valley of Sarnen and Lake of Lungern, and Pilatus in the background; a few steps in the opposite direction reveal the Eiger and Wetterhorn, and other snowy summits of the Bernese Alps, with the gorge of Grimsel on the left, and the Brienzer See on the right.

The descent of the Brünig is romantically interesting, affording fine and varied views of the surrounding Alpine scenery. Soon after passing the splendidly situated hotel, the road divides, that on the right leading past the Brienzwyler Bridge to the beautifully situated village of Brienz (p. 90), where admirers of wood-carving may see that pursuit most industriously and artistically carried on. The left hand road leads to Meiringen, under the wooded ridge surmounted by craggy peaks that bounds this portion of the Aare valley.

Meiringen (p. 80).

MEIRINGEN TO INTERLAKEN.

(By the Scheideck, Grindelwald, Wengern Alps, and Lauterbrunnen.)

The charming district now under notice is one of those portions of Switzerland in which the tourist who can rely on his own powers of locomotion may see the most and realize the greatest enjoyment. He may, however, if so inclined, hire a horse with advantage in some parts of the excursion.

Of course, the time occupied in this détour must entirely depend on the traveller's convenience. He may spend a week or more, and find many points of interest to visit beyond those alluded to in the following brief epitome. But at least two days should be devoted to the trip.

From Meiringen to Rosenlaui is a 3 hours' walk; from Rosenlaui to Scheideck, 2½ hours; from the Scheideck down to Grindelwald, 2 hours. Allowing 2 hours for stoppages at various points of interest, this will make a good day's work for most. On the following day, from Grindelwald to the Little Scheideck will take 3½ hours; thence to the Wengern Alp, half an hour; and to Lauterbrunnen, 2 hours more. Here a horse or a carriage can be hired to Interlaken: or, if the pedestrian be still fresh, he may walk on the remaining 7½ miles. In taking this beaten track no aid from guides is requisite.

The peasantry of this lovely district have become keenly alive to the desirability of preying on the traveller. No native of the Isle of Thanet itself could be more ready in inventing schemes for drawing coins from the traveller's pocket. At every echoing cliff, waterfall, or glacier, somebody is at hand to distract his attention with obtrusive services. Singing-girls, horn-blowers, and itinerant vendors of all sorts of trifles dog his footsteps everywhere. Let patience be cultivated, and a supply of centimes kept in the pocket, for chary distribution in unavoidable circumstances, remembering that the Government advice is to pay nothing, except for pre-engaged services. At any rate, care should be taken to avoid the lavish bestowal of largesse affected by some rich tourists, which has chiefly contributed to develop the system complained of, and sap the sturdy independence and native nobility of the Swiss peasant.

Meiringen (Hotel Sauvage) is a charming Alpine village of 2800 inhabitants, with fine views of snow-clad mountains belted with luxuriant woods, where they bound the long valley that runs eastward from the Lake of Brienz. Along the valley flows the river Aare; and at the village of Meiringen various important Alpine routes converge—viz., to Brienz (p. 79); to Grindelwald over the Scheideck; to Lucerne, by the Brünig (p. 78); to the Grimsel, past the Fall of the Handeck (p. 88); to Engelberg by the Joch Pass; and to Wasen by the Susten Pass (p. 97).

If the interest of the visitor is chiefly centred in art, architecture, or exhibitions, he will find little to please him in Meiringen. He may, if he has an hour or two to spare, look into the shops and buy some wood carvings, or sit on the balcony of the hotel and listen to the tinkle of distant cattle-bells, or the strange, weird cry of the peasants calling the cattle home, or stroll to one of the three brooks that leap down into the valley at the back of the village. The Falls of the Alpbach are best seen in the morning.

The inhabitants of Hasli-Thal—of which Meiringen is the capital—are an active, wiry race, descended from old Swedish conquerors of the soil. Their prowess at the wrestling-matches with the men of surrounding districts at the beginning of August is well established. The women are considered better-looking than is the case with their compatriots generally; and their personal appearance is well set off by the graceful local costume worn on holiday occasions. There is an English church in the village.

The **Falls of the Reichenbach** are only a short walk from Meiringen. The stream comes rushing and tumbling down 2000 feet to the valley below, leap after leap, the three lowest forming the celebrated Falls. Hoardings or huts have been erected, at which fees are demanded at the best points of view. The Lower Fall, behind the Reichenbach Hotel, is illuminated every evening in the season for the benefit of persons staying at that establishment.

From the Falls to Rosenlaui the path gradually rises along the side of the Reichenbach Valley, beloved of artists. During the journey the eye is charmed with ever-varying combinations of rock and grassy slope, woodland and waterfall, with the snowy peaks of the Wellhorn and Wetterhorn piercing the blue sky in front. The latter mountain, as seen from this valley, has been compared to a colossal snow model of the Great Pyramid of Egypt.

At the foot of the Wellhorn, and between it and the Engelhörner, is the **Rosenlaui Glacier**. The path to the foot of the glacier crosses a little bridge over the Weisbach. This is the stream flowing from the glacier to join with others in forming the Reichenbach. It rushes along a deep chasm in the slaty rocks, 200 feet below the bridge. The glacier is small and gradually decreasing, but it is exquisitely beautiful in colour, hemmed in by rocks not friable enough to furnish the usual dirty moraines, and is very easy of access. Any who shrink from more formidable glacier expeditions should at least see the Rosenlaui. The best point of view is from a rock that projects out into the glacier, about 30 minutes' walk from its foot.

The **Baths of Rosenlaui**, in great repute with invalids for the mineral waters, are charmingly situated amongst wood and mountain scenery. An upward walk of 2½ hours, partly through a dense pine wood, conducts to the highest point (6480 feet), where the narrow ridge of rock, about 3 miles in length, known as the **Great Sheideck**, is crossed. The view from this point comprises the lofty and barren crags of the Wetterhorn, the smiling valley of Grindelwald, bounded by the well-wooded Little Scheideck; the Schwarzwald Glacier, and several of the Bernese Oberland peaks. Here is an inn at which a horse can be hired to make the ascent of the Faulhorn in 4 or 5 hours (p. 83). If not inclined to do the Faulhorn, the visitor should walk as far on the road to it as the Grindelalp (where fine views of mountains and glaciers will reward the extra exertion), and then descend to Grindelwald by a path as short as the direct course from the Great Scheideck.

Grindelwald (Hotel de l'Aigle Noir) is a romantic village, inhabited chiefly by those whose vocation it is to tend the thousands of cattle in the adjacent pastures. It is situated in a valley some 12 miles by 4, at a height of 4000 feet above the sea level, and guarded by giant mountains, the Eiger (13,045 ft.), the Mettenberg (10,443 ft.), forming the base of the Schreckhorn, and the Wetterhorn (12,165 ft.). It is chiefly celebrated for its two glaciers, whose "stiffened billows" are far grander and wilder than the Rosenlaui.

These two glaciers descend one on each side the Mettenberg, and supply by their melting the muddy waters of the Black Lütschine. They are the lowest projecting portions of the vast icefield of the Bernese Alps. The **Lower Glacier** affords a capital opportunity of witnessing glacier scenery at a comparatively small expenditure of time and labour. It approaches the valley by a gorge between the Schlossberg (base of *Eiger*) and the Mettenberg. The ravine, it is said, was once extremely narrow, and was the only outlet for an immense mountain lake. This narrow opening was often blocked up, and devastating floods were the frequent result. To remedy this state of things, St. Martin came to the rescue. He pressed his back against the Mettenberg, and pushed the Eiger with his staff, and lo! at one effort the ravine reached its present width. The impression made by the giant's back (**Martinsdruck**), and the hole in the Eiger made by his staff (**Martinsloch**), are pointed out to this day. Through the Martinsloch the sun shines only on February 13th, casting a bright spot of light on the shadow of the mountain below.

In a walk of about three-quarters of an hour from Grindelwald the foot of the glacier can be reached, but little can be seen at this point beyond the moraines or accumulated heaps of rock and other *detritus* brought down by the glacial action. It is desirable to walk two hours further to the Bäregg chalet (5412 ft.), where are facilities for getting on to the glacier, and examining the beautiful forest of spires, called "ice needles," formed by the melting of the ice. If inclined for further exploration, the visitor may (with a guide) cross the **Eismeer** (sea of ice), from which the glacier descends, to Zäsenberg (6076 ft.), where the highest habitation of the Bernese Alps is found. It is a simple stone châlet amidst pastures for goats. The views from the Eismeer are indescribable. Ice and snow of vast extent and in stupendous masses, and a grand amphitheatre of mountain peaks, compose the scene. From the châlet to Grindelwald the descent may be accomplished in 3 hours.

The **Upper Glacier**, which is much smaller than the other, can be sufficiently seen in coming from the Scheideck to Grindelwald. The ice, especially as seen from the artificial cave cut in it, is much purer than that of the Lower Glacier, and the crevasses are more beautiful.

The adventurous traveller with plenty of time at his disposal will find Grindelwald a suitable head-quarters from which to indulge in mountain climbing. Many of the mountains named in the last few pages can be ascended, with proper precautions and good guides. And there are also some less lofty heights, which will amply repay the tourist for the slight detention necessary for their ascent; such, for instance, as the Faulhorn, which is easily accessible to those who have neither nerve nor opportunity for grander exploits.

The **Faulhorn** (8803 feet) can be ascended from Grindelwald in five hours, the return occupying considerably less time. Horses can be made use of for the entire route, or chairs and porters can be engaged at Grindelwald for those preferring that mode of conveyance. There is an inn on the summit, but previous notice should be sent if accommodation for the night is desired. The path leads up, by woods and meadows and châlets, to the hotel on the Ross Alp; then passing the waterfall of Mühlibach, and the châlets of the Bachalp, where cheeses weighing over 150 lbs. are manufactured, we reach the rock-encircled lake known as the Bachalpsee, around which frown the Röthihorn (9060 feet), Simelihorn (9040 feet), and the Ritzligrätli (8281 feet). Presently the path to or from the Great Scheideck is joined, and then the way winds on amongst the *débris* continually descending from the crumbling Röthihorn, till the cone of the Faulhorn is reached.

The view from the top is very fine. On one side we see the whole or parts of the Lakes of Brienz, Thun, Lucerne, Zug, Morat, and Neuchâtel, with their adjacent mountains. Turning southward, we see in the foreground the Wildgerst and Schwarzhorn, with the glacier between, the Röthihorn, the Simelihorn, and the Bussalp; whilst on or near the sky-line we behold the lofty peaks of the Bernese Alps, the most prominent (from east to west) being the Sustenhorn, Wellhorn, Wetterhorn (11,412 feet), Berglistock, Schreckhorn (12,570 feet), Finsteraarhorn (13,230 feet), Eiger, Mönch, Jungfrau, Breithorn, Blumlisalp, etc.

On returning from the summit, the traveller may from the Bachalp ascend the isolated **Röthihorn** (9052 feet), and get a better view than from the Faulhorn as far as the Grindelwald mountains are concerned.

From **Grindelwald to Interlaken** the easiest route is by the carriage road, along the valley of the Black Lütschine to Zweilutschinen, and so to Interlacken (12 miles). But good pedestrians will much prefer the route about to be described. It may be accomplished on horseback, if the rider be willing to dismount at one or two steep, rugged places.

Leaving Grindelwald, the traveller gradually ascends, crossing the rounded spurs at the base of the Eiger, and passing numerous cottages and châlets. Some fine views of the Grindelwald Valley are obtained by occasionally casting a backward glance in that direction. At a height of over 5000 feet above the sea-level, a whey-cure establishment is passed. At length vegetation becomes coarse and scanty, and frequent proofs of the prevalence of avalanches and landslips are witnessed. In about three and a half hours the pass of the

Little Scheideck (6768 feet) is reached. Here there is an inn, the Hotel Belle Vue. The view is superb at any time; and towards sunset, when the Mönch, the Jungfrau, the Eiger, and the Schreckhorn are tinted with a thousand hues, nothing can exceed the glories of the scene. The Oberland peaks are well seen to the south; northward lies the Grindelwald Valley, with its mountain boundaries.

From the Little Scheideck the traveller may, if so inclined, return to Grindelwald by the Lauberhorn (8120 feet), and Männlichen (7694 feet), both peaks of the ridge running northward from the Scheideck; or he may proceed to the Hotel Jungfrau, on the Wengern Alp, by the Lauberhorn, in about two hours. But the direct path descends in about thirty minutes to the sloping pasture known as the **Wengern Alp.** Far below lies the valley of Lauterbrunnen, with the Staubbach like a thread of silver winding from the upper to the lower fall. The Hotel de la Jungfrau is, towards noon, a resting-place for visitors from various directions, when quite an international gathering takes place during the season. Opposite the hotel are the Silberhorn (12,156 feet) on the right, and the Schneehorn (11,204 feet) on the left; and between them, upspringing from a world of glaciers, rises the colossal **Jungfrau** (13,671 feet), in robes of dazzling whiteness, but not revealing her loftiest peak from this point of view. The ascent of this mountain is not considered immensely difficult, but is very fatiguing, and requires good guides. Ladies have on several occasions visited the summit.

From the Wengern Alp the traveller will not only hear the **avalanches,** but also see them, as they break away from the glaciers on the brow of Jungfrau, dash into fragments, and plunge into the ravine called the Trümlethenthal. The sight at this distance is insignificant, but the sound is marvellous as echo after echo takes up the thunders with manifold reverberation. If the traveller wishes for a nearer view of these wonderful phenomena, he must go with a guide and a rope (only needed at one or two points of the journey) down into the Trümlethenthal, cross the branch of the Lütschine at the bottom, anb ascend to the side of a deep channel. Here, in complete security, he may watch the avalanches that have already descended *2000 feet* from the glaciers, dash down for another *thousand feet along* this channel, to reach the accumulation of snow and ice below. The expedition will occupy about three hours going and returning, exclusive of the time spent in watching the avalanches. Particulars as to how best to accomplish the journey should be ascertained at the hotel.

A descending walk of about three hours' length brings the traveller from the Wengern Alp to **Lauterbrunnen.** The course lies at first over grassy slopes, thickly populated by small cattle with their tinkling bells. The immediate descent into Lauterbrunnen valley is by a steep zigzag path down the cliffs. The views *en route* are very beautiful and varied.

LAUTERBRUNNEN

(Hotel du Capricorne)

is a village of châlets, where 1400 inhabitants are so secluded amidst rocks and mountains, that although dwelling nearly 2500 feet above the sea level, the sun cannot visit them till seven a.m. in summer, nor till noon in winter. Lauterbrunnen signifies "nothing but springs;" some twenty or thirty streamlets come down from the surrounding cliffs and mountains.

Of these the finest is the world-renowned **Staubbach.** It is quite possible that the visitor may consider this fall has been over-praised. Its beauty depends, however, very much on the amount of water falling. It is often very small; and as it leaps down over 900 feet—thus taking rank as the highest European waterfall—the water is dissipated into spray before reaching the bottom. Hence the name Staubbach—"Dust-stream." It has been compared to an undulating lace veil, to a bird of Paradise, to the descent of a shower of rockets, etc., etc. Byron compares it to the tail of

> "The giant steed to be bestrode by Death,
> As told in the Apoca'ypse;"

Wordsworth calls it a "sky-born waterfall;" Goethe and several other poets have also sung its praises.

There are no lack of walks and excursions for the tourist who can afford time to linger at Lauterbrunnen. It is a pleasant evening walk to the **Falls of the Trumlenbach,** where the glacier-fed torrent from the foot of the Jungfrau leaps down. *To view the grand,* wild scenery round **Mürren,** half a day *must be allowed.* The road lies through the forest above the *Staubbach Falls,* and the mountain panorama seen on emerging from the forest is beyond description. Mürren itself is gloriously situated, and the view of glaciers, and rocks, and ravines, untrodden save by the daring chamois hunter, is magnificent. From Mürren the Schilthorn (9000 feet) is ascended. The view of mountain-tops from its summit is unrivalled, including the Juras, the Niesen, the peaks of the Bernese Oberland, the Titlis, the Rigi, and many others.

The exploration of the Upper Valley of Lauterbrunnen is well worth the trouble. To *Stechelberg* and Trachsellauinen requires no guide, and can be managed with horses. Beyond that to the Falls of the Schmadribach the path is obscure. The falls are 200 feet in height, and the arch of vapour formed by them is very remarkable.

From Lauterbrunnen to Interlaken is seven and a half miles. The road leads along the valley, whose rocky walls rise to the height of 1000 feet, and past the lowering rock called the Hunnenflüh to *Zweilütschinen.* This town is situated near the junction of the Black Lütschine from Grindelwald with the White Lütschine from Lauterbrunnen. A little further on, the road enters a narrow ravine, with the precipices of the Rothenfluh rising on the left. The *Bösenstein,* with its inscription marking the spot where a fratricide was committed by a local baron, was removed in blasting the rocks to improve the road; but the gloomy spot is still pointed out. Passing on by gôitre-haunted *Mühlinen, Wilderswyl,* and *Matten,* we soon arrive at Interlaken. Between Wilderswyl and Matten we pass the ruins of the Castle of Unspunnen, said to have been in Byron's thoughts as the stronghold of Manfred—the wondrous tale, of which the scenery is mostly laid in the Wengern Alp and neighbourhood.

Interlaken, p. 92.

MEIRINGEN TO THE RHONE GLACIER, BY THE GRIMSEL.

(For the St. Gothard Route, or for the Rhone Valley.)

This cross route takes about eleven hours. From Meiringen to the Handeck Falls, and to return by the same route, takes about as long. A carriage road has been formed a little beyond Imhof, after which there is a bridle path only.

Leaving Meiringen, the Aare is soon crossed (a process which is repeated *many times* during the route), and the summit of the ridge of *limestone,* strewn with granite blocks, known as the Kirchet, or Kirchen, is reached. This ridge, 2782 feet in height, forms the division between the Upper and Lower Haslithal. From the summit there is a lovely view down into the verdant valley of Imgrund.

By paying a small fee at the Inn, a short detour can be made through a woodland path to the **Finsteraar Schlucht.** This is a romantic ravine, cut clean through the Kirchet ridge by the Aare, which foams along three hundred feet below.

As the road winds down the side of the Kirchet, the pedestrian will easily see how to make several short cuts. The first village of any importance in the valley is **Imhof**, near to which diverge the rou'es leading to the Susten and Joch passes respectively. From Imhof a fine excursion may be made to the magnificent **Urbachthal**, with the immense Gauli Glacier at the head of it. The experienced mountaineer may visit many glaciers, etc., from this locality.

Passing on from Imhof, the road leads through a romantic defile, over which towers the Mährenhorn (9593 feet). Refreshments can be obtained at various châlets. After crossing the Aare a time or two, and also various mountain torrents, **Guttanen** is reached. This wretched-looking place, the highest village of the Haslithal, has been four times destroyed in the present century—twice by fire, and twice by flood.

From Guttanen the visitor passes through fine rock and forest scenery, crossing the Aare at the Tschingelbrücke. Here and there the ravages of avalanche and wintry torrent are evident. On the right, the foot of the Weiss Glacier is seen, and mountain-tops patched with snow come into view. After crossing the Aare by the Schwarzbrunnenbrücke, and passing a small cascade, the end of the valley is reached, formed by a rocky height, surmounted by a grove of pines. Up this ridge the path leads amongst rocks where former glacial action is plainly visible.

At **Handeck** are the celebrated **Falls**, where the Aare leaps down 250 feet at a bound. The falls should be viewed from below, and again from the bridge above. Half way down, the river **Erlenbach**, entering at right angles, joins its falling waters with those of the Aare, and the mingling cascades descend into a basin, over which rainbows are seen in the spray between ten and one. This is the third largest, and by many considered the finest, waterfall in Switzerland.

Up to this point rich forest scenery has softened the boldness of the landscape, but now a wild and barren region of desolation is gradually entered. The pine disappears; bushes, moss, and grass form the vegetation, and that not in abundance. **Hahle Platte** is crossed, being the polished granite bed of an ancient glacier. Agassiz studied glacial action here as elsewhere, and has left his name carved on the rock. Opposite, the picturesque waterfall of the Gelmerbach descends from the Gelmer See.

Again the valley narrows, and the savage wildness of the scene increases in intensity. The Aare is crossed again and again; and the Räterisboden, where is the only châlet between Handeck and Grimsel, is soon reached. This hollow basin was given by the French to the innkeeper of Guttanen, who aided them in their attack on the Austrians at the Grimsel in 1799. But the Swiss Government speedily revoked the grant. Between the rocky walls of a mountain glen the traveller still mounts, and, after a time, arrives at the Grimsel Hospice.

The **Grimsel Hospice**, formerly a monastic refuge, and now an inn, was destroyed by an avalanche in 1838, and burnt down in 1852. At the present building, of massive stone, 6148 feet above the sea-level, fifty beds are made up in the season, and a couple of hundred persons are often entertained at the seven p.m. table d'hôte. The hospice stands in the basin called the Grimselgrund. Around are rocks and snow, and a black lake destitute of fish. Beyond the lake is the scanty pasturage of the cows of the establishment.

From this point an easy ascent of the Sidelhorn may be made; the panorama of the Grimsel is very fine. From the rocky height near the hospice, called the Nollen, the **Finsteraarhorn** is visible. This mountain presents a capital expedition for experienced mountaineers with able guides; and, indeed, for travellers of this class, many fine ascents may be arranged from the Grimsel. The **Finsteraar** and **Lauteraar Glaciers** can be visited with comparative ease. The former is twenty-one miles in length, the latter eighteen. On these glaciers Agassiz and others have performed a series of experiments on glacial action. It has been proved that this glacier moves at the rate of eight inches a day, or eighty-five yards a year.

A steep path, which takes about an hour to traverse, leads from the Hospice to the summit of the pass (7103 feet) called **Hauseck.** Here, in 1799, French and Austrians closed in deadly struggle, and the dead were interred in the adjacent lake, henceforward known as the Todtensee. The bare, granite surroundings of *this lake* are sombre enough, but the distant view *of the Weisshorn* and Mischabel is more lovely.

From Hauseck the descent can be made by one path to Obergestelen (p. 75), for the Rhone Valley.

The other path leads by the flowery Maienwand, with splendid views of the Rhone Glacier, Furca, Galenstock, etc., down to the Rhone Glacier Hotel, where there is a table d'hôte at one, after which a diligence runs to Brieg, in the Rhone Valley (see p. 77).

Rhone Glacier to Hospenthal and St. Gothard route (see p. 74).

BRIENZ TO BERNE.

(At Brienz, Hotel de la Croix Blanche. At Giessbach, Hotel Giessbach.)

There is not much in Brienz to detain the visitor. It is a picturesque village of wooden houses, nestling at the foot of the Brienzer Grat; the inhabitants are chiefly occupied in wood-carving, and carry on a considerable trade; and in the Repository a good collection of articles may be seen, and, if so minded, purchases can be made. From the **Churchyard** excellent views may be obtained of the lake and surrounding mountains.

The **Lake of Brienz** is celebrated for the magnificence of its mountain scenery. Except towards the south-west, it is entirely surrounded by high mountains; the Faulhorn, on the south side of the lake, forms a splendid object in the panorama. The lake is 8 miles long, and 2 broad in its widest part. Near the mouth of the Giessbach the depth is 500 feet, but it varies in other parts considerably. It is 10 feet higher than the Lake of Thun, and 850 feet above the level of the sea; it abounds in fish, and the "Brienz-ling," which is salted for the supply of the neighbouring districts, is found in abundance, and is a good fish.

Steamers ply upon the lake between Brienz and Interlaken; and in the season there are special night boats for the illumination of the Falls of the Giessbach (see p. 91).

The journey from Brienz to Interlaken occupies about an hour; from Brienz to Giessbach, about 10 minutes.

Rowing-boats on the lake may be obtained at Brienz or Interlaken. A bargain should always be made with the rowers.

Leaving Brienz by steamer, the lake is crossed, and Giess-*bach is reached.* It must be borne in mind, that from the lake *the Falls* cannot be seen, or the beauty of the scenery surrounding them. Continuing towards Interlaken, there are seen on the right hand (north bank) the villages of Oberried and Neiderried, backed by the Augstmatthorn. Further on, the ruined Castle of Ringgenberg; and further still, the town of Goldswyl. On the left hand (south bank), the charming little village of Iseltwald. Approaching Interlaken the lake narrows; the village of Bönigen is reached; the Aare, as the water is called which connects the Lake of Brienz with that of Thun is entered; and the steamer sets down its passengers at *Bönigen* pier, where a railway takes them in a few minutes to Interlaken (p. 92).

THE FALLS OF THE GIESSBACH.

(Hotel Giessbach. Telegraph for rooms.)

A railway (Drahtseilbahn) will be opened in 1879 from the shore to the Hotel.

The Falls are brilliantly illuminated with Bengal lights every evening, from the middle of June till the end of September—before that time, on Mondays and Saturdays only. Fee, 1½ franc.

In the following account by an American of a visit to the Falls the traveller will find all the information he will need:—

"As the twilight began to gather we landed at Giessbach, and wended our way up a steep declivity to the very fine hotel. After engaging rooms for the night, and partaking of a good supper, we were prepared to see Giessbach Falls illuminated. The hotel is situated on a high bluff of land, which juts out into the lake, and from this eminence you have a fine view of the lakes and mountains, looking towards Interlaken—which place is seen quite distinctly—with a portion of Lake Thun.

"The great attractions, however, at Giessbach, are the cascades, which extend 1300 feet from the mountain top into the lake below. These waterfalls are supplied by two lakes in the mountains, named Hagel and Hexen.

"Issuing from the hotel into the well-lighted, gravelled walks, fringed with flowers and shrubbery, we arrived at an eminence directly opposite the Falls, where seats are provided for the spectators. At a given signal the lights of the garden are all put out, leaving us in almost total darkness, made doubly dark by the shadow of the mountain facing us. Anon, a rocket was sent into the air; then, darker still and murky the interval. Then another rocket whizzed close by us; again, deeper darkness and deeper mystery, by contrast: when—presto! *change!!—each fall,* to the number of twelve, became silvered with intense light!—silvered for a distance of 800 feet up the mountain side.

"The mountain firs and other foliage, lit up with the sudden glare, were wonderfully verdant; with an immediate gloss on it that seemed fairy-like, and with a filmy sheen playing around the outer edges. At the bottom of each fall the foam seemed frosted into so much virgin silver, and bubbled away to sparkle again below; while the water-spray, like silver dust receiving light from the moon's rays, floated away into the deep, mountain shadows. Up, up, up the gorge of the cascades we gaze with much delight, viewing the sparkling little rustic bridges which span with their quaint forms the glistening chasms, at given spaces, to the top. Down came the water in frolicsome curves and splashes, seemingly much pleased with its beautiful glow.

"Lo, and behold again! are we in Fairyland? One of the longest falls turns, or faints, into a liquid purple; another, into a lovely sea-green; and, at the base, the largest fall of all, has dissolved into a stream of liquid ruby, molten and spreading, tinting with a roseate hue the dark stones, and starting by the sight the most prosaic into wonder and delight. Verily, one would think that I had exerted an over-vivid imagination in trying to describe this beautiful exhibition; but, the truth is, our language cannot depict the gorgeous effect of an intense effulgence of light over a large body of water—especially if that water is dancing, foaming, and meandering over a mountain side 800 feet high, garnished with a dense, varied foliage, hid in the gloom, then breaking into blaze, gilding or silvering every web-like twig, illumining every lichen-covered rock, piercing with light every nestling nook of the deep shade, exposing the tangled network of vine and tree-branch, and rousing beetle and bird. We saw the same Falls on the next morning looking innocent of the last night's varied glow—as lovely and limpid in the natural light of a fine day as would satisfy the most veracious poet or painter seeking for the truly picturesque. So beautiful seemed the scene after the night's theatric debauch, so tender seemed the daylight, that the tampering with Nature's slumber appeared, after all, but profanation."—W. J.

INTERLAKEN.

(*Hotel* Victoria and Hotel Ritchard. These hotels command fine *views of the* Jungfrau and other Alps of the Bernese Oberland.)

The lakes of Brienz and Thun are but a short distance

apart, and, as its name implies, Interlaken lies between them. It is thought that formerly the two lakes were joined together, until separated by deposits brought down by streams flowing into them.

Interlaken has been described as the Leamington, or Cheltenham, or Harrogate of Switzerland. It was once a truly Swiss town; it is gradually becoming a little Paris or Brussels. Fashion and gaiety find their homes here, and the pleasure-seeker will vote the town to be one of the most charming in Switzerland. Many of the houses are built in the most perfect and accomplished Swiss style. Interlaken consists of a principal one-sided street, beside which are the hotels, pensions, and boarding-houses. With the exception of the hotels, nearly all the houses are of wood, with overhanging eaves, galleries, shingle-roofs, and ornamented with quaint carvings and inscriptions. Some of these houses bear date 250 years ago, and yet look as sound as ever, though they are never painted.

From the door of the hotel, in the quiet of the eventide, may often be heard the peculiar sound produced by an avalanche from one of the neighbouring mountains. For in the vicinity of Interlaken there are "giant mountains, massive glaciers, rushing cataracts, picturesque villages, green oases, and the ever changeful combinations of Alpine nature in her most lavish mood."

At Interlaken there are many temptations to spend money in articles of Swiss manufacture, from the most minute figure in wood, or the horns of the chamois, to good-sized drawing-room tables, and other large articles of household furniture. The whey-cure is one of the institutions of Interlaken.

The principal avenue of communication in Interlaken is the **Höheweg**, one of the finest promenades in Switzerland, with splendid views of the Jungfrau. Here stands the **Cursaal**, with its Reading Room, Restaurant, Billiard Room, and its constantly recurring Balls, Concerts, and other amusements. At a short distance is the **Monastery**, an ancient pile surrounded by beautiful walnut trees. In the more modern part, called the Schloss, dating from 1750, the Government offices are located. The best view of the town is from the Hohbühl across the bridge.

Opinions differ as to the enjoyment of a lengthened stay in Interlaken. While one traveller of a merry, social, fashion-loving turn of mind will revel in its promenades, billiard-rooms, and *concert-halls*, and such like, the thoughtful, meditative man will turn aside, glad to find a more secluded spot elsewhere. It is undoubtedly a capital place as a centre for excursions; and the tourist may branch off here to visit the Wengern Alps, Grindelwald, and other places of the Bernese Oberland, described fully at p. 80.

Whether the whole of this détour be undertaken or not, no one should miss the delightful drive from Interlaken to Lauterbrunnen, and the Falls of the Staubbach. It is a charming valley, and a description of it will be found on p. 86.

Excursions may also be accomplished in a day, or less, to (1) Kleine Rugen, and Heimweh Fluh, returning by the Unspunnen; Hohbühl, Vogtsruhe, Untere Bleicki, Goldei, Lustbühl, Zwerglöcher, Eck, etc. (2) The Thurmberg and small lake of Golzwyl. (3) To the Beatenhöhle.

Longer excursions. (1) Schynige Platte, 6180 feet high, with a fine view of the Snow Mountains. (2) To Lauterbrunnen, Staubbach Falls, thence by mule up to Mürren, and back to Interlaken; or over the Wengern Alp from Lauterbrunnen to Grindelwald, and back to Interlaken. (3) To Grindelwald, thence over the great Scheideck to the Baths of Rosenlaui and Rosenlaui Glacier, thence to Interlaken by Brienz and the Giessbach Falls.

LAKE OF THUN.

From Interlaken by railway to Därligen, and then by steamboat, on the Lake of Thun, to Thun (the former station of the steamers of this lake was Neuhaus, a walk or omnibus drive of two miles through a long grove of poplars).

On both sides of the lake is a constant succession of rustic villages, and dotted here and there, on the hill sides, are châlets, villas, and gardens, backed by the snowy giants of the Oberland. On the southern shore are two isolated mountains named the Niesen (7,700 feet), and the Stockhorn (7,200 feet), "striking," says Dr. Forbes, "from their sharp and peculiar outline; the former rising up like a vast symmetrical broad-based pyramid, the other shooting out diagonally into the western sky its huge terminal horn." At a greater distance, the loftier Jungfrau, Mönch and Eiger tower on high.

The lake is ten miles and a half long, and two miles broad, and is nearly 1800 feet above the sea level. As we steam on, we notice on the right a perpendicular cliff, forming the base of the Beatenberg. Here is the cavern of St. Beatus, who, says tradition, was the first to introduce Christianity into these parts; of course, no old-fashioned saint could have made his abode in the side of such a cliff, situate in such a place, with a cascade issuing from it, without having some strange legends also attached to it. It is reported that a dragon originally occupied the cave, but was turned out much in the same way as St. Saba ousted the lion. St. Beatus had also accomplished the art of navigating the lake on his cloak, without any other external assistance.

After passing the little perpendicular headland known as the Nase, we soon afterwards see on the opposite (left) bank the castle of the descendants of Erlach, the hero of Laupen.

In about an hour after starting, we reach the mouth of the Aare, at which point we have a beautiful view of the Niesen and Blümlisalp chains of mountains, the latter in their garb of never-melting snow.

THUN.

(Hotel Belle Vue and Grand Hotel de Thoune).

If the tourist wishes to proceed direct to Berne without stopping at Thun, he will alight at

Scherzligen, the landing-place being close to the railway station.

Thun has above 5,000 inhabitants; it is traversed by the river Aare; and its principal street is its principal curiosity. "There is a sort of terrace some ten or twelve feet high, on the flat roof of which are the shops, while the carriage-way is bounded by the cellars, of which the terrace is the roof." The sights of Thun are few, and therefore it is best to ascend to **the church** by a covered way of 218 steps, where a magnificent view is obtained; one of the most striking objects from here is the Stockhorn, whose bell-shaped summit differs from everything else within range of our view. The late Emperor Napoleon III. was a resident in Thun for eight years, when a Captain in the Swiss Artillery, the house he occupied is now known as the Café Maulbeerbaum.

Near the church is seen the tower of the **Castle of Kyburg**, where the old Counts of Thun once dwelt. The square tower, with its high pointed roof, known as the Berne Gate, is a remnant of the ancient fortifications. The **Federal Military College** at Thun is the Sandhurst of Switzerland. Reviews in connection with this establishment are held in the neighbourhood in the summer. Some curious old Gothic windows distinguish the **Beguinage**, near the **Town House.** The Jacobishübeli, or Pavilion of St. John, is a short distance from the town. The view excels that from the churchyard in beauty and extent. The majestic Jungfrau forms a prominent feature in the scene.

Charmingly situated at the junction of the river Aare with the lake is the modern erection known as the Schloss Schadau, with extensive and well-ordered gardens, to which, on Sunday evenings, the public are admitted.

Thun is extremely picturesque, but is not regarded by all travellers as the best halting-place on the journey. Those so minded can speedily proceed by Central Swiss Railway to Berne, the journey of about three quarters of an hour is short, but delightful, with views that require incessant watchfulness from both sides of the carriage.

Berne, p. 98.

THUN TO LEUK AND SUSTEN, BY THE GEMMI PASS.

Carriage road to Kandersteg 22½ miles; thence over the pass to the Baths of Leuk, a bridle-path 5½ hours. From thence to Susten (8 miles), there is a good road.

To Kandersteg it is a charming drive through pasture lands and orchards, crossing the Kander, and passing Moos, **Mühlenen, Reichenbach,** and Frutigen. At the latter place the road ascends the Kander valley, and passes the azure waters of the picturesque **Blaue See,** and the Felsenburg Tower, near Mittelholz, to Kandersteg.

At **Kandersteg** the panorama of the Birrenhorn, Blümlisalp, Doldenhorn, Gellihorn, and other mountains, is superb.

Soon after leaving Kandersteg, the road ascends at the base of the Gellihorn, and in about three hours the Inn of **Schwarenbach** is reached.

Hence the path leads by the dirty waters of the **Daubensee** to the summit of the pass (7553 feet) known as the **Daube** or **Gemmi,** at the base of towering limestone rocks forming the Daubenhorn (9449 feet). From an eminence close by the pass, the view is very grand. The Baths of Leuk are seen far below, and around is a fine mountain panorama, comprising the Mischabelhörner, Weisshorn, Bruneckhorn, Matterhorn, Dent Blanche, etc.

Descending amidst grand scenery, by a skilfully constructed path on the side of the almost perpendicular rock, 1800 feet in height, the **Baths of Leuk** are reached (Hotels des Alpes and Belle Vue). There are twenty-two mineral springs here. The bath house is a unique sight. Male and female patients sit up to their necks in one common bath, attired in fanciful flannel dresses. There are small floating tables, at which the patients sip coffee or read the newspapers for hours together, amidst a lively din of conversation in all languages. Visitors are allowed to view this curious scene.

The road to Leuk and Susten crosses the Dala and passes Inden. The route is very attractive, and presents fine views of the Dala ravine and opposite mountains, and of the Rhone Valley as far as Martigny.

At **Leuk**, where the culture of the vine commences, there is a fine old castle on an eminence. **Susten**, on the other side of the Rhone, is on the high road from Sierre to Brieg (see p. 77).

BASLE TO BERNE.

From Basle to Aarburg (p. 57).

At Aarburg the line to Lucerne diverges to the south-east. Stations, *Niederwyl*, *Morgenthal*, *Roggwyl*, *Langenthal*, *Bützberg*. At **Herzogenbuchsee** (which is a junction with the line to Solothurn, Bienne, Neuchâtel) inquire whether carriages must be changed. The train generally waits from ten to fifteen minutes at this station. Then stations *Riedwyl*, *Wynigen*, **Burgdorf**, or *Berthoud*, where Pestalozzi introduced his educational system in 1798. The town is pleasantly situated, and carries on a good trade in cheese. It commands fine views of the Bernese Oberland. A diligence runs from Burgdorf to Langnau (p. 107). Stations, *Lyssach*, *Hindelbank*, *Schönbühl*, *Zollikofen*, junction, with branch line to Bienne (p. 113). Between Zollikofen and Berne is the most interesting part of the railway journey, the chain of the Oberland being seen from end to end. The approach to Berne by way of the Bridge across the Aare is very striking.

BIENNE TO BERNE.

This journey is performed in about an hour and a quarter.

At **Brügg** cross the Zihl, and at **Busswyl** cross the Aare, by a bridge 800 feet in length. The succeeding stations are *Lyss* (*Aarberg*, four miles south, with ancient castle of the

Counts of Aarberg, etc.), *Schüpfen*, *Münchenbuchsee*, and *Zollikofen*.

Zollikofen is the junction with the Central Railway from Olten. At a short distance are the Fellenberg educational institutions at **Hofwyl.** Passing the lofty, three-arched Bridge of Tiefenau, and the Castle of Reichenbach, where the hero of Laupen, Rudolph von Erlach, was murdered by his son-in-law, the railway next reaches the Drilling Ground, passes the new workmen's quarter, and crosses the Aare by a curious, two storied bridge into Berne.

BERNE.

(Hotel Belle Vue.)

Post and Telegraph Office, near the railway station, west part of town. Branch Office in the Kramgasse.

Omnibuses run from the station to the principal hotels. Fare, 50 c.; extra charge for luggage.

Cabs for one or two persons to drive in the town, 60 c.; three or four persons, 1 fr. 30 c.; whole day, two persons, 12 frs.

The **English Church** is in the Chapel of the Brge r Spital.

PRINCIPAL SIGHTS, AND TIMES FOR SEEING THEM.

Arsenal.—p. 105.
Bear-pit.—p. 106.
Bürger-Spital (City Hospital).—p. 105.
Cathedral.—Interior, 30 c.; tower, 50 c. See tariff at entrance.
Casino, with Reading-room, etc.—Near the Federal Council Hall.
Clock Tower (12 o'clock best time).—p. 100.
Federal Council Hall (*Bundes Rathhaus*).—1 franc. Sessions of "the House," open to the public. The *Kunstsaal*, Picture Gallery (see below).
Fountains in various places.—p. 101.
Museum.—Free, Tuesday and Thursday, 3 to 5, and Sunday, 10 to 12. At other times, 1 franc for two or three persons, p. 105.
Picture Gallery (Kunstsaal).—Federal Council Hall, Upper Floor. Free from 9 to 4, except Saturdays. From Sept. 15 to Oct. 15, trifling fee; p. 102.

Berthold, Duke of Zähringen, having occasion to overawe his refractory nobility, built a castle, around which a town sprang up; and this is said to have been the origin of Berne, deriving its name, its coat-of-arms, and the ubiquitous bear in its public places, from the fact of its founder having slain one of that species in the neighbourhood. The town was about a century old when Frederick II. made it an imperial city. Consumed by fire in 1405, it arose from its ashes on a grander scale. Berne united itself with the Swiss Confederacy in 1352, and in 1849 became the Federal Capital.

Berne occupies an elevated position a hundred feet above the river Aar, which nearly surrounds the city. This river is itself 1500 feet above the sea-level at this point. The city is one of the most ancient in Europe, and at every turn the visitor is reminded of past ages. The main street, nearly a mile in length, extends from the Nydeck Bridge to the Porte de Morat; the smaller streets are mostly parallel to the main street, and connected by transverse streets and places, so that the town has a very regular appearance. The streets, being mostly built in one direction—from east to west—have the two sides respectively distinguished as the Côté du Soleil, and the Côté de l'Ombre. The whole town slopes towards the Nydeck Bridge, the part below the Clock Tower being called the Lower Town, whilst above that structure lies the Upper Town. A stream from the upper end of the town runs through channels in the centre of the chief streets, only partially covered in. The fountains are numerous, and many of them beautiful; they form a striking ornament of the city. The houses are mostly of grey sandstone, with iron balconies, containing seats, usually covered with cushions of crimson, or some other bright colour. The houses, moreover, are generally so constructed, as to form an arcade over the footway. In cold, snowy weather this has its advantages; but as was found to be the case in the Regent Street Quadrant, the shops are rendered dull and gloomy. This leads to the almost universal practice in Berne of exposing the goods outside the shop; so that *if you step in to purchase an article, it is highly probable that you will have to step outside to select it.*

Some handsome promenades, affording grand prospects of the surrounding country, have been formed on the site of the ancient fortifications of Berne.

On **Market-days** (Saturday and Tuesday) the streets of Berne are thronged with townspeople and peasantry. On Tuesday especially the scene is very lively. Pleasure as well as business is made a matter of importance. Few better opportunities could be found for studying the manners, costumes, etc., of the Swiss peasantry. Long drays, drawn by ponderous bullocks, and laden with farm produce, are passing continually. The stalls are innumerable; very conspicuous are those for the sale of cattle-bells; for here all the sheep, goats, and cattle wear bells. Meanwhile, provisions of all kinds are being sold—eggs, poultry, game, vegetables—going at prices that would delight the soul of an English housekeeper; and the whole scene is one of busy interest and enjoyment.

The visitor will of course be struck with the shaggy animal which the good city of Berne so delights to honour. Bears figure prominently on the city arms—on the gates, and fountains, and other monuments—modelled in clay, or more expensive materials, they abound in the shops; and besides all this, a few favoured specimens in the flesh are kept in a municipal bear-pit.

The principal street in Berne extends the whole length of the town, from east to west. It is known as the **Gerechtigkeitsgasse** in its eastern portion, and subsequently as the **Kramgasse, Marktgasse,** and **Spitalgasse.** The curious arcaded shops, and the fountains, towers, etc., combine to render this street very interesting. On market-days (see above) it is the centre of Bernese life and enjoyment. At the extreme western end of the street stands the **Ober Thor,** or **Morat Gate,** with its two colossal bears in granite standing like sentinels on either side. Between the Spitalgasse and Marktgasse stands the **Käfigthurm,** or Bird-cage Tower, now used as a prison. Between the Marktgasse and the Kramgasse, in the very centre of the city, stands the noted **Clock Tower.** When the founder of the city reared this tower, it guarded the outer wall.

The following curious exhibition takes place whenever the clock strikes:—At three minutes before the hour a cock crows and flaps his wings; presently some bears march in procession round an old man, and the cock crows again. Then a fool strikes the hour on a bell with a hammer, whilst the old man checks off the strokes with his sceptre, and turns his hour-glass. A bear nods approval, and a final bout of cock-crowing ends the performance.

At the other end of the Kramgasse is the **Bärenbrunnen**. It displays a bear holding a pennant, and fully equipped for battle, with sword, and shield, and helm, and breastplate.

The **Fountains** of Berne are very numerous. The **Schützen-Brunnen** represents a Swiss archer and a young bear. But perhaps the most curious of these erections is the **Kindlifresser-Brunnen**, near the Kornhaus. It represents a monstrous Ogre encircled by bears placidly devouring a baby, with a number of little ones at his girdle and in his pockets, waiting their turn.

The Protestant **Cathedral**, or **Münster**, of Berne is a handsome Gothic structure, dating from 1421, and constructed in part by *Matthias von Steinbach*, son of the builder of Strasburg Cathedral. The varied parts of the delicately-traced parapet of the roof are the most striking of the exterior beauties of the edifice. The sculpture on the west portal represents the Last Judgment; also a number of prophets and apostles. Opposite the entrance is a fine **bronze statue** of Rudolph von Erlach, with the inevitable bears at the corners of the pedestal.

The **Tower** of the Cathedral, still unfinished, is 213 ft. in height, and commands a good view from the gallery, reached by 223 steps. The entrance to the tower is by a door on the west of the chief portal.

On entering the Cathedral, the tariff of charges is seen, clearly written in German, French, and English. The **Interior** is grand and striking in its plain simplicity. In the choir windows are fifteenth-century stained glass pictures, representing the Doctrine of the Eucharist and a Scene from our Saviour's Life; and there are some beautiful carvings of prophets and apostles on the choir stalls.

The **Organ** is one of the finest in Europe, and should, by all means, be heard, if possible. It is played daily at 6.30 p.m., 1 franc being charged for admission.

There are two **monuments** of historical interest in the Cathedral—one to the founder of the city, the Duke of Zähringen; and another to Friedrich von Steiger, and those who fell with him fighting the French at Grauholz, in 1798. The exquisite **marble group** representing the Entombment of Christ has under it the inscription: "To all those Bernese who fell in the battle of 1798 for God and Fatherland, this statue of the Greatest of all Sacrifices is devoted as an everlasting memorial." On the adjacent walls are tablets with the names of the 18 officers and 683 soldiers who perished on that occasion.

The **Münster Platz**, or Cathedral Terrace, covered with shady chestnut groves, is a deservedly favourite promenade with both residents and visitors. On one side it is supported by a stone wall, rising almost perpendicularly from the bank of the Aare, 108 feet below. An inscription on the parapet sets forth how, in 1654, a horse ridden by a young student was frightened by some children, and dashed over the precipice. The horse was killed, the rider only damaged; he recovered, and became pastor of Kerzerz. A bronze statue of Berthold von Zähringen stands on the terrace. The view of the Oberland scenery from this terrace baffles description. On all who behold it it seems to make a lasting impression. The Wetterhorn, Schreckhorn, Jungfrau, Doldenhorn, Stockhorn, and other peaks, are conspicuous features of the scene. From the West Pavilion the visitor looks right across to the Finsteraarhorn, Eiger, Mönch, and Jungfrau. Especially wondrous is the prospect when lit up with the *alpglühen*—that marvellous glow which rests on the mountains just after sunset—as if the reflection of a huge conflagration shone on them.

There is a **Roman Catholic Church** in Berne, but the interior is uninteresting, and there are iron gates to prevent the visitor from walking round to inspect what little there is to see.

The finest building in Berne is the **Bundes Rathhaus**, or Federal Council Hall. In this magnificent edifice, 874 ft. long by 170 broad, are located the Public Offices and the various Departments of State. Here also are the halls in which the Swiss Diet or Parliament assembles. Two deputies from each of the twenty-two cantons form the Upper House, or Senate; whilst the House of Representatives is much larger, its members being returned by the cantons in proportion to their population. The debates, which usually take place in July, are open to the public.

On the upper floor of the building is the **Kunstsaal**, or Saloon of Art, open, free, from Monday to Friday inclusive, except from September 15th to October 15th. The works here exhibited are chiefly by native artists.

The positions of the pictures are sometimes altered, but the numbers are retained. The objets d'art are numbered from

1 to 197; and these numbers include sculptures, etc., as well as paintings. The following is a list of the principal:—

Room I.

1. The Flight into Egypt . . . . *Albano.*
2. Madonna and Child . . . . . *Barbieri.*
3. Dutch Landscape . . . . . *Both.*
4. The Alchemist . . . . . . *Brekelenkamp.*
5. The Walpurgis Night . . . . *P. Breughel.*
8—12. Portraits . . . . *Düntz.*
22. A Sketch . . . . *J. Jordeans.*
24. Flight into Egypt . . . . *Parmeggianino*(?)
29. The Triumph of Mars . . . . *Rubens.*
35. The Last Judgment . . . . . *Ibid.*
37. Allegorical Tableau . . . . . *Werner.*
39. Justice Crowning Virtue and Condemning Vice . . . . . . *Ibid.*
43. Battle of Morgarten (p. 51). . . *Volmar.*
46. Judith with Head of Holofernes . . *Floris.*
53. Höhenweg at Interlaken (p. 92) . . *König.*
54. The Reichenbach (p. 81) . . . *G. Volmar.*
56. Landscape . . . . *Wüst.*
59. Battle of Morat. . . . . . . *K. Rieter.*
61. Swiss Ambassador before Louis XIV.
62. Portrait of Rod. d'Effinger . . . *Dietler.*
67. David with Head of Goliath . . *Imhof.*
70. Monument of Madame Langhaus at Hindelbank (p. 97) . . . . *Sonnenschein.*
73. Infant Sleeping . . . . . . *Ibid.*

Room II.

88. Collection of Swiss Costumes . . *Reinhardt.*
94. Mont Cervin . . . . . . *J. Meyer.*
95. The Scheidegg . . . .
96. Jungfrau and Valley of Lauterbrunnen . *G. Lory.*
102. Portal of Berne Cathedral . . . *Löhrer.*
107. Group of Cats . . . . . . *G. Mind.*
117. Arch of Constantine, Rome . . *Sonnenschein.*
120. Statuette. The Foundation of the Swiss *Confederation* (p. 67) . . . . Doret.

Room III.

121. The Last Day of the Ancient Republic of Berne . . . . . . *Walthard.*
124. The Cascades at Terni . . . *Bonstetten.*
129. Falls of the Giessbach (p. 91) . . *R. Volmar.*
130. Infant asleep . . . . . . *Dubufe.*
133. John Huss bidding adieu to his Friends *Piris.*
135. Episode in the Battle of Morat . . *Girardet.*
139. View near Berne . . . . . *Dalton.*
143. Lake of Brienz. A Spring Morning . *Veillon.*
150. Hagar and Ishmael . . . . . *Imhof.*
151. Moses . . . . *Ibid.*
152. Ruth . . . . *Ibid.*

Room IV.

154. Falls of Schmadribach (p. 87) . . *Snell.*
155. Elijah in the Desert . . . . *Geyer.*
161. Valley of Lauterbrunnen (p. 86) . . *Diday.*
162. Châlet in the Bernese Oberland . . *Ibid.*
164. The Dying Husband . . . . *Meuron.*
165. Scene from "Faust" . . . . *Walthina.*
167. View near the Handeck (p. 88) . . *Calame.*
168. Cascade near Meiringen . . . *Ibid.*
172. Mountain Scene. Canton of Glarus . *Steffun.*
179. Landscape near Geneva . . . *George.*
180. Villa Pamfili, Rome . . . . *Meyer.*
181. The School Examination . . . *Anker.*
182. The Little Friend . . . . *Ibid.*
185. Maternal Solicitude . . . . *Schimon.*
186. Saying Grace . . . . . *Vautier.*
187. View in Rotterdam . . . . *Ulrich.*
196. Rebecca . . . . *Imhof.*

Before leaving the Federal Palace, the visitor should not omit to ascend to the roof. Of all the many sublime views of the Bernese Oberland, seen from various parts of the city, the panorama beheld from this vantage point is the grandest and most extensive.

In front of the building a Fountain will be noticed, with a statue representing Berne.

At the back of the Bundes-Rathhaus is a **terrace**, affording *a mountain view* even finer than the prospect from the Münster

Platz. The highest mountain (to the eye) on the left, is the Wetterhorn. Standing alone, a little more to the right, is the Schreckhorn. Still further to the right, at the end of a group, sharp and rugged, is the Finsteraarhorn. Then follow the stupendous mass of the Eiger, Mönch, and Jungfrau.

Near the Bundes-Rathhaus is the **Museum.** This building is open free from 3 to 6 p.m., on Tuesdays, Thursdays, and Saturdays; and on Sundays from 10 a.m. to 12 noon. At other times a fee of one franc is required.

The front of the building is adorned with statues of Swiss celebrities. The **zoological department** abounds in stuffed bears of all sizes and ages, and also contains many other animals, including specimens of the rare lynx and steinbok, a gigantic wild boar, chamois with three horns, etc. Very interesting is the noted *Barry*, the dog that saved fifteen lives during his career at St. Bernard. In the ornithological department, the lämmergeier (king of Swiss birds), is especially noticeable.. There is a very complete exhibition of Swiss geological specimens, fossils, etc., with plans in relief. Some Roman and mediæval antiquities of interest, form another collection, in which the spoils from Grandson, and Morat, are striking.

The **University,** founded in 1834, is on the S. side of the Museum. On the other side is the **Town Library,** containing 40,000 volumes, amongst which Histories of Switzerland abound. The **Butter Market** occupies the space below the building.

Close to the Bernerhof there is in course of construction an **Academy of Arts,** for painting and sculpture. It is erected in memory of Rudolph von Effinger, a native of Berne.

At the end of the street leading northward from the Clock Tower is the **Zeughaus,** or Arsenal. Many of its chief curiosities were taken away by the French, but sufficient remain to make a visit interesting. Some may find it pleasing to contemplate the axes, warranted to have cut off a hundred heads each. Here also are the halters prepared for the Swiss by Charles the Bold, and many ancient specimens of arms and armour.

There are many charitable institutions in Berne, of which the administration and efficacy are well spoken of. The **Bürger Spital,** or city hospital, near the Railway Station, bears the inscription, "Christo in pauperibus" (To Christ in his poor). The **Waisenhaus,** or orphan asylum, is near the hospital. A new **Maternal Hospital,** near the Observatory, is nearly ready *to be opened.*

The **Kornhaus** is a fine building near the Arsenal, used till 1830 as a storehouse in case of famine. An immense shield is conspicuous on the wall, supported (of course) by bears.

The immense **Zucthhaus** (Prison and Penitentiary), and the **Post Office**, are a little to the north of the Railway Station.

There are four bridges across the Aare, and in order to accommodate the new quarter of the town of Berne, which is rapidly rising into importance, it is proposed to build a new one nearly in a line with the Belle Vue Hotel and the Mint. The **Nydeck Bridge** is at the extreme eastern end of the main street of the town. From this bridge the town is seen spreading out like a fan or the tail of a bird, as far as the gates of Morat and Aarberg. The structure, 900 feet in length, consists of three arches, crossing the river Aare at an altitude of 100 feet.

After crossing the bridge, we come upon the **Bärengraben**, or Bear Pits, opposite to the old road leading to the Tower and Bridge of the Porte d'en Bas. In these pits a few bears are kept at the expense of the State—shuffling about after the manner of bears in captivity, and swallowing the donations of visitors, all unconscious of their heraldic dignity. About twelve or fourteen years ago an English officer fell into one of the pits, whilst attempting to cross the wall between, and was killed before he could be rescued.

Not far from the Bear Pits is the **Rose Garden**, a pleasant spot to visit if time allows. After leaving the bridge and the bears' den, the turning to the left leads to the new **Cavalry Barracks** and **Military School**. From 150 to 200 horses are always kept here. Visitors can always get leave to inspect the stables.

These, then, are the chief points of interest in the city of Berne, claiming such notice from the passing visitor as his time permits. If able to sojourn awhile in the town, so much the better. Its local attractions and glorious surroundings can then be more fully appreciated and enjoyed. The immediate environs are truly delightful, excursions to many renowned localities can be readily made, and it is *en route* to everywhere.

Crossing the magnificent railway bridge, we find the slopes of the Aare charmingly utilized as **Botanical Gardens.** About half a mile further on is **Schänzli**, a favourite place of resort where refreshments can be obtained, and musical entertainments attended. The view is magnificent, including the roofs and spires of Berne, and the far-spreading glories of the Oberland and Stockhorn Alps.

A quarter of an hour's walk northward from the Railway Station, through the Aarberg Gate, conducts to the **Enge**, a high rocky peninsula, forming a pleasant promenade and a good point of view. Continuing by a charming forest path through the **Engewald**, we reach the Castle of Reichenbach. Here dwelt Rudolph von Erlach, who led the Bernese to victory over the Burgundians at Laupen, in 1399. Here also the same hero was murdered by his daughter's husband, whose debts he had refused to pay.

Another noted position from whence to obtain fine views, is the long hill to the south of the town, called the **Gurten**, on the summit of which is an inn. The panorama visible from this point is a hundred miles in extent, including portions of the Oberland, Stockhorn, Freiburg, and Jura mountains, and portions of the Lake of Neuchâtel.

A glance at the map will show that from the position of Berne, and the facilities for railway travelling in several directions, it is very easy for sojourners in the town to make excursions to a great number of places. These will be mentioned in connection with the routes to or from Berne. It will only be necessary for the visitor to find Morat, Laupen, Hindelbanck, Fribourg, or whatever place he wishes, in the index, and its connection with Berne, and its local attractions will be readily seen.

Berne to Thun and Interlaken (p. 94).
Berne by Herzogenbuchsee and Olten to Basle (p. 97).
Berne to Bienne, Neuchâtel, etc. (p. 97).
Berne to Fribourg and Lausanne, etc. (p. 108).
Berne to Leuk, by the Gemmi Pass (p. 96).

BERNE TO LANGNAU, ESCHOLZMATT, AND LUCERNE.

(By railway 3½ hours.)

Berne to Gümlingen junction, on the Berne and Thun Railway (see p. 96).

From *Gümlingen* the rail passes, with good views of the Stockhorn chain on the right, to the thriving industrial town of *Worb*, with its old castle, and thence by stations *Tägertschi* and *Konolfingen*, and round the base of the Hörnberg, to Zäziwyl, a prosperous place. At *Signau* there is a ruined castle above the pleasing village. Passing *Emmenmatt*, and crossing the Emme *and the Ilfis*, *Langnau* is reached.

Langnau is the chief town in the Emmenthal, an industrious and prosperous valley, some thirty miles by twelve in dimensions, and famous for its widely-exported cheese, its lovely green pastures, its picturesque wooden houses, and its fine cattle.

Langnau was, until very recently, the terminus of the railway from Berne, and the remainder of the journey had to be accomplished by diligence in eight to ten hours. Now the railway is continued to Lucerne, and it is one of the most important of the new lines lately opened in that enterprising country. A glance at the Railway Map will show how greatly it facilitates the connection between Zürich, Lucerne, Berne, Lausanne, and Geneva. The route is almost the same as that traversed by the diligence, namely, the Emmenthal and the Vale of Entlebuch.

After leaving Langnau, the next important station is **Escholzmatt**, a rambling little town, the first in the Entlebuch. **Schüpfheim**, the chief village of the valley, was destroyed by fire in 1829, and since rebuilt. Many pleasant excursions may be made from here. The villagers in the neighbourhood are celebrated for their strength and skill in the national wrestling matches. So also are the people of **Entlebuch**, a village charmingly situated at the foot of the Bramegg, and having on the west the Napf, from the summit of which splendid views are obtained. Here the two torrents, the Emme and the Entle, unite, and add much to the picturesqueness of the place.

Beyond **Wohlhusen**, or Wohlhausen, the line takes a sharp curve round the base of the Bramegg to *Malters*, after leaving which station a short run brings the traveller to **Lucerne**, p. 58.

BERNE TO LAUSANNE (BY FRIBOURG).

(Railway, 30 miles—about 4 hours.)

The journey is made through a fine open country, abounding with charming landscapes. Passing *Bümplitz* and *Thörishaus*, and crossing the Sense river, we arrive at *Flamatt.*

From Flamatt a diligence runs to **Laupen** (5 miles), where the Burgundians and their allies were defeated by the Swiss, under Erlach, in 1399. The commemorative tower was erected in 1853.

Then stations *Schmitten* and Guin-Balliswyl, where the Sarine is crossed on a cast-iron viaduct, 260 feet above the water, and 1094 feet from one abutment to the other. Fribourg comes into view.

The station for Fribourg is at some distance from the town. Omnibuses await the arrival of passengers. On approaching by the Suspension Bridge the view is exceedingly picturesque. The town, with its romantic medley of quaint houses, and towers, and battlements, and gateways, is finely situated on a steep eminence above the Sarine Valley, and forms a more imposing spectacle when viewed from a little distance than when closely explored.

FRIBOURG.

(Hotel, Grand Hotel Zæhringen.)

This town is the capital of the canton of the same name, containing a population of 11,000, of whom 1200 are Protestants. It was founded by Duke Berthold von Zähringen in 1175. It is a curious town, outwardly and inwardly. Go to the upper part of the town, and everybody and everything is German; to the lower part of the town, and everybody and everything is French. It is a very hilly town; the streets are steep, and built one above the other; so that in one part the upper street is carried on arches of stone over the roofs of the houses in the street below.

There are three things which *must* be seen in Fribourg, and many more which may if time permit. First, an old lime-tree, fourteen feet in circumference, its branches supported on stone pillars. It faces the Town Hall and Council Hall; and as the old tree is fruitful in bearing a good story, sit down beside it and read the following:—

"When the memorable battle of Morat was being fought, the townspeople of Fribourg stood in the square anxiously waiting for tidings of how the day sped. There was one young fellow in the battle who remembered that the hearts of many of his friends and fellow-citizens were beating painfully in that time of suspense; and as soon as the contest was over, he ran from the field of blood, jaded and fatigued though he [illegible] to bear to them the joyful news that the Swiss had been victor[illegible]s. Away he sped over hill and dale, and, sliding down a [illegible]y slope, he grasped a twig which would not bear his weight, but came out by the roots. Rising from the [illegible], on and on he sped, till he reached the square of Fribourg, where the old men and maidens, invalids and women, were standing [illegible] pale faces and clasped hands, waiting his approach. Bre[illegible]ss and exhausted, the blood flowing from the wounds he had received on the field of battle, he could only raise his voice to shout out the word 'Victory!' and fell dead in their midst. The twig, which he still clutched in his hand, was planted on the spot where he fell; and now that fine old lime-tree stands there as a beautiful memento of the love and courage of that gallant young soldier and the victory of Morat." This happened in 1481.

Then the **Cathedral**, a Gothic building, dating from 1285—1500, with a fine tower 280 feet in height. The visitor will be struck with the remarkable bas-relief over the entrance, "The Last Judgment"—an angel weighing mankind *in batches*, devils carting off the condemned, etc., etc. The **organ** is one of the finest in the world; there are two performances upon it each day, and a pleasant hour may be spent here in listening to its strange and marvellous music. Some wonderful wind and storm effects are introduced by the organist. The bust under the instrument is that of *Aloys Mooser*, the builder. The organ has 67 stops, and 7800 pipes, some of them being no less than 32 feet in height.

Third, the **Suspension Bridge** thrown across the Sarine, a small river, which runs through, or rather below, the city; for the principal streets are 200 and 300 feet above it. This Suspension Bridge, the longest in Europe, has a span of 964 feet; and as you stand in the centre of it, looking down into the wild, rocky ravine, you have one of the most striking views that can be seen. This bridge was completed in 1834, at a cost of nearly £24,000. It is light and elegant, and yet amazingly strong.

Across the Gotteron ravine is another bridge, 746 feet long, and 305 feet above the water; it is fastened into the solid rock, but looks, from its slight and delicate make, like a mere chain thrown from one side to the other of the gorge.

Amongst the other objects of interest in Fribourg, we may enumerate the **Cantonal School**, which, previously to 1848, was a Pensionnat for 400 pupils, taught by the Jesuit fraternity. The **Jesuit Convent**, suppressed in 1847, was founded by Father Canisius in 1584. The Rathhaus, with its curious clock-tower; the statue of the Monk Gerard; the very perfect remains of ancient fortifications; and the general construction and architecture of the city.

Leaving Fribourg by the railway, we see Mont Moléson on the left across the Sarine. Then stations, *Matran, Neyruz, Cottens, Chenens, Villaz-St.-Pierre*, and **Romont.** The town (population, 1600) is 2230 feet above the level of the sea. There is an old castle here, dating from the 10th century, including in its construction an adapted Round Tower, similar to those seen in Ireland. Another Round Tower stands isolated outside the town. The Church was erected in 13th century.

At Romont is the junction for Bulle (45 miles), the chief town of the Gruyère cheese district. The village of **Gruyère**, with its 9th century castle, is about two miles from Bulle.

The next station after passing Romont—and, if the day be fine, catching a glimpse of the head of Mont Blanc—is Siviriez. Then Vauderens, Oron, Palézieux, and **Chexbres.** Hence an omnibus conveys passengers to Vevay, in about an hour's time (fare, 1 franc). Leaving Chexbres, the train darts through a tunnel, after which a splendid view is obtained of the Lake of Geneva. *Grandvaux* and *La Conversion* (for Lutry) are next passed; and then, passing on to the line from Geneva, the train enters Lausanne (see p. 134).

Lausanne to Geneva (p. 132). Lausanne to Villeneuve (p. 133).

BASLE TO NEUCHÂTEL, LAUSANNE, AND GENEVA.

The new direct route, via Delemont, abounds in picturesque scenery. It follows the course of the Birse and Diese rivers, and pierces the chain of the Jura with numerous tunnels. Another route is via Herzogenbuchsee and Soleure.

From Basle to Olten and Herzogenbuchsee (see p. 97).

Herzogenbuchsee, the junction for Berne. Inquire whether it is necessary to change carriages. Stations at *Inkwyl, Subigen,* and *Derendingen,* then, as Soleure is approached, the Hotel on the Weissenstein becomes conspicuous.

Soleure (pop. 7000), in German, *Solothurn,* is a bright, clean town, the capital of the canton. It is a quaintly interesting place, of Roman origin; for, under its name of *Salodurum,* it was a flourishing colony in very early days. It was once a strong fortress; its ramparts (turned into boulevards) form an agreeable promenade. Fountains and statues abound. The **Cathedral,** or St. Ursus Münster, dates from 1762, when it replaced an earlier erection of the eleventh century. Gideon wringing out the Fleece, and Moses striking the Rock, form two striking fountains on either side of the flight of steps, leading to the façade. St. Ursus was one of the Theban Legion. The **Arsenal,** near at hand, contains a good show of French,

Austrian, and Burgundian standards, and armour. It is the best collection of the kind in Switzerland. The most ancient building in Soleure is the **Clock Tower**, a rough pile of masonry, bearing an inscription assigning its erection to the fifth century B.C. It is, however, believed to be of Burgundian origin. At the striking of the clock there is a performance of automatic figures similar to that of Berne. Amongst the other sights of Soleure we may note the **Jesuits' Church**, with a Crucifixion by *Holbein* (1552), the Roman antiquities in the **Hotel de Ville** and in the **Public Library**, the splendid collection of fossils (15,000 from the Jura) and minerals, etc., at the **Museum**; and the Franciscan Church, which possesses a picture by *Raphael*. At No. 5 in the Bieler Strasse is the house where the Polish patriot Koscziusko died in exile, in 1811.

Among other charming walks in the vicinity of Soleure we may note that to the **Hermitage of St. Verena**, a pious maiden, who accompanied the Theban Legion. The path lies through the pretty ravine known as the St. Verenathal. Near the village of **S. Nicholas** is the Hermitage where the saint resisted the devil, *à la* St. Dunstan, on one occasion only escaping being carried off by clinging tightly to the rock. The marks of her finger-nails are still shown. In the vicinity is the **Wengenstein**, one of those immense granite boulders frequently seen on the Jura slopes, a memorial of the glacial epoch.

But the chief attraction of Soleure to most is the **Weissenstein**, which rises to the height of 4213 ft., 8 miles to the north of Soleure. The view is more extensive than from the Rigi. The town of Soleure, the valley of the Aare, and the lakes of Neuchâtel, Bienne, and Morat, and a vast assemblage of mountains, including Mont Blanc and the Jungfrau, the Schreckhorn, the Wetterhorn, the Titlis, and the Rigi are comprised in the scene. **The ascent** of the Weissenstein is perfectly easy either by the long winding road or by a steep path through the woods. Carriages pass to and fro several times a day; for, as the pension at the summit is town property, every facility is afforded for reaching it. At this pension the Swiss air-cure and whey-cure are to be experienced in perfection, and all around are ample opportunities for pleasure walks and rides. The **Röthe** (4587 ft.) and the **Hasenmatt** (4754 ft.), in the vicinity, afford even more extensive views than the Weissenstein.

Leaving Soleure, the railway runs between the river Aare and the Jura mountains, and passes the stations of *Selzach*, *Grenchen*, and *Pieterlen* to Bienne (Germ., Biel).

Bienne was a free and independent town from 1250 to 1798. An interesting collection of Lacustrine antiquities belonging to Colonel Schwab can be seen by visitors. Leaving the town to the S.E. some beautiful avenues are passed, and the **Lake of Bienne** (Germ., *Bielen See*) is reached. This is a miniature affair in comparison with the more celebrated Swiss lakes, being only about 10 miles in length by 2 in breadth. From **Neuveville** (Germ., *Neuenstadt*), or, indeed, from any village on its banks, a boat can be hired to the small island of **St. Pierre**. Hither, in misanthropic mood, came J. J. Rousseau, in 1765, after being ejected from Paris and stoned by the street boys of Motiers. Of the peace and tranquillity of this island home he has written enthusiastically. The room occupied by him in the little inn is still preserved as he left it, except that tourists innumerable have scrawled their names all over it.

[From Bienne, Basle may be reached by a romantic journey through the defiles of the Val Moutier (Germ., *Münster Thal*).]

The train to Neuchâtel runs along the N.W. coast of the lake, stopping at *Twann* (Fr., *Douanne*) and *Neuveville*. From the latter station, on the right, is seen the Chasseral, rising in three terraces to the height of 5800 ft. The view from the summit embraces a considerable extent of Switzerland, the Black Forest, the Vosges, and the Alps.

The stations of *Landeron*, *Cressier*, *Cornaux*, and *S. Blaise* are successively passed, and then the Lake of Neuchâtel comes into view. This lake is 24 miles in length by 5 in breadth.

NEUCHÂTEL.

(Grand Hotel du Lac and Hotel Bellevue.)

Neuchâtel is the capital of the small canton of the same name, which chiefly consists of six or seven valleys amongst the ridges of the Jura. From being a Burgundian province in the eleventh century, this province has since had many masters. German, Prussian, French, or petty local potentates have at various times ruled its destinies before its final settlement as a canton of the Swiss Republic.

The town of Neuchâtel is pleasantly situated on the Jura slopes, rising from the lake, at its base, in the form of an amphitheatre. The general aspect of the place is peculiarly inviting, the streets being open and admirably clean, and the principal buildings substantial in appearance. Scholastic institutions of the first class abound, both in the city and in the surrounding localities, and it is scarcely possible to walk abroad without recognizing by eye and ear groups of English pupils.

Neuchâtel is renowned for its wine and its watches. Of the former, both in red and white varieties, large quantities are exported; the latter are produced in vast abundance, and, it seems, can be produced at a smaller cost here than at Geneva.

The town is built at the mouth of the Seyon, which has been diverted from its former course, and made to pass by a tunnel through the rocks to the lake. On a bank of *débris* brought down from the old channel, a fine terrace skirting the lake, and known as the **Promenade du Gymnase**, has been constructed. This is adorned with rows of lime, chestnut, and other trees, in luxuriant growth. One remarkable clump of trees, probably 90 to 100 feet high, is to be seen near the Bellevue; and skirting a basin of the lake, is a magnificent grove of trees, all of gigantic dimensions, under which are placed seats overlooking the water. On the terrace first-named is an ingenious contrivance for distinguishing the various mountains in the vicinity. A brass plate, forming half a circle, has the names engraved on its outer margin, and a style, fixed by a pivot, works from one end of the half-circle to the other; when the side of the style coincides with a line on the brass plate opposite—we will say Mont Blanc—spectator looks along the style and over a "sight" something like that on a rifle, and, if the weather is clear, it distinctly marks the mountain we have mentioned. The panorama of the lake, the Jura mountains, and the more distant summits of the Oberland Alps, white with snow, is very pleasing.

The **Schloss**, on the hill, formerly the residence of the princes of the province, is now used for the Government offices.

The Temple, or **Church**, is a Gothic building dating from the twelfth century. In the choir is a remarkable monument, erected in 1372, by one of the Counts of Neuchâtel, comprising fifteen life-sized figures. Farel the reformer, who was buried on the terrace outside, and General Zastrow, one of the Prussian Governors of the town, have also monuments in this building.

The **Gymnasium** is the large new educational building in *connection with* which Professor Agassiz has been so earnest a *worker. It* comprises a Museum of Natural History, Lacustrine relics, etc. Open free on Sundays and Thursdays, from 11 to 12 o'clock. At other times ½ franc is charged.

In the same building is the Public Library, containing 30,000 volumes, and a vast number of autograph letters of J. J. Rousseau, dating between 1760 and 1770.

In front of the Gymnase is a statue of David Pury, originally a poor boy, who in the course of his life amassed a fortune of over four million francs, the whole of which he left to his native town. The cantonal Hospital was built from the fund thus created.

The Pourtalès hospital owes its origin to the munificence of a private citizen. It is open to applicants of any religion or nationality.

The Observatory is a recent erection for the benefit of the watchmakers of the town.

Picture Gallery. In the Hotel Dupeyron, formerly the Palais Rougemont, is a very good collection of modern Swiss pictures. Admission, ½ franc. Sundays from 1 to 4, free.

In the Entrance Hall is a collection of casts.

Rooms 1 and 2 contain, among others—

8. A Young Savoyard . . . . . *Berthout.*
12. Rosenlaui Glacier (p. 81) . . . . *Calame.*
13. Monte Rosa (p. 164) . . . . . *Calame.*
16. A Huguenot Family surprised by Soldiers . . . . *Girardet.*
18. Cromwell and Mrs. Claypole . . *Girardet.*
19. A Father's Blessing . . . . . *Girardet.*
22. The Ne'er-do-Well. . . . . . *Girardet.*
24. The Vintage of 1834 . . . . . *Grosclaude.*
32. View of Rome . . . . . . *Meuron.*
33. Lake of Wallenstadt (p. 47) . . . *Jecklin.*
37. View between Isentwald and the Faulhorn . . . . *Meuron.*
40. Henry II. of Longueville in the Castle of Colombier . . . . . . *Moritz.*
50. St. Paolo fuori le Mura, after the fire of 1823 . . . . *Robert.*
57. A Flemish Bridal Procession in the 17th century . . . . *Tschaggeny.*

In the 3rd Room are portraits, and in the 4th Room sketches and water colours.

Amongst the excursions from Neuchâtel, that to the

Chaumont,—a spur of the Jura chain—is the best. There is a fine view of the Lakes of Neuchâtel, Bienne, and Morat, and the towns of Soleure, Berne, and Fribourg, and the fertile country between.

The **Pierre à Bot** (toadstone), is an immense mass of granite, above 14,000 cubic feet, in a wood above the town, probably deposited by a melting iceberg, when the condition of things in this part of the world was very different from the present.

Visits to the Gorge of the Seyon, Chanélaz with its Hydropathic establishment; or longer expeditions to the Creux du Vent or Chasseral can be undertaken by those protracting their stay at Neuchâtel. Steamboat expeditions to Yverdon or Morat can also be made.

BIENNE—CHAUX-DE-FONDS AND NEUCHÂTEL.

The traveller wishing to vary the above route and make a visit to La Chaux-de-Fonds, may do so by taking a train thence from Bienne, and after visiting Le Locle, proceed to Neuchâtel.

Or the visit to Chaux-de-Fonds may be made (as is more frequently the case), from Neuchâtel to Le Locle, either by railway 2¼ hours, or by diligence, 4 hours. The best excursion is, rail to Chaux-de-Fonds and Le Locle, and diligence from thence by Les Ponts to Neuchâtel.

The **views** from the railway between Neuchâtel and Hauts Geneveys are magnificent.

Stations, *Corcelles*, *Chambrelien*, *Coffrane*.

Hauts Geneveys. The views from here are the finest on the line, and Mont Blanc is seen to perfection. Passing through a long tunnel, *Convers* is reached, and the next station is **La Chaux-de-Fonds** (Hotel de la Fleur de Lis), which is a large scattered town, resembling an assemblage of villages, in a bleak bare valley, over 3000 feet above the sea, and very imperfectly supplied with water. The inhabitants (about 18,000), are almost exclusively engaged in the manufacture of watches and clocks, which is carried on in the dwellings of the workpeople, each of whom devotes himself to the manufacture of one particular piece of the machinery.

There are always to be found commercial travellers in the hotels, a brisk trade being done here. Sometimes as many as 200,000 watches are manufactured here in the course of the year.

There is not much beyond the inspection of the industries of the people to detain the tourist.

An uninteresting run past *Eplatures*, and the traveller arrives at

Locle (Hotel Jura), another town almost as populous as La Chaux-de-Fonds, where nearly all the men are watchmakers, and the majority of the women are employed in the manufacture of lace. A tunnel through the limestone rock forms a channel for the *Bied*, which in former days inundated the plain, and worked much havoc. The Bied, below its exit from the tunnel, leaps down a chasm 100 feet deep, and joins the Doubs, the water of the fall being utilised for turning the mills.

The Saut du Doubs is quite a curiosity in its way, and should be visited by the tourist with leisure, as the scenery around is very beautiful, and the fall itself is picturesque.

From Locle by diligence, *via Les Ponts, Montmollin, Corcelles*, and *Peseux*, to *Neuchâtel*.

FROM NEUCHÂTEL TO LAUSANNE

the railway crosses the river Seyon, and then enters a tunnel. On emerging, be careful to notice the charming prospect of lake and mountain. Near the Castle of Beauregard, a lofty viaduct spans the ravine of Serrières, and we rapidly reach *Auvernier*. Here the Pontarlier railway diverges, and after passing *Colombier* (noted for its white wine), we arrive at *Boudry*, the birthplace of Marat, at some distance from its station.

Boudry is the place for the ascent of the Creux du Vent, where a strange phenomenon is to be seen. There is a basin like a crater at the top of the mountain, and when the weather changes, clouds of vapour roll within it, but do not quit the hollow. A gunshot produces a rattling echo like a volley of musketry. An idea of the phenomenon in miniature is produced by filling a tumbler with smoke from a cigar, and witnessing the action of the atmosphere upon it, causing it to surge and roll like the sea.

At *Bevaix* we again reach the lake, and follow its banks to Yverdon. At the next station, *Gorgier St. Aubin*, we see the small town of Estavayer on the opposite bank of the lake. Passing *Vauxmarcus* on the right, with castle, and château of La Lance, formerly a monastery, on the same side, we reach *Concise*, and then *Grandson*. At Grandson there is a picturesque old castle, overgrown with ivy. The town is memorable for its siege, by Charles the Bold, in 1476, when the populace were cruelly massacred after being induced to surrender by promises of safety. Roused by this atrocity, the Swiss collected their forces, rushed on the Burgundians, and totally routed them. A collection of antiquities is kept at the old castle.

Skirting the S.W. end of the lake, we have fine views of the Jura mountains, and crossing the river Thièle, speedily reach **Yverdon.** At Yverdon, Pestalozzi lived from 1805 to 1825, and elaborated his practical methods of teaching "the young idea how to shoot." The ancient castle was the scene of his labours. It now contains a Museum, with Lacustrine curiosities, Roman antiquities, a Town Library, and Public Schools.

There is much picturesque scenery in the neighbourhood, affording many delightful walks, or drives, or longer excursions. The Chasseron may be visited by way of the town of St. Croix, which annually produces 50,000 musical boxes; also the Aiguille de Beaulmes, or Mont Suchet, both over 5000 feet.

Yverdon is a very good place to stay at for those who wish to explore the scenery of the Val d' Orbe. This excursion can be effected by taking the train to Chavornay (15 minutes), and then taking the diligence to the old Burgundian city of Orbe, or by going on to Chavornay and then taking the branch line by La Sarraz to the Val Orbe district.

From Yverdon the railway passes along the Thièle Valley, with fine views of the Jura, and other mountain scenery. The stations of *Ependes*, *Chavornay*, and *Eclépens la Sarraz* are passed, and then *Cossonay*, on its wood-embowered hill. Near Bussigny is a branch line to Morges and Geneva (p. 133), that to the left leading to Lausanne (p. 134).

Lausanne to Geneva (p. 133).

PONTARLIER TO LAUSANNE, BY VALLORBES.

Travellers between Paris, Dijon and Switzerland, or *vice versa*, will find the **New line of Railway** from Pontarlier to Lausanne of great convenience. Formerly the tourist had to travel to Neuchâtel, and thence to Lausanne, the journey being two sides of a triangle. The new line is the base of the triangle, and it is an easy problem to solve how great a saving is thus effected.

The line is a continuation of that from Cossonay (see above) to Vallorbes, and will no doubt be one of the most popular of the many new Swiss railways.

Leaving **Pontarlier,** a French town on the Doubs, where

passengers' luggage is examined, the line for a short distance runs in the same course as that to Neuchâtel. It then diverges southward, and continues, through pleasant scenery, to **Jougne.**

Vallorbes, the former terminus of the line, is a considerable village, and its inhabitants are nearly all watchmakers. **Romainmotier** has an old Abbey Church. dating from 750. Margaret of Austria was married here to Philibert, Duke of Savoy (1501).

La Sarraz, a well-to-do village, with a fine old castle, is the last station on the line, which soon after joins that from Neuchâtel to Lausanne, and proceeds to Cossonay (p. 118), and thence to Lausanne.

LAUSANNE TO MARTIGNY.

From Lausanne the railway runs through the Lavaux vineyards, and past the coal-mine at Pully to **Vevey,** and then past the stations of **Clarens,** *Vernex-Montreux*, *Veytaux-Chillon* (for **Chillon**) to Villeneuve. For further details of this enchanting district, see the Tour of the Lake of Geneva, p. 133.

At Villeneuve the route enters the valley of the Rhone, about four miles wide, with grand scenery on either side; which can, however, be much better appreciated from the road than from the railway. Through a large tract of alluvial soil the Rhone pours its yellow waters to the lake—singularly different in hue from the river that leaves the lake at Geneva. This alluvial land has gradually encroached on the lake; so that the Roman station of Port Valais, once on the shore, is now a mile and a half from it.

The first station after Villeneuve is *Roche*. The top of Mount Yvorne was thrown down by an earthquake in 1584; a white wine of good repute is produced on the scene of the catastrophe.

Aigle (Rom., *Aquila*—Hotel Victoria), is built of black marble from the neighbouring quarries of St. Triphon. From this spot a fine excursion can be made to the beautiful scenery of the Val des Ormonts. Another trip is to **Villard,** a small village, with several pensions, at a height of over 4000 feet, and with splendid views of the Valley of the Rhone.

Near *Ollon S. Triphon* station will be noted a Roman Beacon-tower, 60 feet high, on a small wooded hill.

BEX

(Hotel des Bains),

on the Avençon, is an interesting place, with plenty of accommodation in the way of hotels, pensions, and baths. It is a noted place for the milk and grape cures, and also for bathing in salt water from the mines. The pension-studded environs are charming. The most popular excursion is to Devens and Bévieux, to inspect the salt magazines, evaporating houses, etc., and also to explore the excavations from which the rock-salt is obtained. One of these is a gallery cut into the mountain, nearly 7000 feet in length, 7 feet high and 5 feet broad.

From Bex the railway nears the Rhone, and crosses it by a wooden bridge, to unite with the line from Bouveret. There is a fine view of St. Maurice before dashing into the tunnel that conducts to the station just beyond the town.

ST. MAURICE

(Roman, *Agaunum*) stands hard by where the Dent de Morcles on the east, and the Dent du Midi on the west, closely approach, leaving a gorge only just wide enough for the road and river to pass. At this spot is a **bridge** of the 15th century, reaching from the base of one mountain to the base of the other, with a single arch of seventy feet. The view from the bridge is really superb, but is missed unless the visitor arrives by road from Bex. The old town, which was fortified previous to the Sonderbund War, stands beside the Rhone, with dark cliffs lowering behind.

The ancient **Abbey** is one of the oldest religious houses in Switzerland. Its treasury contains many elaborate specimens of ecclesiastical art in gold, silver, and precious stones. Queen Bertha's famous chalice, and a celebrated episcopal staff of gold, elaborately carved with small figures, and a noted Saracenic vase, presented by Charlemagne, are amongst the most striking. There are also a curious MS. of the Gospels, the gift of the same prince, and various other curiosities.

The **Chapel of Verolliaz**, covered with rough frescoes, is supposed to mark the site of the martyrdom of the celebrated Theban Legion, and their leader St. Maurice, whose name the town now bears. This legion consisted of 6000 men, who had become Christians. In A.D. 302, with the rest of the Roman army, the Theban Legion, one of the most courageous in the world, crossed the Alps. On arrival at this spot, Maximian commanded the whole army to offer sacrifice to Jupiter. The Theban Legion refused to take part. For so doing, every tenth man was mercilessly slain. A second command, and consequent refusal was followed by a second decimation. Again and again the terrible ordeal was repeated, till the whole legion, except a few who escaped, and became hermits, had perished, rather than prove false to the faith of their Redeemer.

Not far from this traditional spot, the visitor may get a splendid view by toiling up over four hundred steps to the hermitage of **Notre Dame de Sax.**

The **Baths of Lavey** (hot sulphurous springs) are on the opposite bank of the Rhone.

The **Grotte aux Fées** is a stalactite cavern of immense length, containing a lake and waterfall, a short walk from the station.

The next station after leaving St. Maurice is *Evionnaz.* The village marks the site of Epaunum, destroyed by a torrent of mud in 563. Near the same locality a similar stream of mud descended to the valley in 1835, bringing down numerous blocks of limestone, etc. As it crept slowly down like a lava-stream, no lives were lost, but much property was destroyed.

Near La Barma village are the Falls known as the **Pisse-vache,** about 280 feet in height, and formed by the descent of the Sallenche from the Glaciers of the Dent du Midi. Above the fall, a fine view is obtained of the Glacier of Mont Velan (12,350 feet), connected with the Great St. Bernard.

VERNAYAZ

(Hotel des Gorges de Trient) is the station for visiting the Pissevache (1½ miles), and also the **Gorge du Trient** (¾ mile beyond Vernayaz). A visit to this imposing ravine, with its rocky precipices, recesses never penetrated by the sun, foaming torrent, waterfall, and wonderful echoes, is strongly recommended (entrance fee, 1 franc).

[From Vernayaz Chamouny may be reached by the Valley of the Trient. The path zigzags up through chestnut woods to **Salvan** (3035 feet). Close by is the **Cascade du Dailly,** which is worth visiting, but with proper inspection of its surroundings, will add two or three hours to the expedition. From Salvan the route forward leads by the Falls of the Trièze, and on through the Gorge of the Triquent, with the steep slopes thickly clothed with pines. Passing Triquent (3261 feet), and Finhaut (4058 feet), the path then descends to **Chatelard,** on the Tête Noire route (see p. 158). This cross route will occupy about four hours, exclusive of time spent at the Cascade du Dailly.]

Leaving Vernayaz, the Castle of La Bathiaz is passed. It was built by Peter of Savoy in 1260, and was long a fortress of the Bishops of Sion; but the Round Tower is of much earlier and unknown date. The Dranse is crossed, and Martigny is reached.

MARTIGNY.

(Hotel Clerc.)

Martigny is an uninteresting town in itself, though its situation as to surrounding scenery is fine. It is an important and busy tourist centre, from its position at the junction of the routes from Chamouny (see p. 157), and the Great St. Bernard (see p. 156), with the routes from Geneva to the Simplon, etc. (see p. 170) Martigny has been twice nearly destroyed by inundations from the Dranse, the last occasion being in 1818. Of the latter calamity, evidences on the walls of some of the buildings are still apparent. The bridge is one of the specimens of the roofed wooden bridges of Switzerland; the monastery sends its inmates in their turns to keep guard at the Hospice of St. Bernard.

From Martigny, or from *Saxon les Bains,* the **Pierre à Voir** ridge (8124 feet) may be ascended in five hours; descent, three hours. The descent to Saxon by sledges is performed in less than half an hour. The panorama of the Alps, from the summit is very fine, including the Jungfrau (E.), the Great Moveron (N.), the Dent du Midi, the Aiguilles Rouges (W.), the Aiguille du Tour, the Great St. Bernard, Mount Velan, the Great Combin (S.), and many other intervening heights.

Visitors not intending to go from Martigny to Chamouny should, if time allows, make an excursion at least to the Forclaz (see p. 159).

BOUVERET TO MARTIGNY.

From Bouveret (see p. 142) the railway passes over ground *formed since the* time of the Romans, to Port Valais, once a *real port on* the shore of the lake. Porte du Sex is next reached, a narrow gap between the mountain and the river, formerly the fortified gate of the Canton of Valais.

Vouvry stands where the unfinished Stockalper Canal, commenced in 1740, joins the Rhone. In passing Evionnaz, notice the view of Yvorne, the Diablerets, and Oldenhorn, on the opposite side of the Rhone Valley. *Monthey* is at the mouth of the **Val d'Illiez**. Up this delightful valley, well stocked with rare plants, for the delectation of botanists, a fine excursion can be made to Champéry. Hence the Dent du Midi can be ascended.

Near Monthey are some huge boulders, in a chestnut wood, evidently deposited by a glacier. Among them is the celebrated rocking-stone, the Pierre Adzo.

After leaving Monthey, the mountains converge towards the river, and the rail from Villeneuve is joined before entering the tunnel leading to St. Maurice.

St. Maurice to Martigny (see p. 121).

Geneva.

German, GENF. *French*, GENEVE. *Italian*, GINEVRA.

Hotels.—Hotel de la Metropole; Grand Hotel de Russie et Anglo-Americaine (with magnificent views); Hotel du Lac. (These Hotels are admirably situated in the best part of Geneva.) Cook's Tourist Office, 90, Rue du Rhone, adjoins the Hotel du Lac.

Theatres.—Ancien Théâtre, Place Neuf; Théâtre des Variétés, Rue Levrier.

The **Post Office** is on the Quai de la Coulouvrenière (7 a.m. to 8 p.m.). The **Telegraph Office** is on the first floor (7 a.m. to 9 p.m.).

The **Passport Office**, Hotel de Ville, No. 28 (9 a.m. to 4 p.m.; Sundays, 9 a.m. to 1 p.m.).

The **English Consul's Office** is at the General Post Office; that of the **United States Consul**, 2, Rue de la Paquise.

Carriages wait on the various Places. The coachmen must give a printed card, with number, name, and address, and the local tariff.

Omnibuses run to Carouge, S. Julien, Mornix Fernay, and, in the season, to the Voirons.

A **Tramcar** runs to Carouge, starting from the Place Neuve, and another to Chêne, from the Cours de Rive.

Steamboats start for the northern and southern banks of the Lake from the pier beside the Jardin Anglais. The express boats from the pier close by the Hotel de Russie. Excellent provisions on all the boats.

Diligences from the Grand Quai, Place du Rhone, and *Leon d'Or*. To Chamouny, once daily. To Sixt, once a-day. *To Thonon*, twice daily.

PRINCIPAL SIGHTS, AND TIMES FOR SEEING THEM.

Academical Museum.—Sundays, 11 a.m. to 1 p.m.; Thursdays, 1 to 3 p.m.; p. 130.
Arsenal.—By permission from Military Office, Hotel de Ville; p. 129.
Athénée (near Rue Beauregard).—Exhibition of Pictures.
Bibliothèque Publique.—11 a.m. to 4 p.m.; p. 129.
Birthplace of Rousseau.—p. 129.
Botanic Garden.—Free all day; p. 129.
Bridge of Mont Blanc.—p. 127.
Cathedral.—½ franc to concierge; p. 128.
Hotel de Ville.—p. 129.
House of Calvin.—p. 128.
English Garden, and other Promenades, Quays, etc.—p. 127.
Observatoire.—First Thursday in month, 4 to 5 p.m.; p. 128.
Rath Museum.—Free on Thursdays, from 11 a.m. to 3 p.m. At other times a gratuity to the guardian; p. 129.
Relief of Mont Blanc.—Daily, from 11 a.m. to 3 p.m. A small contribution required, except on Sundays and Thursdays; p. 127.
Zoological Museum of the Alps.—Daily, 7 a.m. to 6 p.m.
New Opera-house constructed on the same plan as the one at Paris.

Geneva is the most thickly populated town in Switzerland, although it is only the capital of the smallest of the cantons; population, 62,600. The river Rhone separates the town into two parts, and this natural division has almost as naturally separated the inhabitants into two classes, the Quartier St. Gervais being chiefly occupied by folk of the poorer sort. The city, like many others on the Continent, is being rapidly transformed; progress and improvement are noticeable everywhere, both in and around the place. The railways which concentrate here have wrought great changes; for all around acres of fortifications have been cleared away to make room for beautiful private residences, and public buildings, and institutions. The chief manufacture of the town is watches, of which about 100,000 are turned out every year. In the production of these an amazing quantity of gold, silver, and precious stones is made use of. *The visitor will find splendid assortments of watches and jewellery in some of the shops of Geneva.*

Geneva and its lake have an interesting and eventful history, of which, of course, only the most prominent details can be briefly glanced at here. Passing over the ages when the mastodon and his compeers were evidently lords of the rich tropical luxuriance which then characterized this district, we find the mysterious tribes of the Age of Stone dwelling on the shores of the lake, and leaving memorials of their existence in the piles and stakes that supported their rude huts. Then, as history dawns, come the Helvetians and Allobroges, who have left weapons, and chariots, and Druidical monuments in evidence. For a time mighty Rome asserted her sway in these regions; then, as Rome decayed, Teutonic tribes conquered or assimilated the Gallo-Roman element, which, however, has always been prominent in this part of Switzerland to the present time. How Burgundians and Franks occasionally wrested these fair regions from each other we cannot stay to tell. In 1033 the Burgundian Empire broke up, and these States became absorbed into the German Empire. And now Geneva and Lausanne slowly ripened for free institutions and Protestantism, whilst the country districts of Vaud were still intensely feudal and Romanist.

Geneva became a town of the German Empire, governed by a Prince Bishop. By continuous struggling, the Genevese contrived to reduce the episcopal power to a minimum, and to a large extent governed themselves. Meanwhile, another danger threatened; the neighbouring Dukes of Savoy managed to draw Vaud from its allegiance to the Empire, and longed to obtain Geneva also. They got scions of their own house appointed by the Pope to the Genevese bishopric, and much oppression, and strife, and discord resulted for some two hundred and fifty years. At length, to throw off the yoke that was growing intolerable, the burghers of Geneva allied themselves, in 1530, with Berne and Fribourg. It was about this time that the patriot Bonnivard was seized by the Duke of Savoy, and imprisoned in the dungeons of Chillon for six years (p. 141). Fierce war now raged between the Duke and the gallant burghers. In 1536, by the aid of Berne, Geneva was freed, Chillon taken, and Bonnivard and his companions released. In 1580 the struggle was renewed, and raged till 1602. In that year the event known as "The Escalade," a final attempt to take Geneva, *failed.* Savoy now accepted the situation, and left Geneva to *itself, growing* and prospering, and backed up by all the Reformed Countries of Europe.

The Reformed Countries might well be interested in Geneva, for here Calvin had taught from 1543 till 1564, and made the town memorable for ever in the history of religion. The tourist, as he stands by that small square stone in the cemetery bearing the initials, "J. C.," will think of the mighty forces that have been put in motion through that man's work, and of the fruit of seed sown in troublous times in the good town of Geneva.

In 1712 Jean Jacques Rousseau was born at Geneva, and has stamped the impression of his genius on much of the surrounding scenery.

Geneva was made a province of France in 1798, under the name of Léman; it again, however, became free in 1814, and joined the Swiss Confederation. In 1846 the aristocratic Government gave place to a democratic one, and since then affairs have gone smoothly.

The **sights** of Geneva can be readily seen in a single day. Passing from the Place in front of the **Railway Station** (where the large **Hospice des Orphelins** is a conspicuous object), along the Rue des Alpes, and turning up the Rue Levrier, we reach the **English Church**, a small but elegant building, consecrated by the Bishop of Winchester in 1853. Thence the Rue du Mont Blanc will bring us to the **Pont du Mont Blanc**, completed in 1863. There the visitor obtains a good general view of the city, with its broad quays along the banks of the blue and rushing Rhone. But the distant view is very striking, as from this bridge is obtained one of the best possible views of the Mont Blanc chain, in some respects eclipsing that from Chamouny. Between this bridge and the next, the Pont des Bergues, is a small island, called the **Ile de J. J. Rousseau**. It contains a statue of that writer by *Pradier*. At the other end of the Pont du Mont Blanc (left bank) is an open place, where stands the **National Monument**, a bronze group by *Dorer* of Helvetia and Geneva. It commemorates the union of Geneva with the Swiss Republic.

Close at hand is the **Jardin Anglais**, a pleasant and attractive promenade. Concerts and fêtes take place here during the summer months. In a small building in the garden is a **Relief of Mont Blanc**, the finest model in Switzerland of this celebrated group. On Sundays and Thursdays it is open free from 11 to 3; at other times the admission is fifty cents. The model is carved in lime-wood, the artist, Séné, having been ten years engaged upon it. From this garden may be seen, standing just above the waters of the lake, the Pierres du Niton, said to have been used as Roman altars for the worship of Neptune. By some they are considered to be portions of a harder rock than the bed of the lake, from which surrounding softer materials have been washed away; others assign them a glacial origin.

The Quai de Rive will conduct us to the Church of S. Joseph and the **Hall of the Reformation.** The latter was erected by public subscription in memory of Calvin, its chief use being for lectures, etc.

The Boulevard Helvetique stretches across the more modern part of the town. In the vicinity are the **School of Gymnastics,** the **Observatory,** and the **Greek Church.** The latter is an edifice in the Russian style, with a gilded dome; it is noted for its exquisite music.

North of the Rue de la Fontane, is the court of the **Cathedral.** This edifice, dedicated to S. Pierre, dates from A.D. 1124, and is a fine example of the Romanesque style. The Corinthian Porch, added by *Alfieri* at the commencement of the present century, is an incongruous blemish. The **interior** displays some fine wood carving in the stalls, and some stained glass windows, and several **monuments** of interest. That of the Duke de Rohan and his wife, Margaret de Sully, and their son Tancred, is worthy of notice. Rohan was leader of the Protestants in the reign of Louis XIII., and was killed at Rheinfelden in 1638. On two sculptured lions rests a black marble sarcophagus, above which is a statue of the Duke in plaster, the original one of marble having been destroyed in the time of the French Revolution of 1798. The grave of Jean de Brognier, once President of the Council of Constance, is marked by a black tombstone in the nave. The monument to Agrippa d'Aubigné, erected by the town in grateful remembrance of his services whilst in exile at Geneva, will be noticed in one of the aisles. He was a favourite of Henri Quatre, and grandfather of Madame de Maintenon. But perhaps to many, more interesting than any of these pretentious monuments, as a memorial of the illustrious dead, will be the Canopy of the Pulpit. It is the same which hung over Calvin when the Genevese burghers crowded the Cathedral, and drank in the Truth of God from his impassioned lips.

Close by the Cathedral, at No. 11, Rue des Chanoines, is *the house* **where Calvin lived** for nineteen years, and where, in 1564, he died in the arms of the devoted Beza. Turning from thence up the Rue de S. Pierre, we come shortly to the **Arsenal**. Here are preserved many specimens of mediæval arms and accoutrements of the Swiss. The Duke of Rohan's armour is shown; also some scaling ladders, and other memorials of the Duke of Savoy's abortive "Escalade" in 1602. At the end of the Rue de S. Pierre is the **Hotel de Ville**, a good-sized, heavy building in the Florentine style, the square tower dating from the 15th century. In this building an inclined plane takes the place of a staircase, so that it was possible to enter the Council Chamber on horseback. In the Salle de la Reine are some fine pictures. It will be remembered that this edifice is associated with the history of our own time; for here in 1872 sat the Arbitration Commissioners on the Alabama Claims. In front of the Hotel de Ville, in 1762, the Emile of *Rousseau* was burnt by the common hangman. Now the city counts his fame and glory as her own.

In the Grand Rue, at No. 40, is the **house in which Rousseau was born**. The house formerly shown as his birthplace, at No. 27, Rue Rousseau, was the abode of his grandfather.

In or near the Place Neuve are two or three objects of interest. The **Musée Rath** owes its foundation to the Russian General Rath, who was a citizen of Geneva. It contains some good paintings, *i.e.*, some landscapes by *Salvator Rosa*, some pictures by the Swiss artists *Diday* and *Calame*, and the Death of Calvin, by *Hornung*. There are also some beautiful plaster casts by *Pradier*, and a collection of enamels. The adjacent **Conservatoire de Musique** was founded through the liberality of a Genevese, M. Bartholony. Close by is the **Botanic Garden**, founded by the celebrated De Candolle in 1816, and memorable for the horrible scenes enacted here by the Republicans in 1794.

Opposite the Botanical Gardens is the **Acadèmie**, a fine building, erected in 1871. It contains the **Bibliotheque Publique**, which owes its origin to Bonnivard, whose library formed the nucleus of the present collection (p. 129). It contains more than 73,000 volumes, and an immense number of MSS. Amongst these are autograph letters of Calvin, Beza, Luther, Rousseau, S. Vincent de Paul, etc., documents of the Council of Bâle, a MS. volume of the Waldensians, "Noble Lecon," and many other unique curiosities. There is also a collection of precious miniatures. In this institution we may see, amongst the portraits one picture which is a sad reminder of the intolerance so often mixed with earnest belief. It is a picture of Servetus, the Spanish Unitarian, condemned by Calvin. It bears the label, "Burnt at Geneva, to the honour and glory of God." In the same building is the **Academical Museum**, containing the geological collection of De Saussure and the zoological collections of Boissier and Neckar, etc. There is also a collection of medals and antiquities.

The **Eglise de la Madeleine**, in the Place of the same name, is the oldest religious edifice in the city, dating from the 10th century. The doctrines of the Reformation were first taught in this church in 1534. One of the favourite Protestant places of worship in Geneva is the **Temple St. Gervais**, in the Rue du Corps Saint, where, on Sundays, the most popular preachers may be heard. It contains the tomb of the seventeen heroes of the Escalade. The Roman Catholic Church of **Notre Dame**, in the Place Cornavin, was commenced in 1851, and dedicated to the Immaculate Virgin in 1859. Pope Pius IX. presented the statue of the Virgin Mary, by *Forzani*. The windows are from designs by *Claudius Lavergne*.

We have enumerated the chief objects in which the tourist is likely to be interested. There are, of course, other churches, municipal buildings, fountains, etc., the nature of which will readily be ascertained by the inquiring visitor.

With a few exceptions, the streets of Geneva are neither imposing nor picturesque. The quays, however, are broad and handsome, and afford pleasant and much-frequented promenades. The terrace near the Town Hall, known as **La Treille**, affords a splendid prospect; and parallel with the Botanic Gardens is a pleasant walk under a fine avenue of trees, called Les Bastions. The **Plaine de Plainpalais** is the Champ de Mars of Geneva; it is pleasantly surrounded with trees and houses. The **Corraterie** was anciently the rampart where the "Escalade" of 1602 was tried, and failed. A fountain in the Rue des Allemands commemorates this event. In the **Cemetery** of Plainpalais will be found the supposed grave of Calvin, already alluded to, and also the graves of Sir Humphrey Davy and the great botanist, De Candolle.

ENVIRONS OF GENEVA.

In addition to excursions on the lake (to be mentioned presently), several pleasant walks and drives can be enjoyed in the neighbourhood of Geneva. Amongst places most visited is the **Confluence of the Rhone and Arve**, a little below the island where the eagles (heraldic emblem of the canton) are kept in a cage. It is very curious to watch the two rivers as they meet at the junction, but do not blend for a considerable distance; the Rhone, a deep blue, which gives you the idea that anything white steeped in it must come out dyed; and the Arve, a thick, dirty white, struggling side-by-side, until at length they merge into a mottled mass of waters. Voltaire's villa, *Les Délices*, can be viewed on the way to the Confluence.

Geneva abounds in beautiful suburbs and environs, and no difficulty will be experienced in reaching them by those having time at their disposal. Travellers with limited time should secure one of the open carriages on the quays, and drive round to the most picturesque spots. The coachmen are accustomed to such drives, and can be trusted to make the selection according to the time the visitor can spare.

We will just enumerate a few of the chief points of interest: Secheron, with villa of Sir Robert Peel. Varembé, where the Empress Josephine, and subsequently Lola Montez, resided. **Prégny**, with fine villa of M. Rothschild; open by cards from the hotels, on Sundays and Thursdays, from 12 to 3. the **Petit Sacconnex**, with the finest cedars in Europe, about 100 feet in height, and a dozen feet in circumference. The **Grand Sacconnex**, from which splendid views of Mont Blanc, etc., are obtained.

On the Savoy side: the **Campagne Diodati**, residence of Byron in 1816; the promenades of the **Bois de Frontinex**; the Genevese holiday-makers' resort at **Montalègre**. A special excursion on the Savoy side should be made, if possible, to **Mont Salève** (4527 ft.), from which a grand panorama of the lake and adjacent cantons of Geneva and Vaud is beheld. Half a day must be allowed. Cost for two-horse vehicle and driver to the Little and Great Salève, 28 francs.

Fernex, in France, is distant only 5 miles from Geneva. Here Voltaire lived, and built the church with the inscription, "Deo erexit Voltaire." Here is the garden where he used to *compose; also, his* bed, arm-chair, etc.; and the mausoleum which was intended by the Marchioness de Villette to contain his heart.

The **Perte du Rhone**, where the river dives beneath the rocks (10 minutes from *Bellegarde* station); the immense French fortifications, known as the **Fort de l'Ecluse** (half an hour from *Collonge* station; the splendid **Suspension Bridge of La Caille**, over a gorge 700 ft. in depth, which can be visited by the diligence which runs along the road to Annecy, are within excursion distance from Geneva.

Les Voirons, a charming excursion, can be reached by omnibus (p. 124).

THE LAKE OF GENEVA.

(*Lacus Lemanus* of the Romans.)

The Lake of Geneva is the largest in Switzerland, being on the north shore 56 miles long, and on the south 44; it is in shape like a crescent; its surface is 1230 ft. above the sea level, and its depth from 300 to 600 ft. The widest part is near Lausanne, where it is 8 miles across; and the extreme beauty of its scenery is between Villeneuve and Ouchy. The colour of the water is blue; that of other Swiss lakes being green. It has been sung about, written about, preached about; and to select what has been said and sung would fill a large volume. Byron is always quoted, and deservedly, as he is, *par excellence*, the poet of the lake. Everybody knows the lines—

"Clear, placid Leman! thy contrasted lake,
With the wild world I dwelt in, is a thing
Which warns me, with its stillness, to forsake
Earth's troubled waters for a purer spring.
This quiet sail is as a noiseless wing
To waft me from distraction."

And the lines—

"Lake Leman woos me with its crystal face,
The mirror where the stars and mountains view
The stillness of their aspect in each trace
Its clear depth yields of their far height and hue.'

A delightful hour or two in the evening may be spent in rowing on the lake in a good English boat (to be hired for 2 or 3 francs an hour on the Quai du Mont Blanc), or to take a place in the steamer for a short trip, and, if so inclined, select one that has a company of Swiss singers on board, to give a promenade concert.

NORTHERN BANK.

We will now make the circuit of the lake describing all that is of importance, and leave the tourist to visit for himself whatever opportunity and inclination may render desirable, or if unable to do more, survey them as well as possible from the steamer deck, or the window of the railway carriage.

The railway from Geneva along the Northern shore of the lake, has stations at *Chambéry, Genthod-Bellevue, Versoix, Coppet, Céligny, Nyon, Gland, Rolle, Aubonne, St. Prex, Morges, Renens, Lausanne, Lutry, Cully, Vevey, La Tour de Peilz, Burier, Clarens, Vernex-Montreux, Veytaux-Chillon, Villeneuve.* Some of these places are small, but are well known to many English visitors, from having children or friends at the schools which abound all through the district. There are also numerous houses and châlets which belong to or are occupied by English gentlemen. Many exquisite views of the lake are obtained on this route.

The steamboat journey, which is performed between Geneva and Villeneuve in about four hours, is far preferable to the rail, presenting a thousand charms which cannot be seen and leisurely contemplated from a railway carriage. The steamer keeps near the Swiss or Northern side, passing in front of Sécheron, Prégny (p. 131), Chambesy, Bellerive, Genthod (where the two Genevese scholars, De Saussure and Bonnet dwelt), and Versoix. This town was vainly attempted to be nursed into a rival of Geneva by Choiseul, the minister of Louis XV. Looking southward, we have a grand view of Mont Blanc; the peaks surrounding it are the Salève, the Savoy Alps, the Dôle and the Voirons. Northward, the long blue line of the Jura forms the background of the Swiss shore. Above Versoix, is the pass of La Foncile, one of the few carriage roads across the Jura; it passes under the Reculet, the highest summit of the range, and affords magnificent views.

At Versoix we leave the Genevese territory and enter the Canton of Vaud. Soon we reach Coppet, where there is a château belonging to the Duc de Broglie, where Necker, the Finance Minister of Louis, retreated to end his days, and where also his daughter, Madame de Staël, spent the long years of her exile, when banished by Napoleon I. The villages conspicuous on the green hills by Coppet, are Myes and Tannay. The next landing place is by Céligny, which though enclosed by Vaud, is Genevese territory. Close by, the pretty village of Crans is noticeable.

The next stopping place is at **Nyon**, an ancient Roman colony, founded by Julius Cæsar. From this place the ascent of the Dôle is most readily accomplished. The promontory of Promenthoux here juts out, opposite to that of Yvoire in Savoy, and passing these, the lake expands to a much greater width. Above the point of Promenthoux, is the Chateau de Prangins, formerly belonging to Joseph Buonaparte. Prince Napoleon's villa, La Bergerie, is very near.

Passing Dulit, Bursinel, Bursins, and other villages, and numerous pleasant villas, we arrive at **Rolle**, from which to Thonon on the opposite shore the greatest width of the lake is measured. This is an agreeable little town with a small island in the harbour, laid out as a promenade, and adorned with a monument to General La Harpe, a native of the place. We next come in sight of Perroy and Allaman, passing the celebrated vineyard of La Côte, nine miles in length. Between Rolle and Aubonne, on the height above, the Signal de Bouchy should be noticed. One of the most extensive views in Switzerland is obtained from it.

Passing close to the point of S. Prex, and in sight of innumerable villas, and the towering ruins of the **Chateau de Wufflens**, attributed to good Queen Bertha in the 10th century, we arrive at **Morges.** (Hotel des Alpes. Pop. 2800), with its arsenal and cannon foundry close by the lake. Here Mont Blanc is again beheld; a splendid view, one of the finest on the lake. It is, however, quickly lost as we pass on. Morges is a delightful place for a lengthened visit. The picturesquely situated village of S. Sulpice is soon left behind, and the next landing place is Ouchy.

Ouchy (Hotel d'Angleterre). At the Hotel Ancre, Byron and Shelley had to stay two days through stress of weather after boating across from Diodati, and here "The Prisoner of Chillon" was written. Omnibuses run from Ouchy in half an hour, for half a franc, to Lausanne.

LAUSANNE.

(Hotel Gibbon, an excellent house, in the best situation). In the garden-house of the Hotel Gibbon, Gibbon completed his "*Decline and Fall* of the Roman Empire."

Lausanne is the capital of the Canton of Vaud, beautifully situate on hills and intervening valleys. It enjoys the advantage of a salubrious climate, and a moderate temperature in winter; but its streets are badly paved and unpleasant for promenading, and conveyances here are dear and unsatisfactory.

From the steamboat or railway, the town is entered by the Rue de Grand Chene, which conducts to the **Place S. Francois**, the chief place of public resort, containing the Post and Telegraph Offices, etc., and also the **Hotel Gibbon**, in the garden of which the great historian completed his history of Rome. To the left is the **Grand Pont**, a fine structure with a double row of arches, spanning one of the intersecting valleys, and affording a good central view of the city.

The fine old **Cathedral**, whose Gothic towers were seen standing high and dark against the sky, before landing at Ouchy, is the chief sight of the town, and indeed the only one which need detain the tourist desirous of making rapid transit. The most direct approach is by 164 mean-looking steps, ascending from the market place. Like most Protestant places of worship, the Cathedral is not generally open to the public; Thursday only being the day on which it can be seen without application to the sacristan, No. 5 in the little square north of the Cathedral. The simple and massive edifice is one of the handsomest Gothic churches in Switzerland. It is associated with the stirring events of the Reformation, for here in 1536, Calvin, Farel, and Viret met in disputation; from which came about the separation of Vaud from the Romish Church, and the transfer of its allegiance from Savoy to Berne. The Cathedral, originally founded about 1000 A.D., was completed in its present form in 1275, and consecrated in the presence of Rudolph of Hapsburgh, by Pope Gregory X. It is 333 feet in length and 61 in height. It has a central spire and two towers to the west, of which only one is really completed. The beautifully sculptured West Portal (of recent date) and the South Portal, or Porch of the Apostle, claim special notice. The prominent features of the interior are—

Columns "(over a thousand)"
The Rose Window.
Monument of Otho of Grandson.
Tomb of Victor Amadeus VIII. (who was successively duke, bishop, pope (Felix V.), and finally monk.
Monuments of—
  Bishop of Menthonex.
  Russian Princess Orlow.

Duchess of Courland.
Harriet, first wife of Lord Stratford de Redcliffe, by *Bartolini.*
Robert Ellison.
Countess Wallmoden.

There is a fine view from the **Terrace** surrounding the Cathedral; but if the visitor likes to ascend the clock tower (162 feet), a much finer prospect will be obtained.

The visitor who has time to make the round of the town, will find a few other objects of interest. In the Rue Montèe de S. Laurence is the **Musèe Arlaud**, containing some good ancient and modern works of art, open free on Sundays, Wednesdays, and Saturdays, from 11 a.m. to 3 p.m. Near the Cathedral is the old **château**, erected in the 13th century, but since subjected to many alterations. It is in form a heavy square tower, with turrets, and from once being the Episcopal Palace, it has now become the Council Hall. The Barracks are adjacent, and at a short distance are the Academy and College (founded in 1587). In the **Museum**, which is worth a visit, will be found—

Collection of Minerals, given by Emperor Alexander to General La Harpe.
Zoological and Botanical Collections.
Antiquities from Herculaneum, Pompeii, etc.
Relief of the Bernese Oberland.
Antiquities from Aventicum.
Objects from the Swiss Lake Dwellings.
Natural History Collection.

The **schools** of Lausanne are in very high repute, and pupils from Great Britain are found in them in large numbers. Professors of music, drawing, etc., abound. The Public Schools of Design maintain a high standard of excellence. There is an Asylum for the Blind, admirably conducted, which owes its origin to Mr. Haldimand, an Englishman, who, when resident here, took great interest in works of philanthropy and benevolence.

In the Rue de Bourg, which is the central and chief business street, containing most of the principal hotels, there is an **English Reading-room** and Circulating Library, where, for an admission fee of half a franc, the traveller can peruse the *Times, Punch, Illustrated London News,* or other favourite journals from home. The English Chapel is on the road between Lausanne and Ouchy.

THE ENVIRONS OF LAUSANNE

are exceedingly beautiful; an abundance of tasteful country villas enliven the scene. Those fond of a quiet, healthy town, with plenty of opportunity for charming walks in the vicinity, will find their tastes well provided for. One of the most frequented spots is the Montbenon, a fine open promenade on the Geneva road, commanding a lovely prospect of the lake and its surroundings. The Signal is on a hill 2000 feet high, north of the town. The finest view in the neighbourhood is obtained here, the greater part of Lake Leman being visible, and a vast horizon, crowded with mountain peaks. The adjacent forest of Sauvabellin is traditionally linked with the worship of Bel by the Druids. Les Grandes Roches are about a mile and a half on the road to Yverdon, affording a fine view across the lake, including Mont Blanc, which is not visible from the Signal. The Blumer Institution for Delicate Children, at the Chateau de Vennes, on the Berne road, is worthy of attention. The view is grand. The English Cemetery, two miles along the Berne road, contains the remains of John Philip Kemble, the tragedian. At a short distance is the garden he delighted to cultivate, and the house where he died (Feb. 26, 1823).

Several excursions can be made from Lausanne by rail, amongst others, viâ Cassonsay, to the magnificent scenery of the Val Orbe; or to all parts of the lake, from Ouchy.

Leaving Ouchy, the route becomes surpassingly beautiful, the steamer passes Pully and Lutry, and we find ourselves in front of the celebrated vineyards of Lavaux, which extend for ten miles along the lake. An immense amount of labour has been expended in rearing the innumerable low walls which sustain the crumbling soil. Near Cully, which stands in the midst of these vineyards, is the monument to Major Davel, killed during the long struggle between Vaud and Berne. On a terrace of rocks, near S. Saphorin, stands the old castle of Glérolles; and hard by a picturesque waterfall is formed by the torrent of the Forestay. Above, on the height, is the Tour de Gourse, the remains of a stronghold, dating from the 10th century—once a refuge for the neighbouring villagers in times of chronic strife and disturbance. The traveller will be struck with the amount of skill and industry that must have been necessary to construct a carriage road and railway in the narrow limits between the mountains and the lake. On leaving

Glérolles, and catching sight of Vevey, the slopes are more gradual, the valley wider, and the whole landscape softer and more cultivated.

VEVEY

(Grand Hotel Vevey),

(Pop. 7800), the representative of the old Roman *Vibiscum*, is the second town of the Canton Vaud; clean, picturesque, and with a climate free from extremes, either in summer or winter. The town is situated at the end of a narrow valley, down which the Veveyse rushes to the lake. Its exquisite views and pleasant walks in the neighbourhood attract a large number of visitors.

From Vevey may be seen Chillon, Clarens, Villeneuve, and the mouth of the Rhone; in the distance the Alps of the Valois, with the Dent du Midi and Mont Catogne; whilst on the opposite shore of the lake are seen the rocks of Meillerie, with the Dent d'Oche. The best point of view in the town is the Quai Sina; but some spots outside the town afford more extensive prospects.

On the left of the landing-place is the chateau of M. Couvreu, with its beautiful tropical garden, open free from 10 a.m. to 12, on Thursdays, Fridays, and Sundays. At other times the gardener expects a franc.

In the **Church of St. Martin** (15th century), amongst the vineyards above the town, are the graves of Ludlow and Broughton, two of the judges of Charles I.;—it was Broughton who read the sentence of death. In vain Charles II. demanded their extradition; in this quiet town they ended their days. An "Indicateur des Montagnes" will be found here.

The English Church service takes place at St. Claire on Sundays, at 11 a.m., and 3.30 p.m.

Rousseau's favourite inn, the "Clef," has been transformed into a café, with the same name.

Vevey is the centre of the Swiss wine-growing district; the wine called Lavaux being its speciality. An ancient guild known as "L'Abbaye des Vignerons," exists here, whose function it is to promote the interests of the wine-growers, and excite competition by presenting prizes to the most successful. After an extraordinary wine season, a grand festival is held, known as La Fête des Vignerons. It last took place in 1865.

"*The Vintners'* Fête at Vevey," says a recent writer in "*All the World Over*," "is famous everywhere, and though still in vogue, is a genuine relic of the old worship of Bacchus—a deity long revered in this, a vine country *par excellence.*

"The continuance of this fête is characteristic of the conservative and mirth-loving Vaudois. It comes off every twelve or fifteen years in the market-place of Vevey. A large platform is raised, the square is gay with flags and triumphal arches, and thronged with spectators—artisans, little peasant proprietors by hundreds, and strangers from all quarters. The music strikes up, and gives the signal for the grand allegorical procession of the Four Seasons. But first comes a corps of Swiss halberdiers in motley costume, the vintner guilds of Vevey and la Paus, and their abbé carrying a gilt crosier. He opens the proceedings with a speech, and the coronation of the two most successful vintners.

"This little ceremony over, the procession begins. First enters Spring, a young girl in the character of Pales, reclining in a triumphal car. Children and shepherdesses dance around her, haymakers, labourers, and Alpine cowherds sing their Ranz des Vaches. Summer follows—a lady of riper years, impersonating Ceres—in a car drawn by two large oxen, accompanied by children carrying beehives and other appropriate fixtures. With Autumn comes the climax of excitement, as Bacchus, the god of the vine, appears in a chariot drawn by horses covered with tiger skins. This is the signal for wild dances and wilder music, after the fashion of the ancients. He is accompanied by his train, among which Silenus, mounted on his ass, figures conspicuously. Winter ends the cortège, which thus forms a complete series of illustrations of rural life. In this, the cold season, the peasant's work is ended, and he returns to his cottage hearth. So winter stands in their minds for things domestic, and is pictured accordingly. The aged parents lead the way, then come the young couple, bride and bridegroom. Rustic dances by woodmen and huntsmen follow, and the whole concludes with a grand patriotic hymn. The tenacity of life shown by this remarkable fête arises, no doubt, from its being more than a mere recreation and show. It still breathes the true spirit of the people, of whose labours and joys it is a faithful picture." *

The environs of Vevey are replete with interest. **Hauteville**, a mile and a half from the town, is an imposing structure, and affords beyond doubt the finest prospect in the neigh-

* "*All the World Over.*" (T. Cook & Son.) July, 1875.

bourhood. **Blonay**, at a somewhat greater distance from the town, is a romantic castle, which for eight centuries was the residence of the most powerful and distinguished of the old Vaudois families. History and tradition join in confirmation of the spotless honour and renowned valour of the house of De Blonay. When the aristocracy were swept away at the close of the last century, the family was still held in local reverence. It exists in the neighbouring French province of Chablais at this day. The **Pleiades** (4000 feet) is visited for the view from its summit, and also for the Sulphur Baths of **L'Alliaz** at the base. **La Tour de Peilz** is a little village west of Vevey, with an old castle built in 1239 by Amadeus IV., Duke of Savoy; but its two round towers are of very uncertain and possibly far earlier origin. Peilz means skin, and is said to refer to a certain Crusading proprietor, who returned to find his château roofless, and made for it a temporary roof of skins.

Most of the objects mentioned in the preceding paragraph are visible from the steamer as we resume our course on the lake. The vineyards again reappear, and become a conspicuous feature of the landscape. In about a quarter of an hour we arrive at **Clarens**.

Clarens is all poetry, and little else, and Byron must again describe it to us, in the place which none would feel as if they had visited, did they not read it here—

"Clarens! sweet Clarens, birthplace of deep Love!
Thine air is the young breath of passionate thought;
Thy trees take root in Love; the snows above
The very glaciers have his colours caught,
And sunset into rose-hues sees them wrought
By rays which sleep there lovingly: the rocks,
The permanent crags, tell here of Love, who sought
In them a refuge from the worldly shocks
Which stir and sting the soul with hope that woos, then mocks.

"'Twas not for fiction chose Rousseau this spot,
Peopling it with affections; but he found
It was the scene which passion must allot
To the mind's purified beings; 'twas the ground
Where early Love his Psyche's zone unbound,
And hallowed it with loveliness; 'tis lone,
And wonderful, and deep, and hath a sound,
And sense, and sight of sweetness; here the Rhone
Hath spread himself a couch, the Alps have rear'd a throne."

Notice the clump of trees to the left known as the "*Bosquet de Julie,*" the favourite resort of "La Nouvelle Héloise."

Montreux (Langbien's Hotel Beau-Séjour au Lac), the warm winter refuge of the invalid, Glion, Vernex, and Veytaux, embosomed in walnuts, successively appear in sight, and near the latter is the renowned Castle of Chillon.

This Castle, washed by the waters of the lake, which at this point is over 300 feet in depth, was built in A.D. 830, and fortified by the Dukes of Savoy about four centuries afterwards. Apart from its historic interest, it is impressive from its solid walls and towers, and its strangely isolated situation on a rock connected with the bank by a wooden bridge. Over the entrance is the inscription, "God bless all who come in and go out." It well repays a visit to its feudal hall, bedrooms, etc., and the rock-hewn dungeons beneath, in one of which thousands of Jews are said to have been sentenced to death, and forthwith drowned in the lake. The beam where criminals were hung, the torture-chamber, the oubliette, and other horrors, are shown. But the dungeon rendered memorable by Lord Byron's "Prisoner of Chillon" is, of course, the chief point of interest.

"Chillon! thy prison is a holy place,
And thy sad floor an altar—for 'twas trod,
Until his very steps have left a trace
Worn, as if thy cold pavement were a sod,
By Bonnivard! May none those marks efface,
For they appeal from tyranny to God."

The tourist, when he treads the pavement worn down by the feet of the prisoner, or touches the iron ring in the dungeon by which he was bound to one of the pillars, must remember that the subject of Lord Byron's poem is not to be received as a record of the historical Bonnivard. A few facts may not be uninteresting, nor need they necessarily spoil the charm of the fiction.

Francois de Bonnivard was born in 1496 at Seyssel. He was educated at Turin, and at the age of sixteen received from his uncle the rich Priory of St. Victor, and the lands attached thereto. In 1519 the Duke of Savoy attacked Geneva, and Bonnivard, who was of liberal opinions, and opposed to feudal oppression, sided with the Republic. He was captured, and confined by the tyrannical Duke for two years in the Castle at Grolée. No sooner was he released, than he again made a strenuous effort to advance the principles of the Republic. Again, in 1530, he fell into the hands of the Duke of Savoy, and was confined for six years in the Castle of Chillon. During this time the Cantons of Berne and Fribourg were in league with the Republic of Geneva; and when at length the Bernese took possession of the Canton of Vaud, they lost no time in throwing open the doors of the Château de Chillon, and releasing Bonnivard. He returned to Geneva, fought bravely in the cause of the Republic, and died in 1570 at the age of seventy-five. His fine collection of books formed the foundation of the public Library (p. 129).

"On the fact of Bonnivard's imprisonment here, and certain traditions of the residents in the vicinity, Lord Byron founded his short narrative poem of 'The Prisoner of Chillon.' The additional circumstance of two of the brothers of Bonnivard having been imprisoned with him has no foundation, except in the imagination of the poet. The description of their sufferings and death, which forms the most affecting part of the narrative, was probably suggested by Dante's Count Ugolino and his two sons."

The earliest recorded prisoner was a dangerous Bishop of Corbie, shut up here by Louis le Debonnair.

Near the Castle of Chillon a part of the plot of Rousseau's celebrated "Nouvelle Héloise" is laid.

We now speedily arrive at **Villeneuve**, the ancient little town at the head of the lake. Some of the steamers go on to Bouveret.

SOUTHERN BANK.

Between Geneva and Bouveret diligences run to and fro daily along the southern or Savoy side of the lake. Steamers run twice daily to Bouveret in five and a half hours; four times daily to Évian-les-Éaux, crossing thence to Ouchy (see local time-tables).

Two miles from Geneva is Cologny, between which and the lake stands the Villa Diodati, where Lord Byron resided in 1816, and composed the third canton of Childe Harolde and Manfred. The hamlets of *La Belotte* (stat.), Bessinges, Vesenar, Collonge, *Bellerive* (stat.), *Anières* (stat.), and *Hermance* (stat.), are in Genevan territory. Entering Chablais, a district of Savoy, we pass the Savoyard Castles of Beauregard and De Boigne, and the little village of Nernier, on the edge of the water. From the point of Yvoire a deep bay recedes, on which stands **Thonon** (nine miles by road from Geneva), the ancient seat of the Dukes of Savoy.

Evian, *or* **Evian-les-Eaux**, is a fashionable French *watering-place;* the mineral waters have a high reputation for gout, and various other complaints. A company, "under English direction," is engaged in developing the attractions of this charming neighbourhood. Several short excursions can be made; for instance, to the fine ruined Castle of **Allinges**, where S. Francis de Sales dwelt many years; to **Laninge**, or to the Valley of the Dranse. The torrent of the Dranse widens as it reaches the lake, and is crossed by a curious bridge of twenty-four arches. Near the mouth of the river is the pretty village of Amphion, with ferruginous waters.

Another pleasant expedition is to the old Castle of **La Ripaille**, famous for its connection with the eccentric Victor Amadeus VIII. of Savoy, successively duke, pope, and friar. This ruin is seen from the steamer soon after passing Thonon. To this monastery he withdrew for several years with six companions, and founded the order of the Knight-errants of St. Maurice. According to one tradition, they passed their time in carousing, and thus gave rise to the French expression, "*faire ripaille*," or to make merry, very merry. According to another, they led an exemplary life of abstinence, and the name of the convent was derived simply from its situation on the shore, or *ripa*.

It is now a farm, the church is a hayloft, the cemetery a cultivated field. The park of oaks which Amadeus had laid out in the form of a star was allowed to run wild. The vegetation here is extremely rich. An enormous walnut-tree overshadows the ruins; its origin, according to folk-lore, was supernatural indeed. The tree sprang from a walnut containing a diamond brought hither by the Prince of Darkness himself, from the shades below, and buried in the ground. At certain intervals it was said to bear a crop of diamonds, but of late years the tree appears to have given up this good habit. In the numerous superstitions of Chablais and Vaud, hidden jewels and buried gold and silver play a prominent part. The nobles, constantly at war with Berne and Geneva, alternately conquered and conquering, would often find it a measure of prudence in such precarious times to conceal their treasure. Valuables dug up here from time to time prove this to have been their habit. At Evian no landed property is ever sold without some special stipulation as to reserved rights on possible treasure trove; and when, in building, excavations have to be made, a watch is always set on the workmen.

The views across the lake from Evian are very fine.

Passing on we see **La Tour Ronde**, and then the cliffs

of **La Meillerie**, famous for their supposed resemblance to the Leucadian rock. They afford excellent stone for building At one time they ran down straight to the sea, and Evian and S. Gingolph could only communicate by water. The rocks were blasted by Napoleon, to get material for the Simplon Road.

It is in this portion of the lake, where the waters are least disturbed, that the fisheries are chiefly carried on. From hence come those fascinating little boats with double sails, like wings, that strike every traveller who sees them poised like butterflies on the surface. Here, in Rousseau's story, the lover of Héloise lodged, to be in sight of her dwelling-place on the opposite shore.

Six miles further on is **St. Gingolph**, the border village between Valais and Chablais, situated on both sides of a ravine that separates the two countries. For long, the only place of worship was on the Chablais side, so that people were in Switzerland at home, and in Savoy when they went to church.

Excursions from St. Gingolph are made to the **Dent d' Oche** (8000 feet), in four hours; up the Gorge of the Morge, the frontier ravine just alluded to; or by boat to the Grotto of Viviers. Boats can be hired to cross the lake for ten francs to Clarens, Montreux, Chillon, or Villeneuve, or for six francs to Vevey. Three miles beyond St. Gingolph is **Bouveret**, at the head of the lake.

Besides the swift Rhone, cleaving "his way between heights which appear as lovers who have parted," Lake Leman receives about forty rivers and streams. The depth of the lake varies from about 950 feet near the rocks of Meillerie, to 30 or 40 feet in the neighbourhood of Geneva. It covers an extent of about ninety square miles.

The marvellous beauty of this delightful lake has won encomiums from a host of writers. Mr. Laing says, "The snowy peak, the waterfall, the glacier, are but the wonders of Switzerland; her beauty is in her lakes—the blue eyes of this Alpine land. The most beautiful passage of scenery in Switzerland is, to my mind, the upper end of the Lake of Geneva, from Vevey, or from Lausanne to Villeneuve." Again, "the margin of the lake is carved out, and built up into terrace above terrace of vineyards and Indian corn plots; behind this narrow belt, grain crops, orchards, grass fields, and chestnut trees have their zone; higher still upon the hill side, pasture grass and forest trees occupy the ground; above rises a dense mass of pine forest, broken by peaks of bare rocks shooting up, weather-worn and white, through this dark-green mantle; and, last of all, the eternal snow piled up high against the deep blue sky; and all this glory of Nature, this varied majesty of mountain-land, within one glance!" "It is not surprising that this water of Geneva has seen upon its banks," he adds, "the most powerful minds of each succeeding generation. Calvin, Knox, Voltaire, Gibbon, Rousseau, Madame de Staël, Byron, John Kemble, have, with all their essential diversities and degrees of intellectual powers, been united here in one common feeling of the magnificence of the scenery round it. This land of alp and lake is indeed a mountain-temple, reared for the human mind on the dull unvaried plains of Europe."

It is from Geneva and the lake—especially that celebrated view near Morges—that the traveller realizes the supremacy of Mont Blanc, more than he can do even at Chamouny, when in its immediate presence. No one should be content with the scenery at the Geneva end of the lake, which is comparatively uninteresting. Its grandeur is only fully perceived from Morges or Ouchy.

GENEVA TO CHAMOUNY.

(To Sallanches, 32 miles; to Chamouny, 50 miles.)

The journey from Geneva to Chamouny is along a good carriage-road. The diligences take 10 hours. From Sallanches (reached in 6½ hours) the remainder of the journey may be performed on foot easily and pleasantly by good walkers.

Early application at the office is desirable to ensure seats. The diligences of the Messageries Imperiales are arranged for affording the best views of the country, the after-part being open; and there are also two seats in front. When places are taken, they must be described and entered in the register of the office, and on the pay-bills of the conductor. This prevents all grumbling and confusion, as parties can only take their allotted places. Diligences start from Geneva three or four times daily; the exact time must be previously ascertained at the Hotel or Diligence Office (p. 124).

A pleasant suburban road from the New Quarter of Geneva leads to the large village of **Chene.** On the right, Mont Salève, the Castle of Mornex, and the Jura mountains are seen; and on the left the Voirons. At the river Foron, the French (formerly Savoyard) territory is reached, the first village in which is **Annemasse** (Custom House). The high conical mountain called the Môle (6128 ft.), here comes fairly into view, and forms a prominent object for miles. The Castle of Etrambière is passed on the right, at the foot of the Petit Salève. The road follows the valley of the Arve. This stream, as the banks abundantly testify, is sometimes a broad and furious torrent. The Menoge river is crossed by a broad lofty bridge. After passing **Nangy**, the Château de Pierre, the property of an Englishman, is seen on a small fir-clad eminence. **Contamines** is passed on the left, and the two ruined towers of the ancient castle of Faucigny stand out conspicuously. The bold mountain scenery bounding the Arve valley, now becomes very enjoyable.

Bonneville is one of the most considerable towns on the road, though its population has much declined of late years. (From this place there is a good road—17 miles—traversed by diligence in 4 hours to Annecy, where the rail can be taken to Aix-les-Eaux.) At the foot of the town, the Arve is crossed by a stone bridge; and on the river side, close by, is a monument over ninety feet in height, erected in honour of *Rex Carolus Felix* of Sardinia, as an expression of gratitude for favours conferred on the town by the execution of works to prevent inundations of the Arve. To the summit of the Brezon or the Môle is a four hours' excursion from Bonneville.

Through a fertile district between the Môle and Brezon, we pass on to **Vougy**, where the Giffre, from the Sixt Valley, joins the Arve, and then to **Scionzier**, by which lies the romantic Reposoir Valley.

The village of **Cluses**, newly built since the fire of 1844, is chiefly inhabited by watchmakers. Near this town, the Brezon precipices seem almost to overshadow the route, and the fertile valley seems to be closed in by the mountain. But the road is continued through a narrow gorge. Beyond La Balme, two small cannons are planted, for the purpose of awakening the echoes. The entrance to a grotto is seen on the side of the rock to the left, which penetrates into the heart of the mountain to the extent of 1800 feet. Mules wait here to take visitors to the cavern. A couple of hours will be occupied if the visit is *undertaken. Passing* **Magland** and on to **St. Martin**, *several fine cascades* and waterfalls attract attention on the left; *the finest of* these is the graceful Nant d'Arpenaz, dreadfully beset, however, with specimen dealers, cannon firers, and various sorts of beggars. The rocks on the same side of the road are exceedingly fine, and the low flat on the right show signs of the effects of the overflow of the Arve, to which the country is subject. At Sallanches, the diligence used to terminate its course, and passengers were transferred to small carriages, because of the hilly and stony roads before them. Now there is a new good road all the way, but it is not so interesting as the old. The diligence used to come into Sallanches (¼ mile) to allow the passengers to dine and return to St. Martin to pursue the journey. From the bridge between the two towns, fine views of Mont Blanc are obtained. A well-known writer has thus described the scene :—

"Mont Blanc, and his army of white-robed brethren, rose before us in the distance, glorious as the four-and-twenty elders around the great white throne. The wonderful gradations of colouring in Alpine landscape are not among the least of its charms. How can I describe it? Imagine yourself standing with me on this projecting rock, overlooking a deep piny gorge, through which flow the brawling waters of the Arve. On the other side of this rise mountains whose heaving swells of velvet-green cliffs and dark pines are fully made out and coloured; behind this mountain rises another, whose tints are softened and shaded, and seem to be seen through a purplish veil; behind that rises another, of a decided cloud-like purple; and in the next still the purple tint changes to rosy lilac; while above all, like another world up in the sky, mingling its tints with the passing clouds, sometimes obscured by them, and then breaking out between them, lie the glacier regions. These glaciers, in the setting sun, look like rivers of light pouring down from the clouds. Such was the scene, which I remember with perfect distinctness as enchanting my attention on one point of the road."

Sallanches, like most of the towns on the route now under notice, has had its conflagration. It was on Good Friday, 1840, when *everybody* was at church, that the fire broke out.

The road from Sallanches and St. Martin, still recommended to pedestrians, continues along the picturesque banks of the Arve. Chède is passed, near which is a fine waterfall. The road then crosses a plain, which was a lake till choked up by mud and stones in 1837, and Servoz is next reached. Les Ouches is the first village in the valley of Chamouny.

The new road is on the left bank of the Arve; it crosses

the Bon-Nant, and passes the **Baths of St. Gervaix** (5 miles). They are situated in the lovely Bon-Nant ravine, and seem efficacious for numerous disorders of the stomach, nerves, skin, etc. The village of St. Gervaix is a mile from the baths. Excursions to the eastern part of Mont Blanc, or the ascent of the great mountain itself, can be arranged from this place. There is a cross route, 5 hours' walk, by the Col de Voza, with grand views of Mont Blanc, etc., to Chamouny.

The Tête Noire (not the Tête Noire leading to Martigny) is then skirted, and, after passing the Tunnel of Châtelard and Le Lac, the old road is reached at the Hotel des Montets.

CHAMOUNY

(Hotel de l'Angleterre and Hotel Royal)

is situated in a valley, about 28 miles in length from the Col de Balme in the N.E., to the Col de Voza in the S.W. Its north-western boundary is formed by the Aiguilles Rouges and the Brévent; whilst on the south-eastern side, Mont Blanc, with seven glaciers streaming down towards the valley, form its crowning glory. Along the entire length of the valley flows the Arve, with a multitude of mountain-born rivulets flowing into it.

Chamouny is 3446 ft. above the sea. Its permanent population is small, but in the season it is a crowded resort of tourists, for whom the district offers attractions and excursions innumerable. Chamouny was long an almost unknown spot. The monks of St. Benedict came and settled here in the eleventh century, and its occasional notice or inspection by Bishops and Counts of Geneva is historically proved; but it was not till Pococke and Wyndham visited the valley in 1741, and reported on it to the Royal Society of London, that the locality began to be generally known. From that time the fame of the valley has spread, and the tide of eager sightseers has increased, till now in every land Chamouny is justly celebrated for its glorious prospect of the "Monarch of Mountains" and its surroundings, and for the absorbing interest of the excursions that may be undertaken in the neighbourhood.

Applications for the services of any of the 200 intelligent and efficient **guides** of Chamouny must be made at the office of the *Guide* en Chef. There is an official tariff and a code of rules as to the engagement of guides, mules, etc., which must be strictly carried out.

There is an **English Church** at Chamouny, where services are celebrated during the season.

Loppé's collection of **Alpine Pictures** is worth seeing. The collection is at the back of the Royal Hotel.

The following itinerary may be useful to the traveller:—

To visit Montanvert, the Mer de Glace, the Chapeau, and the source of the Arveiron, is an excursion of at least 6 or 7 hours; or a day may be well spent over it.

To the Brévent and back, 7 to 8 hours.

To the Glacier des Bossons and back, about 4 hours.

To the Flégère and back, 5 hours.

To the Jardin and back, 10 to 12 hours. A good day's work.

We will note a few of the principal excursions, and the tourist must combine or select from these according to the time, at his disposal.

Montanvert (6302 ft. above the sea level, or 2858 ft. above Chamouny) needs no guide; anybody will point out the path; and when once found, nobody need lose it. The ascent can easily be done in two hours. On the way, a pine forest, *débris* of avalanches, and other scenes usual in mountain paths, will be passed, and by-and-by you will stand face to face with the

Mer de Glace. "Imagine the ocean to have overflowed the mountains in front of you, and to have descended, boiling, foaming, dashing, bubbling, into the valley, thousands of feet below. Imagine the waters in the height of their wild and furious descent to have been miraculously stopped by the Divine fiat, 'Be still,' and you see before you thousands of sharp and tapering billows, mountain waves arisen and petrified before they burst, snow-crested heights and chasms of the deep. Such is the Mer de Glace. And then imagine the surroundings. To your right, as you look up, are green, precipitous banks, covered with shrubs and plants, and beyond rises Mont Blanc, approached by walls of barren rock, where the snow can find no settling-place. In front and to your left rises a barrier of rocks, and mountains, and peaks that make you cold and dizzy to gaze upon. There is the *Aiguille du Dru*, shooting up alone like an arrow, 6000 feet above the spot on which you stand. There are the dark, awful masses of vertical granite, on which no blade of grass will grow, no bird will rest, no snow will cleave, standing like evil spirits brooding over the haunts of *death*. Then imagine the sounds which give tone to these scenes. There is a crash and a tumble, and thunder is echoing all around, and a thousand weird voices seem chuckling at some sad disaster. It is an avalanche that has fallen in the distance! Listen again. You hear the moan and the strain of glaciers grinding each other to powder in a deadly strife. Again, and you hear the war and tumult of cataracts and torrents rushing madly into the hollow vaults, and delighting to startle their awful stillness!"

Nearly 300 feet above the edge of this sea of ice is an inn, where the night can be spent by those wishing to go forward from this point in the morning. A rude hut once stood here, where Forbes and Tyndal studied glacial phenomena. The "Pierre des Anglais," commemorating the visit of Pococke and Wyndham, is close by.

Everybody should cross the Mer de Glace; it is easy for ladies, or even children, but should not be attempted without a guide, as the steps cut in the ice may easily be missed, and the traveller would as easily get astray and nervous. If intending to return direct from Montanvert to Chamouny, the visitor should first take a walk by the side of the glacier for some distance, and so get a better idea of the wondrous scene.

The descent from Montanvert, after crossing the Mer de Glace, is by the **Mauvais Pas**, cut in the side of the rocks, which once was a formidable journey, but is now bereft of its horrors from having an iron rail along it, to which the traveller can hold, instead of having to take his chance upon the bare rock-ledge. The green mound called the

Chapeau, where some glorious views are obtained over the Glacier des Bois, is next reached. Here there is a grotto and an inn. Descending by the moraine, the visitor soon reaches

The Source of the Arveiron. The stream issues from the Glacier des Bois, and passes through an arch of ice. Sometimes this spot is very beautiful, and at others it has little or no interest, and does not repay the trouble of leaving the direct path to view it. In any case it is dangerous to stand under the ice arch, and instances are recorded in which fatal results have happened.

N.B.—Whatever else the traveller may omit, the round just described, occupying about 7 hours, ought to be taken. Either the Chapeau or the Source of the Arveiron, or both, may, of course, be visited direct from Chamouny, without crossing the *Mer de Glace, if* wished,

To visit **The Jardin** is a good day's work from Chamouny, even by taking a mule to and from Montanvert. From the inn at this place, where it is best to pass the previous night, it is a seven hours' expedition, and the descent to Chamouny may be effected in less than two hours more. This is a very fine glacier excursion. Guides are required, but ladies may readily undertake this expedition, and an idea will be obtained of the glorious rock and glacier solitudes of Mont Blanc, which no shorter excursion will afford. The Jardin itself is an island of about seven acres, a grassy, flower-sprinkled oasis of beauty in the midst of eternal snows and aiguilles.

The **Flégère**, a plateau on the side of the Aiguilles Rouge, (6500 ft.) is ascended for its fine view of Mont Blanc. This excursion can be entirely accomplished on mules, about five hours being required for going and returning. There is a châlet where refreshment, or, if required, beds can be obtained.

The **Brévent** (8000 ft.) presents an almost identical view towards the south-east with that from the Flégère. It takes about four hours to walk up and somewhat less to descend. Many visitors only go up as far as the inn at Plan Praz (3 miles) which can be reached with mules. Here there is a terrace 6772 feet above the sea, connected by a mountain path (3 miles) with the Flégère. An hour's walking brings you to the foot of La Cheminée, where some fifty feet of nearly vertical climbing must be done. There is a longer way round for ladies. The view from the summit (8283 ft.) is a glorious panorama of the Mont Blanc chain, and the hamlet-studded valley of Chamouny from the Col de Balme to the Col de Voza.

The **Cascade du Dard**, the **Glacier des Bossons**, the **Pavillon de Pierre Pointue**, and many other attractions, can be visited by those who can make a lengthened sojourn at Chamouny. Those not intending to return by Martigny should, if possible, spend a day in exploring the **Col de Balme** and **Tete Noire**; a mule path connects the two (p. 158). Those wishing to get a slight notion of the ascent of Mont Blanc, without encountering the dangerous portions, may ascend to the Grand Mulets, and spend a night at the inn.

MONT BLANC.

To realize in some degree the height of this wonderful mountain, compare the following heights of certain mountains in *Europe*.

Malvern Hills	1,444 ft.
Skiddaw	3,022 "
Macgillicuddy Reeks	3,404 "
Snowdon	3,571 "
Vesuvius	3,731 "
Cairngorm	4,050 "
Ben Nevis	4,380 "
Grand St. Bernard (Convent) . .	8,040 "
Peak of Teneriffe	12,358 "
Jungfrau	13,725 "
Monte Rosa	15,540 "
Mont Blanc	15,781 "

It is curious how much higher Mont Blanc appears from the Flégère than it does from the valley of Chamouny, but even there the actual peak of Mont Blanc does not so impress the spectator with the glory and majesty of nature, as do the marvellous peaks around it, varying from 12,000 to 13,000 feet.

The group of mountains known as Mont Blanc is an immense mass of rock, stretching about 13 miles from S.W. to N.E., and about 5 or 6 miles in breadth. The enclosing valleys vary from 3000 to 4000 feet above the sea level. The whole of this mountain mass rises to at least a thousand feet above the line of perpetual snow. Innumerable aiguilles or peaks shoot up from this vast basis, of varying heights, surrounding the mighty monarch himself, who towers to a height of more than 12,000 feet above the level of Chamouny.

The scenery of Mont Blanc is a wonderful combination of Alpine glories on the grandest scale. Lofty peaks, for ever robed in untrodden snow, wide seas of ice, huge crevasses, bright green glaciers, savage rocks, and pine forests (skirting the borders of civilization) make up a *tout ensemble* truly marvellous and impressive.

Dr. Paccard and the guide, James Balmat, were the first to scale Mont Blanc in August, 1786. The celebrated philosopher, Saussure made the ascent in the following year with several assistants, and numerous scientific observations were made on the summit. Since that date, the ascent has become increasingly frequent; and guides and all necessary appliances are to be found either at Chamouny or St. Gervais, for those who feel physically qualified for the undertaking, and are willing to meet the somewhat expensive outlay required.

The Ascent of Mont Blanc occupies from 17 to 22 hours, and the descent about 8 hours. This does not include stoppages. About forty times a year the ascent is accomplished; favourable weather is necessary, and the advice of the guides must be strictly adhered to. It is usual to go on mules to the Chalet de la Pierre Pointue, and then forward to the Grands Mulets (10,007 ft.) to spend the night; the ascent to the summit (15,781 ft.) and return to the Grands Mulets occupies the second day, and the return to Chamouny the third. The Grands Mulets route unites on the Grand Plateau with the route from St. Gervais. Visitors coming from the latter place spend the night at a hut on the Aiguille du Gouter. The view from the summit is far reaching but indistinct.

The chief peaks of importance in the Mont Blanc group, after the summit are the Grandes Jorasses, 13,800; Aiguille Verte, 13,540; Aiguille de Bionnassay, 13,324; Les Droites, 13,322; Aiguille de Trélatête, 12,900; Aiguille d'Argentiere, 12,799; Mont Dolent, 12,566.

TOUR OF MONT BLANC.

(By Chamouny, Courmayeur, Aosta, and the Great St. Bernard.)

Martigny to Chamouny (see p. 157).

Leaving Chamouny by the road, and passing the Glacier des Bossons on the left, the traveller reaches the small, prettily situated village of Les Ouches. Here the mule path is taken leading to the Pavillon de Belle Vue above the Col de Voza. The views of the Chamouny valley from this point are very fine. Hence the path may be taken by Bionnassay to the high road at Bionnay, but it is nearer to keep by Champel, joining the high road at La Villette. This part of the route is very charming, as the valley of Bionnassay is beautifully wooded, and surrounded by mountains of every form and colour. Two miles along the high road from La Villette brings the traveller to Les Contamines, 18 miles from Chamouny. Here the night is usually spent.

From Contamines, Mont Joli can be ascended in four or five hours, and affords good views. Leaving the village to resume the route, the visitor reaches the pilgrim-visited Church of *Notre Dame* de la Gorge. Here the road terminates, and the *path leads* through a rocky, pine-clad defile, and crosses the mountain torrent near the waterfall, emerging on an elevated plain. **Nant Borrant** (4560 ft.) is next reached, and then the **Chalet de la Balme** (an inn). Crossing the **Plaine des Dames**, where a conical heap of stones is said to be the memorial of a lady who perished here in a snowstorm, the path winds up to the **Col du Bonhomme.**

Hence the traveller may descend by the **Col des Fours** to **Mottet**, or to the Alpine village of **Chapiu.**

From Chapiu, the visitor may proceed to Pré St. Didier by the Little St. Bernard. In bad or doubtful weather this should be preferred to going forward by the Col de la Seigne.

At Chapiu (36 miles from Geneva) the night is usually passed. The route to the **Col de la Seigne** is through Mottet. From the summit of the Col de la Seigne are obtained glorious views of the Mont Blanc precipices towering over 11,000 feet above the grandly elevated valley known as the **Allée Blanche.**

From the Col to Courmayeur is a six hours' walk, a mingling of snow and rock and pasture land. The Lac de Combal, the Glacier de Miage, the majestic Glacier de Brenva with its huge Moraine, the Chapelle du Glacier (with its hermit), and the Baths of La Saxe are passed on the way.

[With guides from Contamines, Courmayeur may be reached in one day by ascending direct from the former place to the Pavilion of Trélatête, traversing for some distance the Glacier of Trélatête (don't omit the rope, even if guides smile at it), and then crossing the Col du Bonhomme (9204 ft.), higher up than previously indicated. The Glacier de Lancettes must then be crossed, and thus the Col de la Seigne reached without passing through Chapiu and Mottet.]

Courmayeur (56 miles from Chamouny), at an altitude of 4211 ft. above the sea, is in the summer a well visited little Piedmontese watering place. Excursions can be made to the **Glacier de Brenva**, to the **Glacier de Miage**, or to the **Cramont** (9081 ft. above the sea), with fine scenery on the route, and glorious views of Mont Blanc from the summit. From the **Mont de Saxe** (7329 ft.) some good views are obtained.

From Courmayeur the traveller may reach Martigny by the Col de Ferret, 38 miles, or to Aosta, 27 miles; and from thence to Martigny by the Great St. Bernard, 47 miles. There is also a less interesting route by the Col de la Serena (7389 ft.) to St. Remy and the Great St. Bernard.

The first of these routes, viz., Courmayeur to Martigny by the **Col de Ferret**, will take nearly fifteen hours' walking. The Val de Ferret is a prolongation of the Allée Blanche; numerous glaciers and huge mountain masses bound the valley. The Col is 8176 ft., and forms the boundary between France, Italy, and Switzerland; the view of **Mont Peteret** and other mighty buttresses of Mont Blanc is very grand. The descent is by the châlets of La Foliaz, Orsières, and Sembrancher to Martigny.

From Courmayeur to Aosta is a very attractive and interesting journey. It can be traversed by diligence in five hours. The first village of importance is **Prè St. Didier**, on the Doire.

From Prè St. Didier the traveller may visit the **Little St. Bernard**, where is a column indicating the boundary between France and Italy. Here there are very imposing views of the Mont Blanc chain. Hence, passing a **hospice** similar to the Great St. Bernard, a gradual descent brings to the Bourg St. Maurice, from whence there is a diligence to **Chamousset** on the Mont Cenis Railway.

The route to Aosta, after leaving Pré St. Didier, is by **Morgex**, where the Col de la Serena route to the Great St. Bernard branches off. The ruined castle of Chatelard and village of La Salle are passed. Along a steep road above the foaming waters of the Doire, the route lies by Avise, with its old tower, and Liverogne, to Arvier, noted for its good wine, and possessing a thirteenth century castle. **Villeneuve** is next reached, the most picturesque portion of the valley, with the ruined Château d'Argent overlooking the village. After passing one or two chateaux, the Castle of Aosta is seen at the mouth of the Val de Cogne.

Aosta, with a population of about 8000, is a beautifully situated town of importance. The valley produces various metals from its mines, marble from its quarries, and timber in abundance from its vast pine forests. The town was anciently named Augusta Prætoria Salassorum, after Augustus, who garrisoned it with 3000 Prætorian Guards. Amongst the **Roman remains** still left are the town walls and towers, a fine triumphal arch, the ruins of a basilica, a gateway, etc. The cathedral has a curious portal, and some frescoes, mosaic work, etc.

From Aosta to Ivrea (where the rail can be taken for Turin) is 42 miles, traversed by diligence in nine hours, passing Chatillon, *Bard (with the fortress that nearly spoilt Napoleon's grand march in 1800)*, Douna, St. Martin, and Setteino Vittore.

AOSTA TO MARTIGNY BY THE GREAT ST. BERNARD.

This route is amongst picturesque and fertile scenery, by Signaye to the defile of Gignod. Here the southern aspect of the scenery diminishes. After passing **Etroubles** and St. Oyen, cultivation begins to get very scarce, and St. Remy is reached, the last Italian village. From St. Remy, about a two hours' walk will bring the visitor to the noted **Hospice of St. Bernard,** passing a small lake that is frozen nine months of the year, and a column marking the boundary between Italy and Switzerland. The celebrated **hospice** is a stone edifice on the crest of the pass, the highest winter habitation in Europe. The mean temperature for the summer is 48 deg.; for the winter, 15 deg. The institution is said to owe its origin to St. Bernard of Menthon in 962. Across the pass armies have several times marched. It was used by the Romans a hundred years before the Christian era; and in the fearful struggles that closed last century several hundred thousand soldiers, French and Austrian, passed through these sterile scenes.

The approach to St. Bernard suggested Longfellow's noble poem "Excelsior." We welcome another pen to describe the scenery here. "What a bewildering, what a sudden change! Nothing but savage, awful precipices of naked granite, snowy fields, and verdureless wastes! In every other place of the Alps we have looked upon the snow in the remote distance, to be dazzled with its shining effulgence—ourselves, meanwhile, in the region of verdure and warmth. Here we march through a horrid desert—not a leaf, not a blade of grass—over the deep drifts of snow. And this is the road that Hannibal trod, and Charlemagne, and Napoleon! They were fit conquerors of Rome, who could vanquish the sterner despotism of eternal winter."

It is usual to stay the night in the hospice (8131 ft.); no charge is made, but of course no one would avail himself of the accommodation without contributing liberally to the institution. Everybody has heard of the noble work accomplished by the devoted monks and their faithful dogs in rescuing from death in the snow those who would otherwise perish. A piano in the room set apart for visitors was presented by the Prince of *Wales.*

The Morgue will be seen with interest by those who *indulge in visiting* chambers of horrors. (This brief account of the world-famed hospice is deemed sufficient, as the Brethren on the Mount take an interest in giving all particulars of the place.)

From the Great St. Bernard to Martigny is through the desolate Vallée des Morts, and across the Dranse, and past the old Morgue, to the elevated pasture called the Plan de Proz. Here the traveller reaches the carriage road at the solitary inn known as the **Cantine de Proz.**

Mont Velan (12,057 ft.), seen to the east of St. Bernard, can be ascended from this point.

From the Cantine the new rock-hewn road leads, through defile and forest, to Bourg St. Pierre, where there is an old 11th century church. Liddes, Orsières, with its ancient tower, Sembrancher, with its ruined castles, and some other small places, are passed, and then Martigny is reached. From the hospice, 29 miles. A coach runs between Martigny and Bourg St. Pierre.

CHAMOUNY TO MARTIGNY BY THE TÊTE NOIRE.

(23 miles. Time, about 9 hours.)

There are three routes connecting the Rhone Valley with the Valley of Chamouny—1. Martigny to Chamouny by the Tête Noire; 2. Vernayaz to Chamouny by Triquent, Salvan, etc. (see p. 121); 3. Martigny to Chamouny by the Col de Balme.

Except for its one grand, incomparable view of Mont Blanc and the Valley of Chamouny (see p. 159), the Col de Balme route is unequal to the other two in general interest.

Leaving Chamouny for the Tête Noire route, the Arve is soon crossed near the village of Les Praz. The source of the Arveiron (see p. 150), in the Glacier des Bois, is left on the right, and then, passing over by Les Tines, Lavancher, La Joux (on the opposite bank), Les Iles, and Grasonet, **Argentière** is reached, 2¼ miles from Chamouny.

At Argentière the grand glacier of the same name is seen stretching down towards the valley, with the Aiguille du Chardonnet, 12,500 feet high, on one side, and the Aiguille Verte, a thousand feet higher still, on the other.

Here the route by Tour and the Col de Balme diverges to the right (p. 159.)

The path to the left passes through the savage glen of Les Montets, and by the village of Trélechamp to the Col des Montets, at a height of 4819 feet. A cross shows the highest point. From the Col the path leads on amidst frequent traces of glacier and avalanche, and varied combinations of rock and snow, and wood and water, past Poyaz, with its romantic waterfall (1 franc), and then beside the Eau Noire to **Valorcine.**

This village of châlets, with a population under 700, is the largest in the valley. It has walls to keep off its "natural enemies" the avalanches.

From Valorcine, past the fine waterfall of the **Barberine** (1 franc), near its junction with the Eau Noire, and amongst scenery increasingly grand, the Hotel Barberine is reached, and soon afterwards the Hotel Royal du Chatelard.

Here the route by Triquent and Salvan to Vernayaz diverges (see p. 122).

Discarding the old Mauvais Pas on the left, the route to Martigny leads through the rocks of the **Tête Noire.** The highest point of the Tête Noire is some distance to the south of the pass, being 6600 feet above the sea level. The Hotel near the pass is over 4000 feet above the sea level. The Bel-Oiseau, Dent de Morcles, and Grand Moveran, are conspicuous peaks in the vicinity. There is a path from the hotel by which the grand view from the Col de Balme may be combined with the journey by the Tête Noire route.

The general character of the scenery in this portion of the excursion is well described in the following extract from "Swiss Pictures:"—

"Mountains lofty and precipitous, black, jagged rocks, roaring torrents, dark, gloomy ravines, solemn pine-woods, between whose columnar trunks the path winds as through the aisles of a vast cathedral; yet, withal, an exhaustless abundance of exquisitely-tinted flowers, delicate ferns, slopes on which the wild strawberry blushes, and hides beneath the rich green leaves, and on all sides a profusion of verdure, which softens down the ruggedness of the mountain forms, yet leaves their grandeur undiminished......Here are vast heights above, and vast depths below, villages hanging to the mountain sides, green pasturages, winding paths, châlets dotting the slopes, lovely meadows enamelled with flowers, dark, immeasurable ravines, colossal, overhanging walls and bastions of rock, snow-peaks rising into the heavens over all."

Leaving the Hotel de la Tête Noire, the Forest of Trient is

entered, with the river of the same name dashing onward below to join the Eau Noire. At the village of Trient (Hotel du Glacier de Trient) the Col de Balme route is reached.

From Trient the road ascends to the Col de la Forclaz, or Col de Trient (5020 feet). In descending towards Martigny, the Valley of the Rhone as far as Sion is seen spread out like a beautiful picture. The scene is described by one traveller as "one of those flat Swiss valleys, green as a velvet carpet, studded with buildings and villages that look like dots in the distance, and embraced on all sides by magnificent mountains, of which those nearest in the prospect were distinctly made out, with their rocks, pine-trees, and foliage. The next in the receding distance were fainter, and of a purplish green; the next of a vivid purple; the next lilac; while far in the fading view the crystal summits and glaciers of the Oberland Alps rose like an exhalation......The Simplon road could be seen dividing the valley like an arrow."

Still descending amongst forests and pastures, and orchards rich with fruit, the traveller soon reaches Martigny-le-bourg, and then Martigny (see p. 122).

FROM CHAMOUNY TO MARTIGNY BY THE COL DE BALME.

As far as Argentière, and from Trient forward, this route is identical with the last (p. 157). At Argentière leave the Tête Noire route, and proceed to La Tour (Hotel du Rivage), where the carriage-road terminates. Leaving Tour, and its beautiful glacier, and passing the landmark known as the Homme de Pierre, and still ascending beside the rushing Arve, the inn is reached on the Col de Balme. Hence there is a grand prospect of the Mont Blanc range, with aiguilles, glaciers, etc. Opposite to them are seen the Aiguilles Rouges, Brévent, etc. Turning in the direction of Martigny are seen the mountains of Valais and the Bernese Oberland.

From the Col the path leads over sloping pastures, then through the Forest of Magnin, much injured by avalanches, and then through more meadows to Trient, where the Tête Noire route is again joined.

There is a fine mountain footpath connecting the Col de Balme with the Tête Noire, which affords a delightful walk in *clear weather* *(p. 158)*.

MARTIGNY TO ZERMATT

By railway to Sierre. Diligence thence to Visp (p. 77).

At Visp horses can be hired for the first nine miles up the Visp Thal to St. Niklaus. From that place there is a carriage-road (13 miles) to Zermatt.

The whole distance can be easily managed in ten to twelve hours by those who can shoulder their knapsacks, and march on, independent of all conveyances.

The route lies now on one side and now on the other of the river Visp, rushing along a richly-wooded mountain gorge. All the way to Zermatt, peaks and glaciers, rocks, and torrents, and waterfalls, in varying combinations, make the journey a very attractive one. It is year by year becoming increasingly popular. The inhabitants of this lovely valley are, however, a poverty-stricken and dirty race, very much afflicted with goître.

The path leads at first along the right bank of the Visp, between hills clad with flowers, and shrubs, and trellised vines. At **Neubrücke** the river is crossed, and the left bank pursued to **Stalden** (5 miles). Fine views abound here. The town is prettily situated at the junction of the Gorner Visp and Saaser Visp, both being streams from the glaciers of Monte Rosa. The bold dividing ridge between the two valleys consists of the Mischabelhorn, Balferinhorn, etc.

Leaving the Saas Thal on the left, the right bank of the Gorner Visp is followed into the **Nicolai Thal.** The Weisshorn comes into view, and the Jungbach, Riedbach, and other waterfalls, are passed. A forest path conducts to another bridge across the Visp, and shortly afterwards St. Niklaus is reached. **St. Niklaus** (Grand Hotel), charmingly situated on a gentle slope, 3819 feet above the sea level, is a good half-way resting-place for those who wish to break the journey. A night's rest here is more likely to be healthful and refreshing than at Vispach or elsewhere in the malarious Rhone Valley. Numerous excursions and expeditions can be arranged from St. Niklaus by those who can spare time. There is in the village a church whose metallic steeple is seen for miles shining like silver. The Grand Hotel is commodious and comfortable.

Leaving St. Niklaus by the carriage-road which begins here, the valley again narrows, and its mountain boundaries increase in size. Frequent waterfalls dash down from the western precipices; the road crosses the Visp, passes by huge reminders of the 1855 earthquake, amongst woodlands and pastures, to Randa.

Before reaching this spot, the Little Mont Cervin and Breithorn come into sight.

Randa is nearly 5000 feet above the sea level. On the opposite side of the valley the **Biesgletscher**, an offshoot of the Weisshorngletscher, protrudes through a mountain gap; and from its precipitous mass a tributary torrent rushes to the Visp. Parts of this glacier have occasionally broken off, spreading terror and destruction around. An immense portion fell in 1819, when 118 buildings in Randa were destroyed, and the snow and broken ice lay in some parts of the village several feet in depth.

East of Randa is the Grabengletscher, under the Grabenhorn, which is the highest peak of the Mischabelhörner, being nearly 15,000 feet.

In about an hour from leaving Randa, **Täsch** is reached. The route is still upward, till, on crossing a rocky ridge, the first view of the **Matterhorn** is obtained, stupendous and overwhelming in its isolated majesty. By the Spiessbrücke, and one or two other bridges, the road crosses and recrosses, till at length the defile opens, and the rich pastoral valley of Zermatt lies full in view.

The quaint little village of **Zermatt** (pop., 450), overtopped by its hotels, is situated in the midst of woods and pastures, in a mountain-girdled valley, nearly 5500 feet above the level of the sea. The valley and adjacent heights are rich in beautiful and varied wild flowers, interesting mineral specimens, butterflies, insects, etc. Three glaciers feed the torrent of the Visp as it rushes past the village; these are the Gorner from Monte Rosa, the Findelen from the Strahlhorn, and the Z'mutt from the Matterhorn. In the surrounding scenery the artist will find abundant subjects for his pencil.

In the churchyard of Zermatt are the graves of Mr. Hadow, the Rev. Charles Hudson, and the guide, Michael Croz, who perished on the Matterhorn, in 1855. The body of Lord Francis Douglas who fell with them, was never found. Its whereabouts remains an awful secret of that mysterious mountain.

The neighbourhood of Zermatt contains so much that is of absorbing interest, that a visit of a day or two only suffices for a glimpse at a few of the chief attractions.

THE RIFFELBERG AND GORNER GRAT.

This is undertaken by most visitors to Zermatt even if time allows of nothing else being attempted. The route is by the first bridge across the Visp beyond the village, past the little church of Winkelmatten, and then up a steep path through the pine woods. From the openings between the trees the foot of the Gorner Glacier is seen, and the fine waterfall of the Visp rushing out from its icy cradle. Passing the châlet on the Augstkummenmatt, the pine woods are left behind, some bare slopes of short grass are crossed, and two hours of good walking from Zermatt brings the visitor to the broad terrace of the mountain upon which stands the Riffel Hotel (8000 ft.) This is truly a glorious spot. In front, separated only by the deep valley in which lie the Gorner and Furggen glacier, rises the majestic Matterhorn, a silent, solitary pinnacle of bare rock, 5,000 feet from base to summit, enthroned upon a pedestal of snow and ice, which is itself 10,000 feet above the ocean level, standing aloof and seeming to frown defiance on its fellows which lie grouped on every side. It is well to behold this scene, if possible, when the rosy glow of sunrise pervades it with an intense liquid light, revealing its furrowed sides, its seams of snow, its overhanging brow, its ice-bound feet, its treacherous chasms, and its awful precipices, and yet softening its asperity into a loveliness that holds the gazer spell-bound.

Two hours' ascent from the Riffel Hotel, brings the visitor two thousand feet higher to the Gorner Grat. This is one of the very few spots in the Alps where one can obtain an elevation of over 10,000 feet without the slightest semblance of a difficulty. The path is good and well-defined the whole way, and the panorama quite unsurpassed. It is remarkable from the fact that there is an unbroken range of magnificent snow peaks on every side. There is not a single break in the chain. It is an isolated, rocky peak that seems formed by nature to enable one to survey at leisure the marvellous scene around. The huge Gorner Glacier winds round its base at a dizzy depth below; beyond are the snows of that glorious range beginning with Monte Rosa (which seems within a stone's throw) and ending with the Matterhorn. Then the central range of the Pennine Alps with the stupendous summits of the Dent Blanche, the Gabelhorn, the Rothhorn, and the Weisshorn all linked together in one vast chain of snow and ice. Next, far away beyond the Rhone Valley, some distant peaks of the Bernese Oberland; and again to the right, the group of the Mischabelhörner, the Alphubel, the Strahlhorn, and the Stockhorn, which last brings us round again to the snows of the Cima di Jazi, and the Weisthor Pass, which flanks Monte Rosa on the east. Between these mighty peaks lie innumerable glaciers, notably the vast sea of ice formed of the Gorner, the Theodule, and the Furggen glaciers which lies like a map below; its moraines, its snow slopes, and its countless crevasses revealed at a single glance.

F. B. Zincke, in his "Month in Switzerland," thus describes the scene from the Gorner Grat—

"Here you have what is said to be the finest Alpine view in Europe. You are standing on a central eminence of rock in, as far as you can see, a surrounding world of ice and snow. On the left is the Cima di Jazi, which you are told commands a good view into Italy. Just before you, as you look across the glacier, which lies in a deep, broad ravine at your feet, rise the jagged summits of Monte Rosa with, at this season, much of the black rock shining through their caps and robes of snow. Next the Lyskamm, somewhat in the background; then Castor and Pollux, immaculate snow without protruding rock; next the Breithorn, then the naked gneiss of the Matterhorn, a prince among peaks, too precipitous for snow to rest on in the late summer, looking like a Titanic Lycian tomb (such as you may see in the plates of 'Fellowe's Asia Minor'), placed on the top of a Titanic rectangular shaft of rock, five thousand feet high. Beyond, and completing the circle of the panorama, come the Dent Blanche, the Gabelhorn, the Rothhorn, the Weisshorn, over the valley of Zermatt, the Ober Rothhorn, and the Allaleinhorn, which brings your eye round again to the Cima di Jazi."

From the Gorner Grat the visitor may return by the **Guggli**, an eminence with a fine view, but less striking than that just described. Hence a path leading beside the Findelen Glacier may be followed back to Zermatt. Or another path may be taken from the Guggli to the Riffel Hotel, and thence a descent effected to the foot of the Gorner Glacier, an interesting and charming spot where the glacial encroachment is very evident.

THE HÖRNLI

is the first great step in the ascent of the Matterhorn, and *should be visited* by all who desire a nearer view of the giant mountain without attempting to scale it. The route is to the right of the Gorner Glacier, and along the base of the Matterhorn to the mountain lake called the Schwarz-See, where there is a fine view of the Zermatt Valley and its surroundings. Horses can be ridden to this point. Another hour's upward climb brings the traveller to the Hörnli (9492 ft.).

The view of the Matterhorn from this point is amazingly grand. The whole eastern face is close in front, and the treacherous northern face is also in view. Down those awful precipices the unfortunate victims of the first ascent fell a distance of 4000 feet to the glacier which lies on the right. From one's very feet stretches away the wonderful plateau of ice and snow constituting the Furggen and Theodule glaciers. The ridge on which one stands is a mere *arête* in parts, perpendicular on one side, and falling abruptly on the other, many thousand feet to the Zermatt Glacier and the pine woods at its foot. Over the ridge the wind sweeps with icy breath, and a scene of desolation is around. Rain, and sun, and frost have bared, and bleached, and riven the barren crags upon which one stands. One glance takes in the green pastures of Zermatt, 5000 feet below; turning, the visitor sees the topmost pinnacle of the Matterhorn, 5000 feet above. The ridge of Hornli affords a wild and wondrous scene of mingled awe and loveliness, which should be seen by all visitors to Zermatt possessing tolerably stout legs and lungs, but having no ambition to measure their strength with the High Alps.

The return to Zermatt can be varied by descending to the foot of the Zermatt Glacier, and passing along the Zermatt Valley. Beautiful and interesting scenery will reward the extra exertion.

THE CIMA DI JAZI.

This is a mountain of 13,000 ft. in height, which can be reached without danger or difficulty, in about 5 hours, from the Riffelberg. The view is very grand, including the Italian lakes, the Tyrol, the Pennine and Bernese Alps, etc.

MONTE ROSA.

The ascent of this mountain is arduous and difficult. It was first accomplished by Taugwald, in 1849. "Its very vastness, or rather its concentrated massiveness, unbroken by peaks of proportionate size, makes it seem less lofty than it really is;

and its immediate union on either side with a range of sharper snowy summits approaching its own elevation tends still further to prevent a just appreciation of its true character at the first glance."

The five highest peaks of Monte Rosa are arrayed in a connected ridge some 2 miles in length, in north to south. This ridge is crossed at the centre by a ridge of lower summits running east and west. At the point of union is the Signalkuppe, 14,964 ft., the most conspicuous of the peaks from the Italian side. North of this is the Zumsteinspitze, 15,004 ft. A little further north, and connected by a ridge frowning over one of the deepest and most awful of Alpine abysses, is the **Hochstespitze**; the true Monte Rosa, presenting from its summit a wondrous view of mountain peaks. The Hochstespitze, or Gornerhorn, is "a sharp, rocky obelisk," 15,217 ft. in height. Still further north is the Nordende, 15,132 ft.

South of the central point is the Parrotspitze, 14,577 ft., and four other peaks, ranging from 13,800 to 14,200 ft.

The

EXCURSIONS AND EXPEDITIONS

that can be made from Zermatt are too numerous to be fully detailed. Tourists who shrink from danger in any form, and even wish to avoid difficulty or over-exertion, will find no lack of charming and interesting walks to occupy a prolonged stay. For those possessing mountaineering ambition and the requisite physical qualifications, there are no end of peaks and passes. Many of these require more than ordinary experience and skill in Alpine adventure; and none will, of course, be undertaken without making proper inquiries and procuring good guides. We simply enumerate a few of these expeditions:—

The **Matterhorn**, 14,889 ft., was first scaled, in 1865, by Mr. Whymper, the guide Taugwald, Lord Francis Douglas, Mr. Hadow, Rev. Chas. Hudson, and the guide Croz. The four latter lost their lives in commencing the descent.

The **Breithorn**, 13,685 ft., is reached by crossing the snow from the Col on the S. Theodule route (p. 169).

The **Triftjoch Pass**, 11,614 ft., a gap between the Gabelhorn and the Triftthorn, leading to the Val d'Anniviers.

The **Col de la Dent Blanche**, a terrace, 11,400 ft. *above the sea level*; also a route to the Val d'Anniviers.

The **Weissthor Pass**, 10,000 ft., to Macugnagna.

The **Mettelhorn**, 11,188 ft., with good guides, is one of the less difficult ascents. No similar scene of ice and precipitous mountain can be witnessed with equal ease on any known mountain.

The **Lyskamm**, 14,889 ft., was once considered the summit of Monte Rosa.

The **Gabelhorn**, 13,363 ft.

The **Weisshorn**, 14,804 ft.

The **Mischabelhorn**, 14,935 ft., the highest mountain entirely in Switzerland.

The **Adler Pass**, 12,461 ft., and other passes to the Saas Valley.

The **Silber Pass**, 14,040 ft. (passing nine of the Monte Rosa peaks), and other passes into Italy.

In the inns of Zermatt will be seen the regular tariff of charges for guides, for the various excursions and expeditions in the vicinity.

ZERMATT TO VOGOGNA ON THE SIMPLON.

To effect this route without attempting any of the more difficult passes above-mentioned, the tourist must retrace his steps to Stalden. From thence the path leads along the beautiful defile known as the Saas Thal. Glaciers look down from the gaps on the western side, and many a wayside cross tells of the avalanche that has brought death and desolation into the lovely valley. The tourist should turn from time to time to see the prospect down the valley, with the Bietschhorn closing the view. In four hours **Saas** is reached, the chief place in the valley—a good place to sojourn at, and becoming increasingly frequented. It stands on a beautiful green plain, with mountains all round.

"The contrast between Saas and Zermatt," says Zincke, in his "Month in Switzerland," "is very great. At Zermatt the valley ends with great emphasis in a grand amphitheatre of mountains and snowy peaks. At Saas it seems suddenly brought to a close, without any object of interest to look upon. With the mind full of Zermatt, Saas appears but a lame and impotent conclusion. The village, however, is very far indeed from being at the head of the valley. That is to be found at the Monte Moro, 5 hours farther on; and as it includes the Allalein Glacier, the grand scenery of the Mattmark See and of the Monte Moro itself, it has enough to satisfy even great expectations—such as one has, of course, coming from Zermatt."

From Saas many mountain and glacier expeditions can be undertaken. Those whose time is limited may make a very enjoyable trip of about 3 hours to **Fée**, a charming little village, in a lovely green hollow, headed by a vast glacier. By allowing half a day, the **Gletscher Alp**, beyond Fée, may be reached. This is a beautiful spot, bright with rich grass and flowers, almost encircled by the sea of ice.

At Saas a guide for Macugnagna should be engaged. Post-chaises can be procured for ladies. Horses can only be taken to Thäliboden, about half an hour from the summit of the pass.

Leaving Saas, the road passes the waterfall from the Rothplatt Glacier, and under the well-wooded Mittaghorn to *Almagel*. Meigeren is next reached, and then the bridle-path winds among rocks and stones, with the remarkable **Allalein Glacier** apparently closing the valley in front. To pass this glacier, the path zigzags up the mountain side, and then skirts the **Mattmark See**. Here there is an inn (3 hours from Saas), where those should pass the night who wish to enjoy the early morning view from Monte Moro. The Schwarzenberg Glacier is close by.

Still ascending from Mattmark, the châlets of *Distel* are reached in half an hour, where the usual light refreshments can be obtained. The Seewinen Glacier is just opposite.

The summit of the pass of **Monte Moro** is reached in an hour from Distel. The name (like Allalein, Mattmark, and some other names in the neighbourhood) is of Moorish origin, and carries us back some eight centuries, when with the Great St. Bernard and the Engadine it was one of the three great passes into Italy, and was held by the Moors, who levied black mail on all comers. Fragments of ancient pavement are seen near the summit. The immediate approach from the Swiss side is very sterile and desolate, past the icy basin, into which the Thäliboden Glacier descends from the Joderhorn.

By ascending the rocks near the cross on the summit, a really sublime prospect of Monte Rosa is beheld to the south, whilst turning to the north the Saas Valley is seen, with its picturesque surroundings. A more extensive view is obtained from the adjacent **Joderhorn**, including some of the Southern Alps and the Italian plains.

The descent to Macugnagna will take about four hours. The route is very steep; first over a snowfield, then amongst stones and rocks, and then over sloping green pastures, with glorious views of the Macugnagna Valley and Monte Rosa beyond.

Mules can sometimes be procured at Macugnagna for the remainder of the journey to Vogogna; or they may have to be sent for from Ponte Grande, unless the traveller inclines to walk on.

Macugnagna is situated between its glacier and the green pastures, 4400 feet above the sea level, and is girded by majestic mountains. In exploring the glacier, and enjoying the incomparable views of Monte Rosa, whose five principal peaks (p. 165) are all in sight, a day may be well spent. At any rate, the pine-clad eminence, known as the **Belvedere**—an ancient moraine, should be visited without fail. There is no grander view in the locality. If possible, proceed also, with a guide, for a considerable distance on to the glacier, to where a **cascade** leaps down into an icy abyss. The surrounding scene from this point is strangely grand and impressive. From the margin of the sea of ice the rocks of the central chain of Monte Rosa tower proudly up to the height of 7000 or 8000 feet, with connecting ridges to the Cima del Pizzo and Pizzo Bianco on one side, and to the Cima di Jazi and Monte Moro on the other.

Fillar, under the old Weissthor Pass, to the north of the glacier; and **Pedriolo**, to the south of the glacier, where immense blocks (one specimen being 500 feet in girth) have come down from Pizzo Bianco, may be included in a day's round with the previously mentioned points of view.

From Macugnagna, the route to the Simplon conducts by *Borca, Pestarena* (with its mines of gold, silver, and copper), and *Campiole*, to the rocky barrier of the *Morgen*, through a narrow gorge in which the Anza forces its way. Here the Val Macugnagna is left, and with it, for the most part, the German language; henceforward Italian.

The traveller now enters the lovely **Val Anzasca**, combining in its scenery both Swiss and Italian characteristics. At *Ceppo Morelli*, the carriage road commences. Notice the women hereabouts doing men's work, in men's unmentionables. *Vanzone* is next passed—a good stopping-place for those who can spare time for leisurely enjoyment of this delightful valley. The same remark applies to the next town, **Ponte Grande**, which is the principal place in the Val Anzasca, with *good hotel* accommodation and travelling facilities. *Castigilione is next reached*; and then *Pie di Mulera*. Here the view up the richly-fertile and well-wooded valley, with Monte Rosa closing the scene, is very fine; there is also a grand prospect of the Val d'Ossola below in the other direction. The road now runs direct to the Simplon, near Vogogna (p. 170).

ZERMATT TO CHÂTILLON.

(By the S. Theodule Pass.)

This is the most frequented of Alpine Glacier Passes; it is accomplished by many ladies with tolerable ease. The distance is 29 miles, requiring from 12 to 14 hours' walking; or horses may be taken to the foot of the glacier, and again forward from the Fourneaux, in descending the southern side. It is necessary to start at dawn in order to reach the two hours' passage across the snow at the summit before it has softened under the influence of the sun's rays.

From Zermatt the route lies by Zmutt and along the side of the Gorner Glacier; from the Riffel (rather shorter), the path is across the glacier just named. In about a couple of hours, vegetation is left behind, and a pathless, rocky tract is crossed to the foot of the glacier, where those who have ridden so far must dismount.

The **Glacier** has few crevasses; but still the neglect of the rope, in such expeditions, is foolhardy, and has led to fatal accidents.

The summit of the **Theodule Pass** is nearly 11,000 feet above the sea level. The scene is a very striking one. Close around is the broad expanse of ice. Outside this, the scene comprises the wondrous Matterhorn, or Mont Cervin, the Piedmontese mountains, Monte Rosa, the valley of S. Niklaus, with the Bernese Alps beyond; and in the eastern foreground, the Theodulhorn (11,391 feet), the Breithorn (13,685 feet), and the Petit Mont Cervin (12,749 feet).

On this Col, Saussure spent three days in scientific experiments. There is a small hut, where light refreshments can be obtained; it is the loftiest inhabited spot in Europe.

Descending towards the Val d'Aosta, a walk of about three-quarters of an hour across the glacier, brings the traveller to the **Fourneaux**, a rugged tract of rocks and débris. Here horses can be often met with, waiting the chance of an engagement. Green meadows are again reached, and at Giomen, near **Le Breuil**, is a good inn, with horses, etc.

From the plain of Breuil, the descent is by a fine mountain gorge, with a torrent rushing through it. No guide is needed for the remainder of the route. From *Val Tournanche*, the descending valley is very delightful, from the charming combination of rocks and precipices, rushing water, and plentiful foliage. Some interesting remains of a Roman aqueduct are visible at intervals, especially the arches, by the cliff near *Antey*. On reaching **Châtillon**, the tourist is on the high road traversed by daily diligence between Ivrea and Aosta. From Ivrea, the railway can be taken for Turin or Milan; and from Aosta (see p. 155) the St. Bernard and Martigny, or Chamouny and Mont Blanc may be reached.

FROM MARTIGNY OVER THE SIMPLON, TO ARONA.

The **Baths of Saxon** are near station *Gottfrey*. They are noted for the cure of skin diseases, and for gambling. Passing *Ardon*, with its ironworks, we soon near Sion. The traveller is now in a region of ancient castles. Every eminence seems to have had, at one time or other, its own particular fortress. At Sion there are three of these edifices, adding much to the picturesque appearance of the place as it is approached. Here the shale mountains are beautifully terraced like those of the Rhine.

Sion contains, besides its three castles (of which the highest, the Tourbillon, may be visited for the extensive view, an old cathedral, of some interest for frescoes; a Jesuit convent, with a local natural history collection; an old prison, La Tour de Force; and a hospital. The town has had its great conflagration, and some thirty sieges.

[From Sion there is a good four days' ride, by Evolena, St. Luc, Grüben, and St. Niklaus, to Zermatt, which, if desired, can be taken in preference to the Rhone Valley and Visp Thal route (see p. 160).]

The railway passes *St. Léonard* station, and by more ruined castles, mulberry plantations, etc., on to Sierre.

Sierre (Hotel Belle Vue) is picturesquely situated on an eminence in the centre of a good wine district, and has many fine but decaying mediæval buildings, and also some interesting ruins in the vicinity.

Excursions from Sierre can be arranged to the Baths of

Leuk (see p. 96) by omnibus; into the lovely Val d'Anniviers, etc.

Crossing the Rhone, the road lies past hills formerly the resort of brigands, past Alpine villages, glistening church towers, waterfalls, castles, rocks, valleys, snow-mountains, alternations of sterility and fertility, past **Leuk**; **Susten**; **Tourtemagne**; **Viège**, or **Vispach** (whence numerous tours may be made to the glacier region of Zermatt); and then on to **Brigue** (Brieg, Hotel de la Poste), where the railway terminates, and the work of ascent really commences.* The diligence leaves Brigue daily for the Simplon route, and takes about 17 hours to accomplish the journey to Arona. Here we bid farewell to the romantic valley of the Rhone, and enter upon the land which Mr. Laing quaintly epitomizes as one of "avalanches, snows, glaciers, winding roads, with cataracts and precipices below, and clouds and blue sky above, and all the other romance furniture of Alpine scenery.' The road now pursued by us was constructed by Napoleon, after the famous battle of Marengo. The scenery becomes wilder and grander at every turn. Bridge after bridge is crossed, gallery after gallery gone through, houses of refuge passed by, and then comes the stupendous panorama of the Alps, the real grandeur of which is beyond the power of words to paint, and which forms a sight well worth the whole cost of the journey from England. "In the distance is an eagle soaring majestically through the air; below us is heard the distant Alpine horn, or the shepherd's melodious pipe, its notes commingling with the tinkling of numerous sheep bells. Higher and higher we rise, from the very roots of the mountains, the picture varying in beauty at every turn; now the dizzy precipices below, now the craggy heights above, until the **summit of the pass**, 6600 ft. above the level of the sea, is reached. Further on is the hospice, capable of giving suitable refuge to three hundred, managed by pious Augustine monks. The little village of **Simplon** is situated about 1400 ft. below the summit. Through a black and craggy rending asunder of the granite Alps, the descent into Italy is commenced, a foaming torrent below, and straight up, above the gloomy precipices, the lowering clouds of heaven. Marvellous are the winding tunnels which commence after passing the famous **Gorge of Gondo**, said to be the wildest and grandest in the Alps. These gigantic tunnels are hewn out of a solid mass of rock,

* *For further particulars of the above-named places, see Rhone Valley route (p. 77).*

which seemed to impede the further progress of the road, and took eighteen months to excavate—100 men, in gangs of eight, working in turns day and night. On emerging from the tunnel, a scene of stupendous majesty meets the eye. Hissing and roaring, the boiling waters of the Fressinone dash over the rocks above into the tremendous gorge below. On either side rise rocks more than 2000 ft. in height, the whole forming a picture of almost terrific sublimity. More cascades, more fearful ravines, more lofty crags, and then **Gondo**, the last Swiss village. Soon **Iselle**, the frontier town of Switzerland and Italy, is reached. **Crevola**, with its rock gallery, gorge, and bridge, passed, a completely new scene unfolds. "Now the scenery softens," says another writer; "the **Val d'Ossola** expands, a charming relief and contrast to past horrors. Luxuriant verdure, plants, vines, insect voices, mellowing tints, the very air 'breathing of the sweet south,' yes, this is Italy indeed!" There is little to detain us at **Domo d'Ossola** (Hotel de la Ville). More and more delightfully Italian becomes the journey. Nothing can exceed its highly picturesque character, especially as **Fariolo** is approached. After passing numerous granite quarries, and the famous quarry "out of which man's skill has disinterred the whole of Milan cathedral," a perfect maze of vineyards, olive groves, corn-fields, and chestnut plantations arrests the gaze. Here, too, the beautiful **Lago Maggiore** suddenly bursts into view, heightening inconceivably the rich glories of the landscape; and in the distance is seen **Isola Madre**, one of the charming islands which stud the lake. Reaching **Baveno** (where many travellers stay in order to visit the Borromean Isles), the diligence journey is continued over a road almost wholly supported by granite pillars, by the side of the famous lake, and passing numerous villas and gardens, it rattles at full speed through the streets of Arona.

LUCERNE OVER THE ST. GOTHARD TO COMO (CAMERLATA).

(By steamer to Flüelen 2½ hours; thence diligence to Biasca; railway to Bellinzona, and diligence to Lugano. In summer time there are two diligences daily.)

The **St. Gothard Railway** is in course of construction, *but will not* be completed for traffic through from Lucerne to *Como for* some years. There are already, however, one or two portions of the line open, namely, from Biasca to Bellinzona and Locarno, and from Lugano to Chiasso (p. 177).

Leaving Flüelen, **Altdorf** is soon reached; the capital of the Canton of Uri, with a colossal statue of William Tell, marking, it is said, the spot where the Swiss hero stood when he aimed at the apple on his son's head.

A little further on is **Burglen**, at the entrance to the Schächtenthal, the birthplace and home of Tell, with a chapel painted over with scenes from his life and supposed to mark the site of his house. Through the Schächtenthal there is a path to the Baths of Stachelberg.

Crossing the Schächenbach (in the waters of which the hero perished while struggling to save a child) and skirting the meadow forming the popular meeting-place of the canton, **Klus** is reached. Near **Silenen** there is a fine view of the pyramidal Bristenstock (10,085); a castle attributed to Gessler, and the chapel of the "Fourteen saints who help the needy." Several minor places are passed in rapid succession, the road rising gradually, and the scenery everywhere being of the most romantic description imaginable. After leaving Amsteg the road crosses the **Reuss**, which here dashes madly along, foaming and leaping over its rocky bed.

The ascent of the St. Gothard is here commenced; it is not, as many suppose, a single peak or eminence, but a mountainous group presenting many peculiar features. The region now traversed has occupied a prominent position in modern continental history. In the valley of the Reuss and the surrounding neighbourhood, several of the deadliest struggles, occasioned by the outbreak of war between France, Germany, and Russia, in 1799 took place; the French, after their defeat of the Russian general, occupying the road as far as the Hospice of St. Gothard, the building of which was used by them as fuel. Crossing and recrossing the Reuss several times, and passing **Wasen**, **Wattingen**, and **Göschenen**, with its glacier landscape and its wonderful works in connection with the St. Gothard Tunnel, the awe-inspiring defile of the **Schöllenen** is entered, and continues for three miles. In it, amid wild and savage desolation, is the famous **Devil's Bridge**:—

"Winding 'neath rocks impending, and o'er steeps
Dread in their awful altitude, the road
Leads through a pass whose grandeur is a load
Upon the awe-struck mind: the wild Reuss sweeps

From precipice to chasm, where it keeps
Boiling and fretting till it throws abroad
Mist clouds: then, chafed and flying from its goal,
Like fiery steed, o'er crag and crevice leaps.
The thunder rolls among the mountain peaks;
The echoes seem gigantic in their home,
(Now answering deep as voice Promethean speaks;)
Towering aloft where the fleet chamois roam,
'Mid pines and cottages the church oft seeks
To build its shrine where prayerful Switzers come."

Here a tremendous battle was fought in 1799, between the French and Austrians, numbers of whom perished in the abyss beneath. The bridge is a modern structure; the old bridge (the ruins of which, covered with creeping plants, are yet visible) was blown up by the Austrians while being forced by the French, during the conflict.

From the "Paradise Lost" of Milton, to the "Satan" of Montgomery, the certain gentleman who haunts mysterious places, has been the burden of poets' song. The following well-known lines are very graphic:—

"Called the Devil's Bridge:
With a single arch, from ridge to ridge,
It leaps across the terrible chasm
Yawning beneath us black and deep,
As if, in some convulsive spasm,
The summits of the hills had cracked,
And made a road for the cataract,
That raves and rages down the steep!
Never any bridge but this
Could stand across the wild abyss;
All the rest, of wood or stone,
By the Devil's hand were overthrown.
He toppled crags from the precipice,
And whatsoe'er was built by day
In the night was swept away;
None could stand but this alone."

Away, through the granite tunnel of **Urner Loch**, across the peaceful **Valley of Uri**, where winter reigns during eight months out of twelve, to **Andermatt**. As Andermatt is only one mile from the Devil's Bridge, it is a convenient and good place to break the journey at. It is considered to be the chief village of the valley. The **Church** has a very remarkable skull-adorned charnel house. From the **Maria-*trilf* Chapel** there is a fine view. An interesting **Exhibi*tion* of St. Gothard Minerals** opposite the hotel is worthy of notice. Hospenthal (Hotel Meyerhof), about a mile and a half further on, is also a good stopping place. From Hospenthal where the road to the Furca diverges (see p. 74), the road becomes steeper, ascending by numerous windings. The route becomes more and more impressive as we reach the summit of the pass, and the tourist's sketch-book is frequently in active requisition. Near the Albergo del St. Gottardo, 6500 feet about the level of the sea, is the famous Hospice, where superior Newfoundland dogs may be purchased, at somewhat high rates, by those fond of canine companions. A pause is made at the post house for some time while the travellers dine.

It is in the St. Gothard that the Rhine, Rhone, and Reuss have their source. (See p. 7).

Hepworth Dixon, in "The Switzers," says, speaking of the St. Gothard :—

"Her cardinal peak is Galen-stock—the peak now towering on our right,—a fount of light and beauty in this sombre realm, which ancient shepherds, coming up the valleys of the Rhone and Reuss in search of fortune, called the 'Pillar of the Sun.' He is the Saul of the St. Gothard group,—above the tallest of his brethren: Gerstenhorn, Lucendro, Mutt-horn, Spitzberg, Six Madun,—though all these mountains are of Anak breed. Three glaciers hang about his hoary neck, and shiver down his sturdy sides; the Tiefen glacier on his northern flank, the Siedeln glacier on his southern flank, and the Rhone glacier (which has many feeders) on his western flank. These glaciers drip by different ravines, and descend to different seas. Above his summit floats a canopy of cloud, from under which at times leap fire, and wind, and hail—those rival demons of this upper air, which shake and daze the earth in their plutonic and magnetic strife. About his feet, low down among the ruts and wrecks of ice, lie caves of wondrous beauty and uncounted wealth. Three years ago a cave was entered by this Tiefen glacier, when the noblest crystals in the world were found. The rock was topaz. Fragments lay about in heaps, each broken piece a hundred to two hundred pounds in weight. Some fifteen tons of topaz were removed from this great hiding-place of nature in a single year. What sage can count the marvels yet in lurking near this Pillar of the Sun?"

Crossing the Ticino, we approach the spot where the Russian General Suwarrow, seeing his grenadiers waver under the fearful fire of the French, caused a grave to be dug, declaring he would be buried at the place where, for the first time, his soldiers had retreated. The effect was electrical. With a loud cry they furiously charged the French, driving them back to Lucerne; the Devil's Bridge, destroyed a second time by the French, being crossed by means of planks suspended from the soldiers' scarves. Descending the Val Tremola, a wild and dismal valley in which avalanches are not uncommon, we reach Airolo (Hotel de la Poste) where is an ancient tower more than a thousand years old, and where the sound of the Italian language reminds us that we are almost in another country. The route now becomes exceedingly beautiful; picturesque ravines, mouldering ruins, foaming cataracts, huge masses of rock, and other romantic features imparting fresh charms to the landscape. The ravine just beyond, Dazio Grande, is one of the grandest pieces of the whole route. Passing Faido, the scenery becomes more Italian in appearance. The masses of snow which encumbered the roadside have completely disappeared. The rich sunshine sparkles on the roofs of the numerous church towers, cascades leap in a thousand fantastic forms over the time-beaten cliffs, while here and there the mulberry, the fig, and the vine lend fresh attractions to the view. Then in swift succession the towns of Giornico, where 15,000 Austrians were ingloriously routed by 600 Swiss in 1478, Bodio, and Poleggio are passed. At Biasca (Hotel de Biasca) the St. Gothard railway can be taken to Bellinzona and Locarno. A further portion of the line is also open (1876) between Lugano and Chiasso. Resuming the diligence route from Biasca, we reach Osogna, situated at the base of a rocky peak. Two or three small villages follow, then, the junction with the Bernardino route (see p. 181), the Moesa is crossed, and the road, passing Arbedo, where in 1422, 3000 Swiss were defeated by 24,000 Milanese, brings to view the frowning walls and lofty turrets of Bellinzona. (Hotel de la Ville and Hotel l'Ange.) Omnibuses may be taken from here to Magadino (p. 189). The position of the fortress-wall was formerly one of great strength. Nothing can surpass the superb character of the landscape at this point. To reproduce it in full beauty is utterly beyond the skill of the artist, even were he possessed of the genius of a Turner. Near Cadenazzo emerging from the charming valley of the Ticino, through which the traveller has so long been pleasantly journeying, and, after passing through a rich chestnut wood, and by various mountains, and villages, he arrives at **Lugano.** (Hotel du Parc.) Passing by the east side of the **Lake of Lugano, Melide** is reached, where the lake is crossed by means of a stone dam, erected some years since at a cost of 700,000 francs. At **Mendrisio** is seen **Monte Generoso,** "The Rigi of Italian Switzerland." Good hotels abound here. At Mendrisio, Hotel Mendrisio; at Monte Generosa, Hotel de Monteroso; and at Rovio, the Hotel Rovio. At **Chiasso** is the custom house, and here the tourist takes leave of Switzerland, and in a brief period of time finds himself at Como.

COIRE, OVER THE SPLÜGEN, TO COLICO (COMO).

Coire (Hotel Steinbock). In the summer-time there are three diligences daily. The journey to Colico is about seventy-six miles, and performed in about seventeen hours.

For six miles the road is level, and excepting the barracks, esplanade, and agricultural school, there is little to see. Passing through the little village of **Ems,** and crossing the Rhine by a covered bridge (252 ft. long), **Reichenau** is reached at the confluence of the Vorder-Rhein and Hinter-Rhein. In the château, Louis Philippe, then Duc de Chambres, seeking refuge from the fury of the French Revolution, resided from October 1793 to July 1794, under the assumed name of Chabot. The road increases in interest as the journey progresses. Small towns and villages are passed, and on the summits of rocky and barren crags in this romantic region, houses and churches are seen perched like doves on the roofs of high buildings. Dark-brown goats are also browsing on the cliffs; vegetation is rich, and the sides of the road are starred with flowers.

Bonaduz, with its ancient frescoes in the chapel of St. George; **Rhäznüs,** with the handsome residence of the Vieli family, overlooking the Rhine; **Katzis;** and many castles, châteaux, etc., are successively passed. Near Katzis, the Piz Curver, Piz St. Michael, and other majestic snow-clad mountains, are prominent features of the prospect. On approaching Thusis, the castle of Tagstein is seen overlooking the slopes by the pretty village of Massein.

Thusis (Hotel Via Mala) is at the confluence of the *Nolla with the* Rhine, a pretty village on a spur of the Heinzenberg, in the midst of fine scenery. It was burnt down in 1845, and has been much improved in the re-building. From the Nolla, a very remarkable view is obtained. The valley is encircled by a guardian chain of lofty mountains; on the right hand are the ruins of the castle of Hohen-Rhaetien, or Hoch-Realt, found, it is said, by Raetus, chief of the Etruscans, B.C. 587. If so, it is the oldest castle in Switzerland.

The **Via Mala** is now entered. It is a remarkable fissure, three to four miles long, a few feet wide, with precipices of 1500 feet. As seen in Middleton Dale, in Derbyshire, and some other similar ravines, the two sides correspond with each other, suggesting that some vast natural convulsion produced this enormous fissure. From 200 to 500 feet above the stream below, a carriage-road has been hewn out of the solid rock, and protected by strong masonry. At the *Verlorenes Loch*, or Lost Gulf, at Via Mala, where the once impassable rocks are tunnelled for over 200 ft., it is as though the grandeur of nature had been concentrated on this wild spot. The view looking back towards Thusis is probably one of the finest in all the Alpine passes. The traveller will not fail to notice the great skill exercised in engineering this wonderful piece of road. The river is crossed three times, and at the **second bridge** the view either way is grand in the extreme.

Leaving the Via Mala, the valley of Schams (Latin, Sexamniensis—"six streams") is entered. Here the green meadows and neat cottages form a graceful relief, after the gloomy terrors of the awful chasms from which the traveller has just emerged. The peaks of the Hirli are seen to the south.

Passing **Zillis**, with its ancient church, and Donat, a village, with the castle of La Turr (where dwelt the Austrian bailiff whose head Johann Calder plunged into the boiling broth, as recorded in Swiss history), and crossing the glacier stream that comes down from the Piz Curver, **Andeer** is reached. Here are a ruined castle, fine views, and capital opportunities for excursions to some of the adjacent valleys. Passing the ruins of the Bärenburg, a kind of minor Via Mala is entered, known as the **Roffna Ravine**, a wild gorge three miles long, through which the bright waters of the Rhine precipitate themselves in a remarkable series of cascades and falls. Leaving the gorge behind, the spacious snow-fields of the Einshorn reveal themselves; while further on the noble Alpine landscape of the *Rheinwald Thal* bursts into view. The little village of Splügen

(Hotel de la Poste) is 4800 feet above the level of the sea. Here travellers by diligence stop for refreshments. On the Splügen, as on the Julier slopes, numbers of Bergamasque shepherds with their flocks are encountered during the season. An excursion to the source of the Hinter-Rhein can be arranged from this place.

Splügen to Bellinzona, by the Bernardino Pass (see p. 180).

Leaving Splügen, the diligence crosses the Rhine through a long gallery or tunnel, and then, by means of numerous zig-zags, mounts to the summit of the Splügen Pass.

Crossing the frontier, the descent into Italy is commenced. "I have crossed by Mont Cenis Pass, the St. Gothard, and the Simplon," says a recent traveller, "and though each has its own peculiar attraction, yet the Splügen Pass is truly the most magnificent road over the Alps. No one can go over this road and enter into the spirit of it, without feeling that the mind has been enlarged by this communion with Nature in her noble grandeur."

This opinion is held by many who have become acquainted with the characteristics of the different routes. The Splügen Pass was known to the Romans. The present road was constructed by the Austrian Government in 1821.

Passing the **Dogana**, or Italian Custom House, and two or three adjacent houses, whose first-floor windows are often on a level with the surrounding snow, the traveller proceeds by endless zig-zag paths, through numerous galleries, past the waterfall formed by the Madesimo (800 ft. in height), till a halt is made at the tiny village of **Campo Dolcino**, with its church and cemetery. Then through the **Liro valley**, or Valle S. Giacomo, the rugged aspect of which is somewhat softened by the rich luxuriance of the vast chestnut forests below. Rapidly the features of the landscape begin to change their aspect. The region of firs and pines, of overhanging precipices and romantic waterfalls, of frowning rocks and yawning chasms, are left for a land of beautiful vineyards, stately olive groves, and golden cornfields.

Chiavenna (Hotel Conradi), is a capital resting-place. Very charming is the locale of the town. It is situated on the Maira, at the entrance to the Val Bregaglia. There are some ruins of an ancient castle of the De Salis family, which had a *troublous history* in the old days. From the castle garden the views are very fine. The church of S. Lorenzo has a beautiful campanile springing up from an arcaded enclosure, which was formerly the cemetery, or Campo Santo. Those interested in such things may inspect the neatly-arranged skulls and bones in the adjacent charnel houses. There is a very antique sculptured font in the Baptistery.

From Chiavenna, the character of the scenery again changes and all around there are mountains hemming in the valleys, and wild ravines forming singular contrasts to the quieter scenes. The falls of the Maira near here form a perfect picture. Crossing swift rushing rivers, and leaving the realms of eternal snow behind, cornfields, vineyards, and mulberry groves are passed. **Riva** is the last village on the road. The **Lake of Riva** is skirted, and the ruins of the castle of Fuentes—owing its origin to the Spaniards in 1603, and its destruction to the French in 1796,—are passed on the right. The diligence stops at **Colico**, where the steamboat is waiting to convey the tourist across the silvery waters of the beautiful lake, whose distant sails

"For floating birds we take,
Bathing in azure waves their plumes of snow,
Wherein shore, tower, and town their mirror make."

SPLÜGEN TO BELLINZONA, BY THE SAN BERNARDINO PASS.

(By diligence in eight hours.)

Splügen (see p. 178).

The road passes Medels and Nüfenen to **Hinterrhein**, the highest village of the Upper Rheinwaldthal.

[From Hinterrhein a fatiguing expedition of four hours can be undertaken to the source of the Hinterrhein, issuing from an opening in the Rheinwald or Zapport Glacier, at an altitude of 7270 ft. above the sea level. From the adjacent Zapportalp the glacier can be ascended, and good views obtained of the Rheinwald mountains, varying from nine to eleven thousand feet in height.]

After crossing the stream by a three-arched bridge, and wending up the mountain side, the road forward from Hinterrhein conducts through a sterile ravine to the S. **Bernardino Pass** (6770 ft.) This pass, which was known to the Romans received its present name from the chapel erected in the time of St. Bernardino of Siena. The inn (Casa di Rifugio), stands by the Lago Moësola, whose shores are an attractive place for the Alpine botanist. A fine waterfall in the river Moësa is passed, and the bridge, named after Victor Emmanuel, is crossed. To the monarch just named, the construction of this Alpine carriage route is chiefly due. Passing for some distance under a well-buttressed roof, to guard against avalanches, the road then descends the precipitous face of the mountain by windings so cleverly constructed that a quick trot can be kept up all the way.

S. Bernardino is the highest village in the Val Mesolcina. The baths at this place, supplied from the mineral springs are in good repute, and well frequented in summer.

Passing the *Fall of the Moësa, Giacomo,* and *Cebbia,* and commanding many beautiful views, especially from the bridge of S. Giacomo, the road proceeds to Mesocco, from which this delightfully Italian and rigidly Roman Catholic valley derives its name. Maize, vines, mulberry and walnut trees, in luxuriant abundance, clothe the valley, into which numerous waterfalls leap down from the enclosing mountains. The snake-haunted ruins of the castle of Misox add charmingly to the interest of the view in passing Mesocco.

The road in proceeding passes abundant evidences of the fearful ravages of the storm and floods of 1868, when over 250 dwellings and many bridges were destroyed. The beautiful Waterfall of Buffalora is seen soon after passing Soazza. *Cabbiola,* with its waterfalls, *Lostallo* with its vineyards, Cama, *Leggia,* and *Grono,* with the strongly-built tower of Florentina and a frescoed chapel, are successively passed.

At Grono is the entrance to the Val Calanca, extending 18 miles northward to the Adula mountains, and studded with numerous towns and villages.

At Roveredo, the chief town of the lower valley (pop. 1100), are the ruins of the castle of the Trivulzio family. At this town the good St. Charles Borromeo, in 1538, burnt eleven old women and the prior of Roveredo for witchcraft. After passing *S. Vittore,* the last village of the Grisons, and *Lumino,* the first of Canton Ticino, the St. Gothard route is reached, near the bridge over the Moësa (p. 176).

Hence by the battle-field of Arbedo to Bellinzona (see p. 176).

COIRE TO ANDERMATT BY THE OBERALP.

(By diligence in 13½ hours.)

The route is by one of the most picturesque valleys in Switzerland, the Vorder Rheinthal, with castles on the heights along the river as numerous as in Rhenish Prussia itself.

At **Reichenau** (p. 25), 6 miles from Coire, two routes offer themselves as far as Ilanz. The shortest is on the left bank of the river, by Versam, with its lofty bridge, (260 feet above the waters of the Rabiusa,) Carrera, Vallendas, and cretinous Kästbris. to Ilanz. The other and far more picturesque route is by the high road on the right bank, through numerous villages, and with plenty of fine views of mountains, waterfalls, ruined castles, etc. **Tamins, Trins,** and **Flims** are the chief places passed.

Ilanz, on both sides the Rhine, was once an important place, as many fine old houses with armorial bearings testify. The language of the place is Romansch, which is more or less prevalent throughout the valley. Grand views are obtained in this vicinity, especially from some of the neighbouring heights—the **Piz Mundaun** (6775 feet), and others. Excursions to the **Lugnetz Valley,** or the **Vrinthal,** are of great interest.

The road forward crosses the Rhone at Tavanasa, and at Rinkenberg, proceeding through delightful and ever-varying scenery to Trons.

At **Trons** the diligence stops to allow the passengers to dine. There are several attractions to inspect. The **Hall of the Statthalterei** of the Abbey of Dissentis, is adorned with armorial bearings of the magistrates of many generations. The fragment of the sycamore-tree near the village, over 700 years old, marks the spot where the celebrated Grey League was formed, in 1424, to resist the tyranny of the feudal lords (p. 32). The adjacent **Chapel of St. Anna** has curious frescoes and mottoes illustrating the history of the League. The view from the Church of S. Maria, above the village, is very fine.

Rabius is next passed, and then picturesque Somvix on its hill. The Val Somvix is well worth exploring. There is a bridle-path through it, and by the Greina Pass to Olivone, occupying about twelve hours.

Nearing Dissentis, the boldly-constructed road crosses the grand Russeiner Tobel, by a wooden bridge over 200 feet in length, at a height of 160 feet above the stream below.

Dissentis was famous for its Benedictine Abbey, founded in the 7th century by fellow-missionaries of St. Gall, and long the head-quarters of religion and civilization in these remote regions. It is finely situated, 4000 feet above the sea level, having been rebuilt after a fire in 1846, and is now used as a Cantonal School.

At Dissentis, the Mittel-Rhein, or Medelser, joins the Vorder Rhein. The Medelser Glacier is well seen from the **Chapel of St. Acletta**, half a mile west of Dissentis. The **Piz Muraun** (9511 feet) can be ascended in five hours; ladies have accomplished it. The Medelser Thal, Lukmänier Pass, Val Piora, etc., to the south, and the Val Russein, Sandalp Pass, in the Tödi Mountains, etc., to the north, afford good opportunities for explorations, of too protracted and fatiguing a character, however, for the general tourist.

From Dissentis there is a route to Biasca on the St. Gothard route (p. 176); nine hours by a bridle-path across the Lukmänier Pass (6298 feet) to Olivone; thence by diligence to Biasca in three hours. Some portions of this route are similar to the Via Mala.

Leaving Dissentis, the Vorder Rhein is seen, reduced to a mountain torrent, up the left bank of which the road ascends, affording splendid views of the valley behind, and the snow-clad mountains in front.

Passing **Sedrün**, chief village in the Tavetsch Valley, *Rueras*, *S. Giacomo*, and other villages, and the ruins of the Castle of Pultmenga on a rocky hill, **Tschamut** is reached, at a height of 5380 feet above the sea level—the highest place in Europe where corn is successfully grown.

Winding up the Val Surpalix, the road reaches the boundary between the Grisons and Uri, at the summit of the **Oberalp Pass** (6733 feet). The **Oberalp See**, abounding in trout, was the scene of a fierce struggle between French and Austrians in 1799. The road crosses the **Oberalp**, and soon brings the traveller in sight of the Vale of Urseren, with the Furca Inn in the background. By a number of long windings, **Andermatt**, on the **St. Gothard route**, is reached (p. 174).

COIRE TO THE ENGADINE BY THE JULIER PASS.

(By diligence to Samaden in 14 hours.)

This route leads through very fine scenery to the increasingly popular district known as the Engadine.

At Churwalden the whey cure is usually in full operation. From Parpan the Stätzerhorn or Piz Raschill, 8452 feet, can be ascended without a guide. There is a splendid panorama of the adjacent valleys and mountain chains.

At a height of 5088 feet, the Pass of Valbella is crossed. The descending road then leads by the Lake of Vatz, and some smaller lakes, on to Lenz. Thence, still descending, the rapid Albula is reached by Tiefenkasten. This village is finely situated in a basin-like valley.

Hence by *Burvein*, *Conters*, *Schweiningen*, *Tinzen*, and other picturesque villages, and amongst much remarkable hill and valley scenery, rendered still more interesting by occasional waterfalls, churches, castles, etc., the route conducts to Molins (Mühlen.) Here the diligence usually halts for dinner.

The scenery is now increasingly fine; grand rocks and dense woods mingle their attractions. Leaving Molins, the road winds through a wild gorge, with fir and larch-covered cliffs rising on either side. As the road rises, the wildness of the scenery increases, and vegetation becomes poorer, till at *Stalla*, or *Bivio* (5827 feet), even potatoes can seldom be successfully grown.

From Stalla there is an ancient route, now little frequented, over the Septimer pass to Casaccia. It was often trodden by Roman and German armies.

In about two hours from Stalla the summit of the Julier Pass is reached (7503 feet). Here are two round columns, said by some to be Augustan milestones, by others described as Celtic altars to the sun. On the adjacent lofty pastures immense flocks of sheep are fed in summer.

The short descent from the pass into the high valley of the Engadine is very striking. Between the lofty precipices of the Piz Julier and Piz d'Albana on the left, and the Piz Pulaschin on the right, the road descends. The view of Silvaplana and its lake, with the snowy peaks of the Bernina mountains in the background, is exceedingly fine. Silvaplana (see p. 186) is reached in about an hour from the pass, and then Samaden (see p. 186).

COIRE TO THE ENGADINE BY THE ALBULA PASS.

(By diligence to Ponte in 11 hours.)

Coire to Lenz, see p. 184.

From Lenz a fine new road passes Brienz, and then winds down into the **Albula Thal** to **Bad Alveneu**, with its mineral springs. The scenery is very beautiful. The ruins of the Greifenstein frown from a rock above the town of **Filisur.**

The **Bergüner Stein** is a thickly-wooded, deep mountain gorge. High up on one side a rock-blasted road runs 650 feet above the Albula flowing below. **Bergün** lies in a grassy basin, surrounded by snowy peaks. It has an old church and a fine prison-tower.

From Bergün the road winds and curves by various châlets, and several fine waterfalls, formed by the Albula river, up to the rock-strewn valley known as the Teufelsthal. Thence the summit of the **Albula Pass** is reached, 7589 feet above the sea level, closed in by the granite and limestone peaks of the Albulastock. The pass itself is a mass of rocks and *débris* in chaotic confusion.

Winding down from the Pass towards Ponte, fine views of the valley are obtained, with the Piz Languard on the right, and the distant Piz del Diavel (10,259 feet).

THE ENGADINE,

or Upper Valley of the Inn, extends along the river Inn for about fifty-seven miles, and is generally about a mile broad. At its north-east extremity, near Martinsbruck, it is over 3000 feet above the sea level, and rises to nearly 6000 feet at Sils on the south-west. The valley produces in abundance grass and wild flowers. *Voila tout!* Its dry, clear atmosphere and intensely blue skies are proverbial, and it is hemmed in by majestic mountains and glacial scenery. For sketchers, botanists, butterfly-collectors, Alpine climbers, and others, the Engadine is a very paradise. The most interesting part of the valley is the Upper Engadine, south-west of Samaden.

THE UPPER ENGADINE.

(The Maloja to Samaden, 15 miles.)

The **Maloja** is an elevated table-land (5941 feet), separating the Engadine from the Val Bregaglia. In the vicinity are the sequestered, mountain-girdled **Cavloccio Lake**, the elegant Monte d'Oro (10,544 feet), the **Ordlegna Waterfall**, the snowy **Muretto Pass** (8389 feet), leading to Chiesa.

From the Maloja we will briefly describe the prominent features of the Engadine Valley to its termination. Passing by the light green **Lake of Sils** (4½ miles in length), commanded by the Piz della Margna (10,354 feet), and its frowning glacier, the town of **Sils** is reached, with some capital mountain and glacier expeditions in the vicinity.

The **Lake of Silvaplana** is next skirted, and then the town of the same name is reached, pleasantly surrounded by green pastures. Every season this delightful town and neighbourhood is receiving an increasing number of visitors; and its beauties are so unique, that they justify the glowing colours in which they have been painted. (Hotel Rivalta.)

From Silvaplana a capital excursion can be arranged to **Pontresina** (p. 187) by the Pass called the Fuorcla da Surlej (9042 feet).

Silvaplana to Coire by the Julier Pass (see p. 184).

Campfêr is 1¼ miles from Silvaplana, Piz Languard, towering to the south-east.

St. Moritz (6100 feet) is the next place in the valley, the highest village in the Engadine. The **Baths of St. Moritz** are on a grassy plain, one mile from the village. They were highly praised by Paracelsus in 1539. Two hundred and fifty patients can be accommodated at the Curhaus. Variations of temperature must be provided against here, as elsewhere in the Engadine, for snow in August is not infrequent. Many beautiful walks, carriage-drives, and excursions are afforded in the varied and interesting neighbourhood of St. Moritz.

Some other small places, only interesting as supplying starting places for further explorations of the district, are next passed, and then

SAMADEN

(Hotel Bernina),

is reached. This is the chief place in the Upper Engadine *(pop., 550)*; it has several handsome houses and a bank. Here reside the great Planta family, who have been a considerable power in the country for nearly a thousand years. The gravestones of the Plantas, and other great families now extinct, lie thick in the old Church of St. Peter near the village.

From Samaden the **Muottas** (8464 feet) may be visited, with fine views of the Bernina Glaciers, the Lakes of the Upper Engadine, etc. Another excursion is to the **Piz Ot** (10,660 feet). The flora of all this district is very fine.

From Samaden, Pontresina (see below) is often visited by those not intending to take the Bernina Pass. The Piz Bernina (13,294 feet), and other peaks of the grand Bernina chain, are accessible from this place. The beautiful and interesting glaciers of this district, covering about 350 square miles, are now frequently inspected.

PONTRESINA.

Pontresina is only a village of about 300 inhabitants, at an altitude of nearly 6000 feet. Flowers are abundant. It is a first-rate head-quarters for glacial expeditions. (Hotel Krone.)

Amongst the attractions of Pontresina, the chief is perhaps the ascent of the **Piz Languard**, through rhododendron fringed forests, and across bright green pastures. From the summit (10,715 feet, or nearly 5000 above Pontresina) the view is bounded by Monte Rosa and Mont Blanc in the south-west, and north-west by the Tödi, and includes all East Switzerland and a portion of the Tyrol. On the sides of this mountain the botanist may find a rich harvest of rare specimens.

The **Morteratsch Glacier** is a "frozen cataract," six miles in length, 1½ hours south of Pontresina.

The **Roseg Glacier**, like the previous, needs no guide; it is about 2½ hours from Pontresina. There are several other excursions, as to the **Diavolezza**, etc., for experienced mountaineers only.

THE LOWER ENGADINE.

Samaden to Nauders, 11 hours by diligence—not worth while to walk.

Leaving Samaden, a fine view of the lower valley, with the snowy mountains and bright glaciers that encompass it, is obtained.

Passing **Bevers**, under Crasta Mora (9636 feet), **Ponte** is reached, with its old castle.

Ponte *to Coire, by the* Albula Pass (see p. 185).

Passing **Madulein**, and its ruined thirteenth century

castle of Guardavall, and **Zuz**, with its ancient tower, a milder and better cultivated portion of the valley is reached. **Scanfs**, **Zernetz** (fine old church and ancient castle), **Lavin**, burnt down in 1869, *Ardetz*, *Schuls*, **Baths of Tarasp**, *Vulpera*, *Remüs*, *Martinsbruck*, and then **Nauders**, are the chief remaining places in the valley. The diligence ride is interesting and attractive throughout; and at many points the traveller who has time at his disposal may well be tempted to alight and sojourn at one of the village inns, to make explorations on either side of this beautiful and remarkable valley.

THE BERNINA PASS.

(Samaden to Tirano, by diligence, 8½ hours.)

From Samaden to Pontresina by the Flatzbach. From Pontresina the route lies by the **Morteratsch Glacier** (see p. 187), and the **Bernina** Houses (6735 feet). Four miles further on, after leaving the region of trees, and passing the Lago Minore and Lago Nero, **Ospizio Bernina** is reached, pleasantly situated on the Lago Bianco, two miles long, and affording plenty of fish. The Cambrena Glacier is just opposite. To this point excursions are often made from Pontresina and St. Moritz. The Piz Campaccio and Piz Lagalp are accessible peaks in the neighbourhood. At a short distance east is the highest point of the **Bernina Pass.**

Through rock-hewn galleries and by winding curves, the road descends, and fine views are obtained of the Poschiavino Valley, the bottom of which is reached at *Pisciadella.*

Poschiavo, the delightful watering-place of *Le Prese*, *Brusio*, *Campo Cologno*, and *Madonna di Tirano*, are successively reached, and then **Tirano**, with its ancient palaces of the Pallavicini, Visconti, and other noble families. From Tirano, there is a route, 45 miles, through the Valtellina to Colico, by diligence, in 8 hours, passing Sondrio and Morbegno, and joining the Splügen route a little before reaching Colico.

THE STELVIO PASS.

Nauders (see above).

From Nauders the road leads by *S. Valentin auf der Heide*, where Maximilian was defeated in 1499 by a Grisons army half the number of his own; then by **Mals**, with *Knoller's* picture of the "Death of Joseph," in the church. Abundance of fine mountain scenery and many ruined castles, and other objects of interest, are passed, and also the towns of *Prad, Trafoi,* and *Franzenshöhe.*

Eight miles from Franzenshöhe, the summit of the **Stelvio Pass** is reached, 9045 feet above the sea level. A grand view of the Ortler Spitz, 12,900 feet, is obtained from an adjacent eminence. This road is the highest in Europe. It is annually much damaged by the spring avalanches, etc.; but is quite safe from June to September, though it is well to postpone crossing the Pass just after a heavy fall of snow. Through grand and varied scenery the route descends to *S. Maria* and the celebrated **Baths of Bormio**, with their chalybeate springs and beautiful pleasure grounds; and then on by *Bolladore* to **Tirano** (p. 188).

THE ITALIAN LAKES.

(For fuller particulars of the Italian Lakes, see "Cook's Handbook to Northern Italy.")

A visit to these charming lakes can readily be united with a Swiss tour.

A tour of the lakes may be made thus:—Visit Lago Maggiore, and terminate the journey at Luino (see below) Take diligence, or carriage, to Lugano. Make the tour of the lake, and terminate the journey at Porlezza. Hence take omnibus or carriage to Menaggio, on the lake of Como, and if Lago d'Iseo and Lago di Garda are to be visited, terminate the Como journey at Lecco, and take train vià Bergamo.

LAGO MAGGIORE

is about forty miles long, of varying breadth, and unequal scenery. The northern part is finer than the southern, the glory of the lake culminates in the neighbourhood of Baveno and Stresa.

Three steamboats daily run from Magadino to Arona in six hours for five francs.

The chief places on the lake are **Magadino**, unpleasant and unhealthy; **Locarno**, a busy place; pilgrimage church of Madonna del Sasso; **Ascona**, with its ruined castle; **Brissago** (by Mont Limidario, 6550 feet), abounding in orchards of orange, lemon, fig, etc.; **Canobbio**; in the church are frescoes by *Gaudenzio Ferrari;* **Maccagno**; **Luino**, from whence the drive to Lugano is one of the sweetest imaginable; **Cannero**, with the two castled islands opposite, where in the 15th century, the Mazzarda brothers lived a life of murderous brigandage; **Oggebio**, **Porto**, **Laveno**, near the beautiful mountain Il Sasso del Ferro, from whose summit a charming prospect, stretching from Milan to Monte Rosa, is seen; the silk-winding town of Intra, Pallanza (Grand Hotel, Pallanza), Baveno, from either of which the Borromean Isles can be readily visited. From Pallanza also there is a pleasant omnibus route to Lago d'Orta, and from Baveno the Simplon route can be joined (p. 172).

Between Laveno and Intra, and between Pallanza and the islands, glorious glimpses of the Monte Rosa, Strahlhorn, Simplon, and other mountain scenery are obtained.

THE BORROMEAN ISLANDS

are four in number, Isola S. Giovanni, Isola Bella, and Isola Madre (belonging to the Borromeo family), and Isola Superiore, or Dei Pescatori (the fishermen's island).

Isola Bella is a planted and terraced pleasure-ground, on a once bare rock; very fine, but somewhat formal and artificial. The views of the lake and its surroundings are splendid. Admission to the Gardens is one franc; to the Château, with some good pictures, and room where Napoleon slept the night before Marengo, also one franc.

Isola Madre (one franc) is a charming terraced island, with many rare tropical plants.

Isola dei Pescatori is a compact fishermen's village.

Isola S. Giovanni is of no particular interest.

After leaving the Borromean isles, at the principal of which, Isola Bella, the steamer stops without extra charge for landing or embarking, Stresa is next reached.

Stresa (Hotel des Iles Borromées, a magnificent hotel, commanding some of the finest views on the lake) is a pleasant place, surrounded with fine scenery both by land and water. From here the Monte Motterone may be ascended: it is 4174 feet above the lake, and the view equals, if it does not rival, that from the Rigi; the plain of Lombardy and Piedmont, with the Cathedral of Milan, in clear view; six of the Italian lakes, with their picturesque islands and surroundings; the rivers Sesia and Ticino meandering in streams of silver; and on the other hand, the great mountains from Monte Rosa to Ortler in the Tyrol.

Belgirate is the next town passed, and the tour of the lake comes to an end at Arona.

Arona contains a Church of S. Maria, with the Borromeo Chapel; a Holy Family, by *Gaudenzio Vinci*, and some other pictures. The **colossal statue** of St. Charles Borromeo is near the town, sixty-six feet high, on a forty feet pedestal. Facilities exist for the adventurous to mount the pedestal, enter the saint's body, and climb up into his head.

From Arona diligences run to Bellinzona, for the St. Gothard or Bernardino Pass, to Lucerne, or Coire. See local time-tables.

(For the Railway to Genoa and Turin, and the Railway to Milan, see "Cook's Guide to Northern Italy.")

THE LAKE OF COMO

is the grandest and most beautiful of the Italian lakes. It is thirty-eight miles long, and varies from one to three miles in breadth. It reminds sometimes of the Rhine, and sometimes of Lake Lucerne, yet differs from both. A perfect efflorescence of loveliness is this fairy lake. In whatever direction you cast your eyes whilst traversing its waters, the scenic effects are unrivalled. Embosomed amongst lofty mountains towering proudly above the silvery surface; verdant slopes and vine-clad hills, with villas on the margin and on jutting peninsulas; picturesque and charmingly-situated villages; the eye never wearies in its search for the beautiful. Castles, with turreted towers, ever and anon keep peeping out, as the boat proceeds, from the sylvan woods which hide them, a sort of stolen glance. The glowing Italian sky, the azure of which is almost unknown to those who are accustomed to the unkind climate of England; the water of an indescribable blue, the delicious purity of the atmosphere, and the silver streaks of sunlight cast upon the lake heighten the beauty of the scene. The finest prospects are near Bellaggio.

The tour of the lake can be made either from Colico or Como.

Colico is simply a station for diligences. They run twice daily to Chiavenna for the Splugen route; also to Sondrio and Bormio. Steamers from Como twice daily.

Menaggio (Hotel Victoria) is a popular halting-place. The scenery is exquisite. It also contains the **Villa Vigoni**, near the town, with some modern works of art of great beauty; reliefs by *Thorwaldsen;* monument to the son of the late proprietor, by *Marchesi;* and a family group, by *Argenti*. The large silkworm manufactory is of great interest.

From Menaggio to Lugano, by omnibus and steamer, is an easy and *pleasant journey*.

The tour of the three principal lakes may be made thus:—Menaggio to Lugano, Lake of Lugano, Lugano to Luino, Lago Maggiore. For this tour a special circular ticket is provided by Thos. Cook and Son.

Bellaggio (Hotel Grand Bretagne, with the Dependence Hotel Pension, Villa Serbelloni. The hotel is one of the finest in the Italian Lake districts; the Pension is the gem of the neighbourhood.)

Bellaggio is charmingly situated where the lake divides into two arms. The magnificent **park** and gardens of the Villa Serbelloni form one of the finest attractions of the place. Admission one franc to those not staying at the Hotel. At the Villa Melzi are many works of art by *Canova*, *Thorwaldsen*, *Marchesi*, etc.

From Bellaggio to Lecco a steamer runs daily.

Cadenabbia (Grand Hotel Belle Vue) is justly popular with invalids and others. The **Villa Carlotta** contains some wonderful works by *Thorwaldsen*, and *Canova*. **Monte Crecione** can be ascended in about eight hours.

Several places of more or less interest and beauty are passed. Between **Moltrasio** and **Cernobbio** is the **Villa d'Este**, now the Hotel Regina d'Inghilterra, where Queen Caroline, wife of George IV., resided. This is a capital centre for excursions; the grounds are very fine. (Cook's coupons accepted).

Como (Hotel Regina d'Inghilterra, see above)—population, 21,000—lies at the extreme end of this arm of the lake, and is backed by fine hills and mountains. It is celebrated as being the birthplace of Pliny the Elder and the Younger. The latter had several villas in the neighbourhood. Volta, the electrician, and Pazzi, the astronomer, were also born here.

The **Cathedral**, built in 1396, is entirely of marble, and is a remarkably handsome church. The **façade** is very rich. *Statues* of the two Plinys by the principal entrance.

In the interior the principal paintings are—

The Marriage of the Virgin	*G. Ferrari.*
The Flight into Egypt	*Ibid.*
Adoration of Magi	*B. Luino.*
Virgin and Child, with saints	*Ibid.*

There are some fine altarpieces in the church; the one with St. Joseph and the young Saviour is the last work of *Marchesi*, and one of his best.

The Town Hall (Broletto) adjoins the church. It is built of black and white stone, in alternate layers. The Theatre is on the other side of the church.

The churches S. Fedele, 10th century; Del Crocifisso, with miraculous crucifix; and S. Abondio, 11th century, on outskirts of town, are worth visiting.

Notice a massive ruined building, the Porta del Tozze. It is five stories high, and is passed in leaving the town to go towards Camerlata.

From Como to Camerlata is a little more than a mile and a half. Omnibuses run to meet each train.

THE LAKE OF LUGANO

is sixteen miles by about two; the scenery is varied and beautiful. It can be reached from Menaggio on Lake of Como, or Magadino or Luino, on the Lago Maggiore.

Steamers run from Porlezza to Lugano (Hotel du Parc). Behind the latter town is Monte San Salvatore, scalable in two hours. The view is superb.

Monte Generoso, called the Rigi of Italy, is best ascended from Mendrisio, on the road to Como. The view of the Italian lakes and the Alpine chain beyond is unrivalled.

THE LAKE OF VARESE,

reached either from Laveno (Lago Maggiore) or from Como, is about six miles by five. Varese (Hotel Varese) is the principal place, from which the chief excursion is to the pilgrimage church of La Madonna del Monte.

THE LAKE OF ORTA

is best reached by omnibus or diligence from Pallanza, Gravellona, or Arona. It is exceedingly pretty, eight miles long by nearly two broad.

The principal thing to see at the quaint town of Orta is the Sacro Monte, sacred to S. Francis d'Assisi, with its twenty frescoed chapels, passed during the ascent. The island of S. Giulio is a delicious little spot.

LAGO D'ISEO AND LAGO DI GARDA

are both within easy reach by diligence from Brescia. Both are very beautiful. Iseo is sixteen miles by two; the chief places are Sarnico, Iseo (named from a temple of Isis), and Lovere, so enthusiastically described by Lady Mary Wortley Montagu. Lago di Garda is thirty-eight miles by six or seven, and appallingly deep, 1900 English feet having been fathomed in some places, and it may be found to be deeper yet. It is often assailed by storms, and is then as rough as the Mediterranean.

Omnibuses run to the lake from Peschiera and Desenzano. Many very popular and charming places are located on its shore.

(For fuller information as to the Italian Lakes, see "Cook's Tourist's Handbook for Northern Italy.")

APPENDIX.

FESTIVALS, FETES, FAIRS, ETC.

[Some time since, a good article in *Macmillan's Magazine* called attention to the want of a Traveller's Calendar, which should indicate the principal Festivals, etc., on the Continent of Europe. The present list is founded upon the data given in that article, and it is hoped it will be useful to the traveller. The Editor will feel much indebted to those of his friends who will kindly favour him with information of other events of interest to add to the list.]

PLACE.	DATE.	DESCRIPTION.
Adelsberg	Whit-Monday...	Peasants' Ball in the Caverns. Illuminated.
Aix-la-Chapelle	July 10-24	Exhibition of Relics in Cathedral every 7 years. Next Exhibition, 1881.
	Whitsun-week .	The "Niederrheinische Musikfest."
Amsterdam ...	2nd Monday in Sept.	Festivities of the Kermesse commence, and continue for a fortnight.
Annecy (Savoy)	Jan. 29.	Festival of St. Francis de Sales.
Antwerp	Sunday following Aug. 15...	Kermesse, Procession of Giant in Rubens' Car.
		Carnival for three days preceding Ash-Wednesday.
Assisi	Aug. 1 and 2 ...	Grand Festivals.
	Oct. 14	Festival of St. Francis.
Augsburg	April 10	Commencement of Fair, which continues for a fortnight.
Avellino.........	Whit-Sunday ...	Pilgrimage to Monte Vergine. Popular Fêtes. At Mercogliano, dances of peasants. (5 days.)
Bari (S. Italy)...	May	*S. Nicholas.* Pilgrimage to shrine. Miraculous manna exuded.
Basle	Aug. 25	Commemoration of battle of St. Jacques.
Batersalp *(Switzerland)*	July 25th or Sunday following.	Wrestling Matches.

PLACE.	DATE.	DESCRIPTION.
Beaucaire (on Rhone)	July	Great Fair. (Beaucaire is near Tarascon.)
Bergamo	Middle Aug. to middle Sept.	Fair.
Black Forest.	End Aug., beginning Sept.	"Raft Parties" at Wildbad and elsewhere.
Bologna	Dec. 3	*St. Francis Xavier.* Fête at Sta. Lucia.
Bra	Sept. 8	Pilgrimage to Sanctuary of Madonna dei Fiore.
Bremen	Nov. 6	Festival.
Bruges	1st Sun. in Lent	Great day of the Carnival.
	1st Sun. in May	Festival.
Brussels	Jan. 8	*Ste. Gudule.* Festival at Ste. Gudule.
	July 13 or Sunday following.	Procession of miraculous wafers in Ste. Gudule.
	Sept. 23	Requiem Mass in Ste. Gudule. Fêtes de Septembre from 23—26.
Cancello (S. Italy)	July 26	Annual Festival in honour of S. Paulinus, who invented church bells. Games, processions, etc.
Catania (Sicily)	Feb. 3-5	Festival of Sta. Agata.
	Aug. 18-21	" "
Coire (Chur) ...	Ascension Day.	Popular Fêtes.
Cologne		Carnival for three days before Ash-Wednesday.
	Whitsun-week.	The "Neiderrheinische Musikfest."
Courtrai (Belgium)		Carnival for three days before Ash-Wednesday.
Einsiedeln (Switzerland)	Jan. 21	Festival of St. Meinrad.
	Sept. 14	Festival of the Engel Weihe. Mass out of doors. Illuminations.
Engstlenalp (nr. Meiringen)	July 26th or Sunday following.	Wrestling Matches.
Ennetegg (in the Entlebuch)	Lt. Sun. in Aug., 1st Sun. in Sep.	Wrestling Match.
Florence	Easter Eve	Fireworks in Piazza del Duomo. "Lo scoppio del Carro."
	March 25	*Annunciation.* Festival at Annunziata Church.
	June 23	*Eve of St. John.* Races and Fireworks.
	" 24	*St. John Baptist.* High Mass in Duomo. Races. Illuminations.
	Aug. 10	*St. Lorenzo.* Festival in all Churches in Italy bearing his name.
	" 15	*Assumption of Virgin.* Musical Services. Decorations.
	Sept. 8	*Nativity of Virgin.* "Rificolone," and decoration of street altars.
		Carnival preceding Lent.

PLACE.	DATE.	DESCRIPTION.
Genazzano (Sabine Hills)	April 26	Pilgrimages.
Genoa	June 24	*St. John Baptist.* Relics carried in procession in Cathedral.
Genzano (near Albano)	Corpus Christi .	Floral Festival—very picturesque.
Ghent	2nd Sunday in July.	Festival. Kermesse.
Gratz	Aug. 12	Pilgrimage to Mariazell.
Gravina(S. Italy)	April 20	Great Fair.
Hal (Belgium)...	Whit-Monday...	Pilgrimages.
Leipsic	Jan. 1	Fair commences.
	Sept. 29	Fair.
	2nd Sunday after Easter.	Great Fair begins. Lasts three weeks.
Liege	Feb. 10	Musical Festival commemorating birth of Grétry.
Locarno	Sept. 8............	*Nativity of Virgin.* Fair.
Loreto............	Dec. 10	Great Festival at the "Holy House."
Louvain	Feb. 9	*St. Apollonia.* Festival.
	May 26	Pilgrimages.
	2nd Sunday in July.	Festival.
Lucerne	Sunday after Ascension.	Festival at Tell's Chapel. Crowds in boats.
	Thursday before Ash-Wed.	Quaint and curious procession.
Lugo (near Ravenna)	Sept. 1-19	Fair.
Malines	July	Festival of the Guilds every five years. Next in 1879.
	1st. Sun. in July	*St. Rombauld.* Festival.
Manfredonia (near Foggia)	May 8	Pilgrimage to Church of St. Michael.
Mantua	Aug. 15	*Assumption of Virgin.* Pilgrimage to Sta. Maria delle Grazie.
Marseilles......	June 16	Festival of Sacred Heart, commemorating the staying of the plague, 1720.
	Aug. 15	*Assumption of the Virgin.* Procession of the silver statue.
Messina	June 3	Festival of the Madonna della Lettera.
	Aug. 15	*Assumption of Virgin.* Festival of "La Vara."
Meiringen......	1st Sunday in August.	Wrestling matches at the Stadtalp, and on Aug. 10 at the Tannalp.
Milan	May 3	*Invention of the Cross.* Procession through the city.
	Nov. 4............	*San Carlo Borromeo.* Grand Fête. Carnival. Preceding Lent.

PLACE.	DATE.	DESCRIPTION.
Moncalieri (near Turin)	Oct. 29. Nov. 14.	Cattle Fair.
Munich	Monday before Ash-Wed.	The "Metzersprung"—a curious performance.
	Good Friday.	Pergolesi's Stabat Mater at Jesuits' Church.
	Corpus Christi.	Procession of Guilds. Open-air services.
Naples............	1st Sun. in May	Liquefaction of Blood of St. Januarius.
	Sept. 19 to 26.	,, ,, Great Festival.
	Dec. 16	,, Feast of his "Patrocinio"
	1st Sun. in June	Festival of the Constitution. Fireworks at Villa Nazionale.
	Aug. 15	*Assumption of Virgin.* Festival at Capodimonte.
		,, ,, Pilgrimage to Massa Lubrense, near Sorrento.
	Ascension Day.	Fêtes at Scarfati and Carditello.
	Corpus Christi.	Festival at Sta. Chiara. Parade of troops.
	Jan. 17	Feste di St. Antonio Abate. Blessing of domestic animals.
	Sept. 8	*Nativity of Virgin.* Festival of the Vergine de Piedegrotta. A variety of curious entertainments, including the Tarantella dance.
	Dec. 24	"Presepe" (*i.e.*, manger) in all churches and houses.
	Whit-Sunday ...	Festival at Avellino.
	Whit-Monday...	,, Shrine of Madonna dell' Arca.
	Easter Sunday.	Pilgrimage to Antignano.
Nepomuk	May 16	Pilgrimage to birthplace of St. John Nepomuk (between Prague and Nuremberg).
Nivello (Belgium)	Whit-Monday...	Procession.
Ober-Ammergau	1st Sunday in June	And each succeeding Sunday till end of September. Passion Play. Every 10 years. Next representation, 1880.
Ostend............	Corpus Christi.	Blessing the sea.
Padua	Jan. 17	*St. Anthony.* Festival.
Palermo.........	July 11-15	Festival of Sta. Rosalia. Cathedral illuminated on last day of festival.
	Sept. 4	Pilgrimage to Monte Pellegrino.
Paris..............	Jan. 1	*Circumcision.* General holiday. Display of étrennes.
	Nov. 2............	*All Souls'.* Crowds visit Père la Chaise.
Pesth	Aug. 20	Festival of St. Stephen of Hungary.
Pisa	June 16	Festival of "La Luminara." Once in three years.

PLACE.	DATE.	DESCRIPTION.
Prague	May 16-24	*St. John Nepomuk.* Grand Festival. Pilgrimages. Mass on great bridge.
	Sept. 28	Festival of St. Wenceslaus.
Rapallo (near Genoa)	July 2-4	Festival of Madonna dell' Orto. Illumination of the coast.
Rigi	July 22	Pilgrimage to church on Rigi. Wrestling Matches.
	Aug. 5......... ..	Pilgrimage to Chapel Maria Zum Schnee, Klosterli.
	Sept. 6	,, ,, ,,
	Aug. 10	Wrestling Matches at Kaltbad.
Rome	[NOTE.—Many of the festivals have been altered, abandoned, or become irregular, since Rome has become the capital of Italy. Those marked with an asterisk are still observed with great pomp.]	
	Jan. 1	*Circumcision.* "Papal Chapel" (*i.e.*, service at which the Pope is present) at the Sistine. Curious ceremony at Sta. Maria in Campitelli—drawing for patron saints.
	,, 5	Fair of the Befano. St. Eustachio.
	,, 6	*Epiphany.* Ara Cœli Church; procession. Benediction with the Sante Bambino from top of steps. Services in various churches throughout octave.
	,, 17	*St. Anthony's Day.* Blessing the beasts.
	,, 18	Chair of St. Peter. Procession with Pope, in St. Peter's.
	,, 20	*St. Sebastian.* Festival at Sant' Andrea della Valle.
	,, 21	**St. Agnes.* Blessing the lambs, at Sta. Agnese fuori Mura.
	,, 25	**Conversion of St. Paul.* Exhibition of his chains at San Paolo.
	Feb. 1	**St. Ignatius.* The interesting subterranean Church of San Clemente illuminated.
	,, 2	*Purification.* Procession with candles in St. Peter's.
	March 9	*Sta. Francesca Romana.* Fête at the Tor de' Specchi.
	,, 12	*St. Gregory.* Festival at S. Gregorio.
	,, 19	*St. Joseph.* Festival of S. Giuseppe.
	,, 25	**Annunciation.* Papal Chapel. Procession of white mule. Sta. Maria sopra Minerva.
	April 23	*St. George.* Exhibition of relics S. Giorgio in Velabro.
	,, 25	**St. Mark.* Procession from St. Mark's to St. Paul's.

PLACE.	DATE.	DESCRIPTION.
Rome	April 30	*St. Catherine.* Festival at the Minerva.
	May 3	**Invention of the Cross.* Exhibition of relics at Sante Croce.
	,, 26	**St. Filippo Neri.* Papal Chapel, Chiesa Nuova. (The rooms occupied by the saint are open on this day.)
	June 24	**St. John Baptist.* Papal Chapel at the Lateran. Fine musical service, and on previous evening.
	,, 28	*Eve of St. Peter.* Papal Chapel, St. Peter's. Dome illuminated.
	,, 29	**St. Peter.* The Pope performs High Mass in St. Peter's. At Lateran exhibition of relics. Fireworks on Monte Pincio, etc. Throughout the octave the Mamertine Prisons are illuminated.
	June 31	*St. Ignatius Loyola.* Festival at the Gesù.
	Aug. 1	**St. Peter's Chains.* Festival at S. Pietro in Vinculi.
	,, 4	*St. Dominic.* Fête at the Minerva.
	,, 5	*Sta. Maria ad Nives.* Cardinal's Chapel (*i.e.*, service at which the Cardinal is present) at Sta. Maria Maggiore. During the function white flowers are showered from the roof of the Borghese Chapel.
	,, 15	**Assumption of the Virgin.* Sta. Maria Maggiore. High Mass, in presence of the Pope. Benediction from balcony.
	Sept. 8	**Nativity of Virgin.* Papal Chapel at Sta. Maria del Popolo.
	1st Sunday in October.	*Rosary Sunday.* Procession from the Minerva. Fêtes, etc., throughout the month on Sundays and Thursdays at Monte Testaccio.
	Nov. 1	**All Saints.* Feast at S. Lorenzo. Curious scenes in the cemeteries throughout the octave.
	,, 4	**San Carlo Borromeo.* Papal Chapel at San Carlo in Corso.
	,, 22	**Sta. Cecilia.* Festival at Sta. Cecilia. Illumination of Catacomb of St. Calixtus, where St. Cecilia was buried.
	,, 23	**St. Clemente.* Festival and illuminations, Subterranean Church of S. Clemente.
	Dec. 3	*St. Francis Xavier.* Fête at the Gesù.

PLACE.	DATE.	DESCRIPTION.
Rome	Dec. 4	Military Mass at Sta. Maria Transpontina. Fête of artillerymen.
	„ 8	*Immaculate Conception.* Papal Chapel in the Sistine.
	„ 24	*Christmas Eve.* Procession of Holy crib in Sta. Maria Maggiore. Night services at Sistine, Vatican, etc.
	„ 25	*Christmas Day.* Pope performs High Mass at St. Peter's. Festival of the "Presepe" at the Ara Cœli. Sermons by boys for ten subsequent days.
	„ 26	*St. Stephen.* Fête, San Stefano Rotondo. "Te Deum" at the Gesu. Pope and Cardinals present.
	„ 27	*St. John the Evangelist.* St. John Lateran.
	„ 31	*St. Sylvester.* At his church, and "Te Deum" at the Gesù.
	Holy Week ...	Noble ladies wash the feet of pilgrims each evening at the Trinita dei Pellegrini. *Wednesday.* The "Tenebræ"—an interesting service, at which the lights are gradually extinguished while the story of the Passion is rehearsed. "Miserere" sung in the Sistine Chapel. Pope present. *Thursday.* Sistine Chapel, High Mass. Procession of the Pope to the Pauline Chapel, which is illuminated. St. Peter's—the Pope blesses the people from the balcony: washes the feet of thirteen priests; serves thirteen priests at table. "Tenebræ" and "Miserere" in Sistine. Illumination of the various chapels. *Good Friday.* "Tenebræ" and "Miserere." Adoration of relics in St. Peter's by the Pope. *Saturday.* Jews baptized in baptistery of Constantine. In the evening, service at St. Peter's.
	Easter Sunday.	Pope borne to St. Peter's, where he celebrates Mass. Blowing of the silver trumpets. Benediction from balcony. Illumination of dome.

PLACE.	DATE.	DESCRIPTION.
Rome	Easter Monday.	Fêtes, fireworks, etc.
	Carnival	Begins Saturday-week before Ash Wednesday, and continues till Shrove Tuesday. Masquerades and horse-racing daily. On the last evening, lighting and blowing out tapers.
	Ash Wednesday	Ashes are sprinkled on the heads of the Cardinals in St. Peter's. High Mass.
	3rd Sunday in Lent.	Exhibition of relics at San Lorenzo.
	4th Monday in Lent.	Feast of the Santa Quattro Incoronati at their Basilica.
	Palm Sunday ...	The Pope carried round St. Peter's. Consecration of Palms.
	Rogation Days.	Processions.
	Ascension Day.	Papal Chapel at Lateran. Benediction by the Pope from the balcony.
	[The GREAT NATIONAL FESTAS, celebrated with music, illuminations, etc., etc., are—	
	1st Sunday in June.	Celebration of the Constitution.
	Sept. 20	Anniversary of the Liberation of Rome. Processions, etc.
	Oct. 2	Anniversary of the Plebiscite.
	Etc., etc., etc.	

[Every visitor should consult the Calendar, and also local authorities, as there is scarcely a day when there is not some ecclesiastical celebration of interest going forward somewhere in Rome.]

PLACE.	DATE.	DESCRIPTION.
Sachseln.........	July 26	Wrestling Matches. (Sachseln is near Sanden, on the Brunig, Switzerland.)
Schopfheim (Switzerland)	June 29	Wrestling Matches.
	Sept. 29	,, ,,
	1st Sunday in Oct.	,, ,,
Seealp (near Appenzel)	July 6	Or Sunday following that date. Wrestling Matches.
Sempach (near Lucerne)	,, 8	Commemoration of victory on battle-field.
Siena	April 30	*St. Catherine.* Festival.
	July 2 & Aug. 16	Horse Races (Il Palio).
Sinigaglia (S. Italy)	October	Great Fair.
Sorrento.........	Aug. 15	Fête at S. Maria a Castello. Illumination of Positano.
Spezia	,, ...	*Assumption of Virgin.* Festival at the Church of the Madonna di Soviore.

PLACE	DATE.	DESCRIPTION.
St. Moritz (Switzerland)	Sept. 21	Illuminations.
	„ 22	Festival and High Mass at **Abbey of** St. Moritz.
Stadtalp (near Meiringen)	1st Sunday in Aug.	Wrestling Match.
Stuttgart	Sept. 28	Volksfest at Cannstadt.
Tannalp (near Meiringen)	Aug. 10	Wrestling Match.
Tivoli	May 8	*S. Michele.* Festival.
Trent (Trento)	June 26	Festival of S. Vigilius.
Trieste............	Corpus Christi	Processions. Festivals.
Turin	Sept. 8..	*Nativity of Virgin.* Festival on the Superga.
Uetliberg (Zürich)	Ascension Day	Children's Fête.
Varallo (Lake of Orta)	Aug. 15	*Assumption of Virgin.* Pilgrimage to the Sacro Monte.
Venice............	April 25	*St. Mark's.* Grand Festival.
		[Festivals on all the Saints' Days, and a variety of Fêtes of local interest.]
Vienna............	May 1	Popular Fête in the Augarten.
	June 28	Pilgrims leave for Mariazell (reached from Brück on the Semmering Railway).
	July 6	Pilgrims return from Mariazell.
	Sept. 4	*Sta. Rosalia.* Pilgrimage to Rosalien Chapel.
	„ 8	Public Holiday at Mariabrunn, a short distance from Vienna.
	Good Friday ...	Holy Sepulchre in all the Churches.
	Easter Eve	Great Procession of the Court in Imperial Palace.
	Easter Monday.	Pilgrimage to Antignano.
	Corpus Christi .	Processions, Festivals, etc.
Vire (Normandy)	Aug. 10	Fête des Drapiers.
Vlaardingen (Holland)	June 14	Prayers for success of the herring fishery.
	„ 15	General Holiday. Fleet of herring boats set sail.
Wengern Alp	1st Sunday in Aug.	Wrestling Match.
Ypres (Belgium)	1st Sunday in Aug.	Festival.

SWISS ELEVATIONS.

THE following is a comparative account of the height (in feet above the sea level) of some of the well-known places in Switzerland referred to in the present work:—

Piz Languard	10,715
Gorner Grat	10,290
Faulhorn	8,803
Riffel Hotel	8,428
Lauberhorn	8,120
Furca	7,992
Grimsel	7,936
Rothhorn	7,917
Niesen	7,763
Bernina Pass	7,658
Albula Pass	7,589
Julier Pass	7,503
Splügen Pass	6,945
St. Gothard Pass	6,936
Bellevue Hotel, Wengern Alp ...	6,788
Engadine	6,100
Rigi	5,905
Rhone Glacier (lower)	5,742
Mürren	5,347
Zermatt	5,315
Rosenlaui Glacier	5,027
Andermatt...	4,900
Maderaner Thal	4,500
Comballaz	4,416
Rosenlaui	4,397
Tête Noire Hotel	4,003
Grindelwald	3,773
Chamouny	3,445
Brünig Pass	3,379
Engelberg	3,291
Lauterbrunnen	2,730
Meiringen	2,224
Interlaken	1,837
Lucerne	1,437
Geneva	1,230

IMPORTANT NOTICE.

THOMAS COOK AND SON'S *tickets are available for one or more passengers to travel by any train any day, and do not compel the holders to travel in parties.*

Programme of Routes.

TIME AND COST OF A TOUR.

IN order to help the Tourist to arrange a route, to show how time may be economized, and, above all, to give him some notion as to the APPROXIMATE COST of a tour to Switzerland, we append a few examples. It must be borne in mind, however, that the costs of travelling are liable to constant change, and therefore the Tourist will do well to consult the last number of "COOK'S EXCURSIONIST" (published monthly, price 2*d.*); or, if he cannot from that source obtain the exact information required, if the precise itinerary of the tour contemplated be forwarded to Messrs. COOK & SON, Chief Office, Ludgate Circus, E.C., with stamped directed envelope for a reply, a special quotation will be sent by first post.

In CALCULATING EXPENSES, nothing will be said here about hotel accommodation, or about the luxuries of travel. Of course, it depends entirely on the taste of the individual, and his habits, as to whether expenses in this respect be great or small. What we wish to denote is the *actual travelling expense* and the actual expenditure of time, necessary for a tour in Switzerland. A tour may be a very expensive matter as regards time and money, if the traveller thinks well to make it so; but this is by no means a necessity. A fortnight, three weeks, or a month, will suffice, as regards time; and the travelling expenses will be within the means of all ordinary Tourists. Full particulars as to hotel accommodation will be found on

Whenever in the following illustrations guides or carriages are mentioned, the expense is not included in the estimate given, except in the case of the Tête Noire or Col de Balme.

ROUTE NO. I. A FOURTEEN DAYS' TOUR.

Allowing time to visit Geneva, Chamouny, Mont Blanc.

1st day.—London to Paris, via Calais, 11 hours.

2nd day.—Paris to Geneva, 13½ hours.

3rd day.—At Geneva.

4th day.—Trip on the Lake.

5th day.—Geneva to Chamouny by diligence.

6th day.—Chamouny. Ascend to Montanvert; cross the Mer de Glace to the Chapeau; descend to source of the Arveiron. (Guide over Mer de Glace; trifling fee.)

7th day.—At Chamouny.

8th day.—Chamouny to Martigny, by the Tête Noire or Col de Balme.*

9th day.—Visit Gorge du Trient; rail to Lausanne.

10th day.—Lausanne and environs.

11th day.—Lausanne to Berne, breaking the journey in order to spend a few hours at Fribourg.

12th day.—Berne to Neuchâtel, 3½ hours.

13th day.—Neuchâtel to Paris.

14th day.—Paris to London.

Approximate cost: First class throughout, £11 10s.; second class, £9.

ROUTE NO. II. A FORTNIGHT'S TOUR.

Allowing time to visit the finest scenery of the Bernese Oberland.

1st day.—Leave London for Paris by morning train, 11 hours, via Calais.

---

* In going to Martigny from Chamouny the Tête Noire is the preferable route. From Martigny to Chamouny the Col de Balme is recommended.

2nd day.—Paris to Basle by Troyes and Mulhouse, 12½ hours.

3rd day.—Explore Basle in early morning; then Basle to Lucerne, 3½ hours.

4th day.—In Lucerne (ascend Rigi or Pilatus).

5th day.—Tour of the Lake of Lucerne.

6th day.—Lucerne to Meiringen, over the Brünig Pass.

7th day.—On foot to Falls of the Reichenbach, Rosenlaui Glacier, Great Scheideck, Grindelwald, Little Scheideck.

8th day.—Wengern Alp, Lauterbrunnen and Staubbach Falls; carriage from thence to Interlaken.

9th day.—Spend morning in Interlaken; return ticket to Brienz, to visit Falls of the Giessbach.

10th day.—Interlaken to Därligen by train; Därligen to Thun by boat; Thun to Berne by rail.

11th day.—In Berne.

12th day.—Berne to Geneva, breaking journey at Fribourg or Lausanne, 5 hours.

13th day.—In Geneva.

14th day.—To Paris.

15th day.—Paris to London.

Approximate cost: First class throughout, about £11; second class, £8 10s.

No provision is made in this estimate for mule, or other means of conveyance from Meiringen to Interlaken.

Route No. III. A Fortnight's Tour.

1st day.—London to Paris (via Dieppe).

2nd day.—Paris to Basle.

3rd day.—Basle to Schaffhausen, 3½ hours; Falls of the Rhine.

4th day.—Schaffhausen to Constance, 2 hours; Lake of Constance.

5th day.—To Zürich, choice of routes.

6th day.—At Zürich.

7th day.—Zürich to Lucerne, 2 hours; at Lucerne.

8th day.—Trip on Lake of Lucerne to Flüelen and back.

9th day.—Lucerne to Brienz; over the Brünig Pass; stay at Falls of the Giessbach.

10th day.—Interlaken.

11th day.—Rail to Därligen: steamboat on Lake of Thun; rail to Berne.

12th day.—In Berne.

13th day.—Rail to Paris by Neuchâtel, Pontarlier, and Dijon.

14th day.—In Paris.

15th day.—To London.

Cost: First class throughout, £11 7s.; second class, £7 15s.

ROUTE No. IV. A THREE WEEKS' TOUR,

Visiting Falls of the Rhine, Bernese Oberland, Chamouny, and Mont Blanc.

1st and 2nd days.—London to Basle (via Dieppe and Paris).

3rd day.—Basle to Schaffhausen.

4th day.—Schaffhausen to Zürich.

5th day.—Zürich to Lucerne.

6th day.—Ascend Rigi.

7th day.—Trip on Lake to Flüelen and back.

8th day.—From Lucerne to Meiringen, by the Brünig Pass.

9th day.—On foot to Falls of Reichenbach, Rosenlaui Glacier, Great Scheideck, Grindelwald, and Little Scheideck.

10th day.—Wengern Alp, Lauterbrunnen (see Staubbach Falls): carriage from thence to Interlaken.

11th day.—In Interlaken. Falls of Giessbach.

12th day.—Rail to Därligen; boat to Thun; rail to Berne.

13th day.—To Lausanne, visiting Fribourg, *en route.*

14th day.—Trip on Lake to visit Vevey; Chillon; thence to Bouveret for Martigny; stop *en route* to visit Gorge du Trient.

15th day.—Martigny to Chamouny by Col de Balme, or Tête Noire.

16th day.—At Chamouny.

17th day.—Diligence to Geneva.

18th day.—Geneva.

19th day.—Geneva.

20th day.—To Paris.

21st day.—To London.

Cost: First class throughout, £12 19s.; second class, £10 8s.

Route No. V. A Three Weeks' Tour,

Visiting Belgium, the Rhine, and Switzerland.

Leave London for Antwerp by evening train; arrive there in early morning of

1st day.—At Antwerp.

2nd day.—To Brussels, 2 hours. Brussels.

3rd day.—Trip to Waterloo, etc.

4th day.—Brussels to Cologne, 7 hours.

5th day.—Up the Rhine to Bingen or Mayence.

6th day.—To Heidelberg.

7th day.—Baden-Baden.

8th day.—To Strassburg; visit Cathedral, etc., and then proceed to Basle.

9th day.—At Basle.

10th day.—Basle to Lucerne, 3½ hours. Lucerne.

11th day.—Lucerne; trip on Lake to Flüelen and back.

12th day.—Lucerne; ascend Rigi or Pilatus, etc.

13th day.—From Alpnach to Brienz by diligence; steamer from Brienz to Giessbach; stay night there, and see the Falls illuminated.

14th day.—Steamer to Interlaken.

*15th day.*At Interlaken; trip to Grindelwald, etc.

16th day.—Interlaken to Berne.

17th day.—Berne to Lausanne.

18th day.—Ouchy to Geneva by boat.

19th day.—Geneva.

20th day.—To Paris.

21st day.—To London, via Calais.

Cost : First class throughout, £14 ; second class, £11

ROUTE NO. VI. A THREE WEEKS' TOUR,

Visiting Belgium, the Rhine, and Switzerland.

1st day to 10th day.—As in Route V.

11th day.— Ascend Rigi, etc.

12th day.—Lucerne to Flüelen by steamboat; diligence to Andermatt.

13th day.—By the Furca Pass to Brigue ; rail to Martigny.

14th day.—By the Col de Balme or Tête Noire to Chamouny.

15th day.—At. Chamouny.

16th day.—At Chamouny.

17th day.—To Geneva, by diligence.

18th day.—Geneva.

19th day.—Trip on the Lake of Geneva.

20th day.—To Paris.

21st day.—To London, via Calais.

Approximate cost : First class, £15 ; second class, £11 18s.

ROUTE NO. VII. A MONTH'S TOUR,

Visiting the principal places in Switzerland leisurely.

Same as Route No. IV.

Cost, same as Route No IV.

ROUTE NO. VIII. A MONTH'S TOUR,

Including a visit to the principal places in Switzerland and the Italian Lakes.

1st day.—To Paris (via Calais).

2nd day.—To Basle.

3rd day.—To Schaffhausen.

4th day.—Zürich.

5th day.—By rail to Coire.

6th day.—Diligence to Chiavenna, over the Splügen.

7th day.—Chiavenna to Colico, diligence; Colico to Bellaggio by steamer.

8th day.—At Bellaggio.

9th day.—To Como.

10th day.—To Menaggio, boat; and Lugano (Lake of Lugano), diligence.

11th day.—Lugano to Luino, diligence; thence to Laveno, Baveno, or Stresa, on the Lago Maggiore.

12th and 13th days.—Still in the same neighbourhood.

14th and 15th days.—From Baveno, by the Simplon Pass, to Brigue.

16th day.—Rail to Martigny.

17th day.—By Col de Balme to Chamouny.

18th day.—At Chamouny.

19th day.—At Chamouny.

20th day.—Diligence to Geneva.

21st day.—Geneva.

22nd day.—Lake of Geneva to Lausanne.

23rd day.—To Berne.

24th day.—Lake of Thun to Interlaken.

25th day.—Interlaken; boat to Giessbach Falls.

26th day.—Over the Brünig to Lucerne.

27th day.—Lucerne. (If there should be thirty-one days in the month spend two days here.)

28th day.—To Basle.

29th day.—To Paris.

30th day.—To London.

Cost: First class throughout, for one calendar month, £18 11s.; second class, £15 10s.

Route No. IX. A Four Weeks' Tour,

Visiting Holland, Belgium, the Rhine, Black Forest, and principal places in Switzerland.

Leave London by evening train for Antwerp, arriving there in early morning of

1st day.—Antwerp.
2nd day.—Antwerp.
3rd day.—To Brussels, 2 hours.
4th day.—Brussels; drive to Waterloo, or train.
5th day.—Brussels to Cologne, 7 hours.
6th day.—Up the Rhine; ascend Drachenfels; stay at Coblenz.
7th day.—Up the Rhine: to Bingen or Mayence, breaking journey at St. Goar.
8th day.—To Heidelberg, by rail.
9th day.—Baden-Baden.
10th day. *11th day.* } In Black Forest. Take Baden-States rail from Offenburg to Hausach, Villingen, Singen, and Schaffhausen.
12th day.—Schaffhausen.
13th day.—Zurich.
14th day.—Zurich to Zug and Lucerne.
15th day.—Lucerne. Ascend to Rigi or Pilatus.
16th day.—Lake of Lucerne to Alpnacht. Diligence to Brienz and steamer to Giessbach.
17th day.—Giessbach to Interlaken and Berne.
18th day.—Berne to Martigny.
19th day.—Over the Col de Balme to Chamouny.
20th day.—Chamouny.
21st day.—Chamouny.
22nd day.—Diligence to Geneva.
23rd day.—Geneva.
24th day.—Trip on Lake of Geneva.

25th day.—Geneva to Neuchâtel.
26th day.—To Paris.
27th day.—In Paris.
28th day.—
29th day.— } To London.
30th day.—

Fares: First class, £13 19s.; second class, £11 14s.

Having now shown how to plan a tour for a given time, it may assist the intending tourist to show a few other specimens taken at random from a great number of combinations provided by the tickets of Thomas Cook and Son. It should be clearly understood that these are but specimens, and are in nowise arbitrary arrangements, as the traveller can be supplied with tickets throughout, for any other route he may have decided to follow.

It is the more necessary to point this out as, formerly, a book of tickets issued by Thomas Cook and Son necessitated a continuous journey in the order of issue. This is not now the case. Take, for example, a point connected with the Bernese Oberland. Formerly they had no tickets which would harmoniously combine the Rhone Valley with the lines leading to Interlaken, Lauterbrunnen, and Grindelwald. They are now able to supply tickets from various points—Geneva, Berne, or Basle to Interlaken; from thence travellers may make their own way over the range of the Alps by the Baths of Leuk, or any other Alpine route which they desire to take to the Rhone Valley, where the tickets again come into operation, taking them up the valley of the Rhone to the Furca or Simplon Pass, or to Martigny, St. Bernard, and the Chamouny district. The great advantage of this system is that there need be no unused coupons, and that the selection may be made in accordance with the wishes of the traveller; and, in the event of a coupon not being required, it will be taken back subject to the conditions on which unused tickets are accepted. It may be well just to mention that their list of tickets for Switzerland, including railways, steamboats on the lakes, and diligences on the Alpine roads leading into Italy, amounts to the number of about threescore and ten, and these can be combined for the selection and choice of travellers, on certain conditions as to the number of coupons which they will be required to take.

Paris and Switzerland.

A.—London to Paris, Dijon, Macon, Culoz, Geneva, and back. Available for one month. Going and returning via Dieppe: 1st class, £8 19s.; 2nd class, £6 12s. Going and returning via Calais: 1st class, £10 19s.; 2nd class, £7 18s.

B.—London to Paris, Dijon, Pontarlier, Neuchâtel, Berne, Fribourg, Lausanne, Geneva, Culoz, Dijon, Paris, and London, or *vice versa*. Available for one month. Via Dieppe: 1st class, £7 16s.; 2nd class, £5 15s. Via Calais: 1st class, £9 16s. 2nd class, £7 11s.

C.—London to Paris, Dijon, Pontarlier, Neuchâtel, Berne, Lausanne, Vevey, Martigny, Tête Noire or Col de Balme to Chamouny (one mule or one guide), thence diligence via Sallanches to Geneva, rail to Culoz, Dijon, Paris, London, or *vice versa*. Available for one month. Via Dieppe: 1st class, £9 7s.; 2nd class, £7 4s. Via Calais: 1st class, £11 7s.; 2nd class, £9.

D.—London to Paris, Fontainebleau, Dijon, Macon, Culoz, Geneva, Lausanne, Fribourg, Berne, Thun, Interlaken, Brienz, Brünig, Alpnach, Lucerne, Olten, Bienne Neuchâtel, Pontarlier, Dijon, Paris, London, or *vice versa*. Available for one month. Via Dieppe: 1st class, £9 6s.; 2nd class, £6 17s. Via Calais: 1st class, £11 1s.; 2nd class, £8 13s.

E.—London to Paris, Belfort, Basle, Lucerne, Alpnach, Brünig, Brienz, Giessbach, Interlaken, Thun, Berne, Lausanne, Geneva, Culoz, Dijon, Paris, London, or *vice versa*. Available for one month. Via Dieppe: 1st class, £8 17s.; 2nd class, £6 14s. Via Calais: 1st class, £10 16s.; 2nd class, £8 9s.

F.—London to Paris, Belfort, Basle, Lucerne, Alpnach, Brünig, Brienz, Giessbach, Interlaken, Thun, Berne, Lausanne, Vevey, Martigny, Tête Noire or Col de Balme, Chamouny, Geneva, Culoz, Dijon, Paris, London, or *vice versa.* Available for one month. Via Dieppe: 1st class, £10 8s.; 2nd class, £8 3s. 6d. Via Calais: 1st class, £12 8s.; 2nd class, £9 19s. 6d.

G.—London to Paris, Belfort, Basle, Lucerne, Flüelen, Hospenthal, Furca Pass, Brigue, Visp, Sierre, Martigny, Tête Noire or Col de Balme, Chamouny, Geneva, Culoz, Dijon, Paris, London, or *vice versa.* Available for one month. Via Dieppe: 1st class, £11 16s. 6d.; 2nd class, £9 9s. 6d. Via Calais: 1st class, £13 16s. 6d.; 2nd class, £11 5s. 6d.

H.—London, Paris, Dijon, Pontarlier, Neuchâtel, Berne, Thun, Interlaken, Brienz, Brünig, Alpnach, Lucerne, Flüelen, Hospenthal, Furca, Brigue, Visp, Sierre, Martigny, Tête Noire or Col de Balme, Chamouny, Geneva, Culoz, Dijon, Paris, London, or *vice versa.* Available for one month. Via Dieppe: 1st class, £11 11s.; 2nd class, £9 8s. Via Calais: 1st class, £13 10s.; 2nd class, £11 4s.

THE RHINE, BLACK FOREST, AND SWITZERLAND.

I.—London, Harwich, Antwerp, Brussels, Cologne, Rhine steamer to Mayence, Worms, Heidelberg, Baden-Baden, Offenburg, Hausach, Villingen, Singen, Schaffhausen, Zürich, Zug, Lucerne, Alpnach, Brienz, Interlaken, Thun, Berne, Fribourg, Lausanne, Geneva, Paris, Rouen, Dieppe, London, or *vice versa.* 1st class, £11 19s. 6d.; 2nd class, £8 18s. 9d.

Same route between Brussels and Paris, but going and returning via Calais: 1st class, £14 10s. 6d.; 2nd class, £11 0s. 9d.

Going via General Steam Navigation Company's route to *Antwerp:* 1st class, £11 8s. 9d.; 2nd class, £9 0s. 9d.

PARIS, THE BLACK FOREST, SWITZERLAND, AND THE JURA.

K.—London, Newhaven, Dieppe, Paris, Nancy, Strassburg, Kehl, Offenburg, Villingen, Singen, Constance, Rorschach, St. Gall, Winterthur, Zürich, Zug, Lucerne, Bernese Oberland, Berne, Bienne, Chaux de Fonds, Neuchâtel, Pontarlier, Dijon, Paris, Rouen, Dieppe, London, or *vice versa. Available for two months.* 1st class, £11 10s.; 2nd class, £8 2s.

Same route beyond Paris, but going and returning via Dover and Calais: 1st class, £14 5s.; 2nd class, £10 15s.

LUXEMBURG, BLACK FOREST, SWITZERLAND, AND PARIS.

L.—London, Harwich, Antwerp, Brussels, Luxemburg, Metz, Strassburg, Kehl, Offenburg, Villingen, Singen, Schaffhausen, Winterthur, Zürich, Zug, Lucerne, Alpnach, Brienz, Interlaken, Thun, Berne, Fribourg, Lausanne, Geneva, Culoz, Macon, Dijon, Paris, Rouen, Dieppe, Newhaven, London, or *vice versa.* 1st class, £11 13s.; 2nd class, £8 12s.

Going to Brussels via Calais; returning from Paris via Calais and Dover; same route between Brussels and Paris. 1st class, £13 19s. 6d.; 2nd class, £10 13s. 6d.

Many "CIRCULAR TOURS" are issued in combination with those quoted above. Take Tour B for example. It only takes the traveller within sight of Mont Blanc. But by combining with that tour "Circular ticket Geneva to Lausanne," the tourist can go by diligence to Chamouny; be provided with a guide or mule (one of each is best if there are two in a party, or two mules and one guide if there are three) over Tête Noire or Col de Balme to Martigny. Rail to St. Maurice and Bouveret; thence by steamer on the Lake of Geneva to Ouchy, or by railway through to Lausanne, whence the journey may be continued by the tickets in Route B. For a delightful addition to the tour, such as is given in this circular tour, the additional cost is only £1 11s., first class throughout, or £1 9s. second class.

HOTEL ACCOMMODATION COUPONS,

ORIGINATED AND ISSUED BY

THOMAS COOK AND SON.

THE HOTEL COUPON business, which was commenced as a friendly arrangement of mutual interest to ourselves, to Hotel Proprietors, and Tourists, has far exceeded our most sanguine anticipations; and as its benefits become better known, they will be more highly appreciated by all who are interested in the success of the scheme.

The European Hotel Coupons are issued at the uniform rate of 8s. per day, and are arranged as follows:—1st Coupon (yellow).—*Breakfast*, specifying of what it shall consist. 2nd Coupon (red).—*Dinner at Table d'Hôte*, with or without Wine, according to the custom of the Hotels. 3rd Coupon (blue).—*Bed room* including *lights* and *attendance*.

These are the ordinary features of Continental Hotel life, all else being regarded as extras, and as such they are left to be paid for by Supplemental Coupons or cash.

The coupons are accepted at full value at one principal Hotel in each of the chief cities, towns, and places of Tourist resort, in Switzerland, Italy, on the banks of the Rhine, and at a great many places in France, Germany, Holland, Belgium, Austria, etc.; also for meals on board the Great Eastern Channel Steamers and the Rhine Steamers.

SUPPLEMENTAL AND EXCEPTIONAL ARRANGEMENTS.

IN LONDON Tourists may be accommodated *en route* to or from the Continent at Cook's British Museum Boarding House, 59, Great Russell Street, Bloomsbury, at 6s. per day, for Bed, Breakfast, and Tea with meats. (Hotel Coupons accepted at their full value in payment.)

Hotel Coupons are also accepted at the London and Paris Hotel and Refreshment Rooms, NEWHAVEN WHARF, Coupons are accepted for meals on board the GREAT EASTERN CHANNEL STEAMERS, and on the RHINE STEAMERS.

SPECIAL COUPONS are issued for VIENNA, available at the Hotel d'Union, and Hotel Metropole at 13s. per day.

For PARIS, Hotel Coupons at special rates are issued for the Grand Hotel and for the Hotel Bedford.

In PARIS, the other Hotels in Messrs. COOK AND SON's connection are not equal in appearance and style to those of the Continent generally; but the proprietors having long evinced a kindly interest in promoting the comfort and convenience of Excursionists and Tourists, the Coupons are allowed to be accepted at the London and New York Hotel, Place du Havre; Hotel St. Petersbourg, 35, Rue Caumartin; at the Hotel Beretta (late Londres), 8, Rue St. Hyacinthe, Rue St. Honoré. For these Hotels accommodation cards are also issued at the rate of 8s. per day, including meat for Breakfast. SPECIAL COUPONS are issued on the Grand Hotel, at 16s. to 28s. per day, and on the Hotel Bedford at 12s per day.

At ROUEN, Mrs. Daniells, widow of the late Interpreter at the Station, who keeps a small Hotel, the Victoria, near the Station, wishes to accept Coupons from parties breaking their journey there.

ADDITIONAL CHARGES are made on the Coupons as follows:

At BADEN-BADEN, at the time of the Races, 2 francs per day.

At ROME, from the 1st of December to the end of April, from 1 franc to 3 francs per day, according to the class of rooms, are now agreed to as extra charges; but new arrangements may have to be made in consequence of Rome being now the capital of Italy. Whatever change is made, notice will be given thereof.

For Rome, an additional series of Hotel Coupons can be had, providing for three meals per day, and other accommodation, at the Hotel d'Allemagne, at an extra charge of 2s. per day.

At the RIGI KULM Hotels, 1 franc extra is required on the Bedroom Coupon. All these extras can be paid by Supplemental Coupons or Cash. Travellers wishing to spend the night at this Hotel must give at least one day's notice by letter or telegram to the Manager, stating that they hold "Cook's Coupons," and wish rooms reserved.

GIESSBACH.—The Dinner Coupons can only be accepted at this Hotel when the passengers remain for the night.

CONDITIONS and terms of REPAYMENT for unused Coupons are printed in the Coupon Books.

ANY COMPLAINTS which parties have to make as to the use of the Coupons, or the conduct of Hotel Proprietors or Servants, to be addressed, in writing, to Messrs. THOMAS COOK & SON, Ludgate Circus, Fleet Street, London.

COUPONS CAN BE OBTAINED at the offices of Messrs. THOMAS COOK & SON, Ludgate Circus, and 445, West Strand, London; 11, Ranelagh Street, Liverpool; 43, Piccadilly, Manchester; Stephenson Place, New Street, Birmingham; 1, Royal Exchange, Leeds; 8, Exchange, Market Street, Bradford; Change Alley Corner, Sheffield; 15, Place du Havre, Paris; 22, Galerie du Roi, Brussels; 40, Domhof, Cologne; 90, Rue du Rhône, Geneva; 1B, Piazza di Spagna, Rome; and also at the Hotels Swan, Lucerne; Trois Rois, Bale; Trombetta, Turin; Victoria, Venice.

REPAYMENTS FOR UNUSED HOTEL COUPONS, less 10 per cent., can only be made at the Chief Office, Ludgate Circus, Fleet Street, London, and no agents are authorised to repay for any not used.

HOTELS IN THE EAST.—A special Series of Coupons is provided for the East Levant, and we append List of Hotels.

For SCOTLAND AND IRELAND also a special series is provided, as per Programme.

EUROPEAN AND EASTERN HOTELS

Where Cook's Coupons for Hotel Accommodation will be accepted.

HOTELS IN FRANCE AND FRENCH SAVOY.

Aix les Bains—Hotel de la Paix.
Allevard les Bains—Grand Hotel des Bains.
Amiens—Hotel de l'Univers.
Amphion (Lake of Geneva)—Grand Hotel des Bains.
Angouleme—Grand Hotel du Palais.
Annecy—Hotel d'Angleterre.
Avignon—Hotel de l'Europe.
Bagneres de Bigorre—Hotel de France.
Bagneres de Luchon—Grand Hotel des Bains.
Biarritz—Grand Hotel Garderes.
Bordeaux—Hotel de France.
Boulogne—Grand Hotel Christol.
Calais—Hotel Dessin.
Cannes—Hotel Beau Site.
Chambery—Hotel de l'Europe.
Chamouny—Hotel de Londres, and Hotel d'Angleterre. Hotels Royal, Imperial, Union, Couronne & Palais de Cristal.
Cherbourg—Grand Hotel de l'Univers.
Cintra (Portugal)—Hotel Victor.
Dieppe—Hotel Queen Victoria. Grand Hotel des Etrangers.
Dijon—Hotel Jura.
Fontainebleau—Hotel de Londres.
Gorges du Fier—Châlet Hotel.
Grenoble—Hotel Monnet.
Havre—Grand Hotel de la Banque.
Hendaye—Grand Hotel Chapny.
Hyeres—Hotel des Iles d'Or.
Lisbon (Portugal)—Hotel Braganza.
Lyons—Hotel de l'Europe.
Macon—Hotel de l'Europe.
Marseilles—Hotel du Louvre et de la Paix.
Mentone—Hotel Grande Bretagne. Hotel de Menton. Hotel de Turin.
Modane—Grand Hotel International. Station Buffet.
Nice—Grand Hotel.
Pontarlier—Hotel de la Poste.
Paris—Grand Hotel (Special Coupons). Bedford Hotel (Special Coupons). Londres et New York, Place du Havre. St. Petersbourg, 35, Rue Caumartin. Londres, 8, Rue St. Hyacinthe.
Pau—Grand Hotel Gassion.
Perpignan—Grand Hotel de Perpignan.
Rouen—Smith's Albion Hotel.
Semnoz Alps—Chalet Hotel de Semnoz.
Toulon—Grand Hotel.
Tours—Grand Hotel de Bordeaux.
Vichy—Grand Hotel des Bains.

ALGERIA AND TUNIS.

Algiers—
Batna—Hotel de Paris.
Blidah—Hotel d'Orient.
Bona—Hotel d'Orient.
Constantine—Hotel d'Orient.
Guelma—Hotel Auriel.
Oran—Hotel de l'Univers.
Soukahras—Hotel Thagaste.
Tlemcen—Hotel de France.
Tunis—Hotel Bertrand.

HOTELS IN SICILY, etc.

Catania—Grand Hotel.
Malta—Dunsford's Hotel.
Messina—Hotel Victoria.
Palermo—Hotel de France.
Syracuse—Hotel Victoria.
Taormina—Hotel Timeo.

SWITZERLAND AND THE ALPINE DISTRICTS.

Aarau—Hotel de la Cigogne.
Aigle—Hotel Victoria.
Airolo—Hotel de la Poste.
Alpnacht—Hotel Pilatus.
Altdorf—Hotel Furka.
Andermatt—See Hospenthal.
Axenfels (Brunner) — Grand Hotel Axenfels
Baden (Switzerland)—Hinterhof.
Bale—Hotel Trois Rois, and Central Station Buffet.
Bel Alp—Hotel Bel Alp.
Bergun—Hotel Piz Dela.
Berne—Hotel Belle Vue.
Bellinzona—Hotel de l'Ange, and Hotel de la Ville.
Bex—Hotel des Bains.
Biasca—Hotel de Biasca.
Briens—Hotel de la Croix Blanche.
Brigue—Hotel de la Poste, and Station Buffet.
Brunnen—Hotel Adler.
Chamouny (Savoy)—See under "Hotels in France."
Chaux de Fonds—Hotel de la Fleur de Lis.
Constance (Baden)—Hotel Hecht.
Coire—Hotel Steinbock.
Davos Platz—{ Hotel Kuranstalt. / Hotel Belvedere.
Disentis—Disentis Hof.
Einsiedeln—Hotel du Paon.
Engelberg—Hotel Sonnenberg.
Falls of the Rhine (Neuhausen)—Schweizerhof.
Fluelen—Hotel Croix Blanche et Poste.
Fribourg—Hotel Zæhringen.
Frutigen—Hotel Bellevue.
Furka—Hotel Furka.
Geneva—{ Hotel de la Metropole. / Hotel du Lac. / Hotel de Russie.
Giessbach—Hotel Giessbach.
Granges (Soleure)—Hotel du Lion.
Grindelwald—Hotel de l'Aigle Noir.
Hospenthal—Meyerhof.
Interlacken—{ Hotel Victoria. / Hotel Ritschard.
Kandersteg—Hotel Gemmi.
La Tour—Hotel du Rivage.
Lac Noir (Fribourg)—Hotel des Bains du Lac Noir.
Lausanne—{ Hotel Gibbon. / Hotel d'Angleterre, Ouchy.
Lauterbrunnen—Hotel du Capricorne.
Leukerbad—Hotels des Alpes and Belle Vue.
Locarno—Grand Hotel, Hotel de la Couronne.
Locle—Hotel Jura.
Loeche les-Bains—Hotel des Alpes.
Lucerne—Hotel du Cygne (Swan)
Lugano—Hotel du Parc and Station Buffet.
Lungern—{ Hotel du Lion d'Or. / Hotel Brunig. / Hotel l'Oberwald.
Martigny—Hotel Clerc.
Meiringen—Hotel du Sauvage.
Mendrisio—Hotel Mendrisio.
Monte Generoso—Hotel de Monteroso.
Montreux—Langbein's Hotel Beau-Séjour au Lac.
Morges—Hotel des Alpes.
Morschach (Lake Lucerne)—Hotel Frohnap.
Neuchatel—{ Grand Hotel de Lac. / Hotel Bellevue.
Pilatus—{ Hotel Klimsenhorn. / Hotel Bellevue.
Pontresina—Hotel Krone.
Ragatz—{ Hotel Quellenhof. / Hotel Ragatz.
Rigi-Kulm—{ Hotel du Rigi-Kulm. / Hotel Schreiber.
Rigi-Staffel—Hotel Rigi-Staffel.
Rorschach—Hotel Seehof.

Rosenlaui—Hotel Rosenlaui.
Rovio—Hotel Rovio.
Salvan—Hotel des Gorges du Triege.
Samaden—Hotel Bernina.
San Moritz—Hotel Engadine.
Sarnen—{ Brunig Hotel. Hotel de l'Oberwald.
Schaffhausen—See Falls of the Rhine.
Schonfels (Zug)—Hotel Schonfels.
Schuls—Hotel de la Poste.
Schweiz—Hotel Rossli.
St. Gall—
St. Nicholas—Grand Hotel.
Sierre—Hotel Belle Vue.
Silvaplana—Hotel Rivalta.
Sion—Hotel and Pension Silas.
Spiez—Hotel Spiezerhof.
Splugen—Hotel de la Poste.
Stansstad—Hotel Burgenstock.
Susten (near Leuk)—Hotel de la Souste.
Territet-Montreux—Hotel des Alpes.
Thoune (Thun)—{ Hotel Belle Vue. Grand Hotel de Thoune.
Thusis—Hotel Via Mala.
Trient—Hotel du Glacier de Trient.
Vevey—Grand Hotel Vevey.
Vernayaz—Hotel des Gorges de Trient.
Viesch (Eggischorn)—Hotel des Alpes.
Villeneuve—Hotel Byron.
Visp—Hotel de la Poste, and Station Buffet.
Vissoie—Hotel d'Anniviers.
Zermatt—Hotel du Montervin.
Zurich—Hotel Belle Vue.

HOTELS IN BLACK FOREST.

Albruck—Hotel Albthal.
Brennet (Station)—Hotel Werrathal.
Belchen (High Mountain Station)—Rasthaus Belchen.
Donaueschingen—Hotel Schutzen.
Feldberg (High Mountain Station)—Hotel Feldbergerhof.
Furtwangen—Angel Hotel.
Gernsbach—Bath Hotel.
Hochen Schwand—Hotel Maier.
Holsteig (Hollenthal)—Golden Star Hotel.
Hornberg—Hotel Baren.
Lorrach—Hirsch Hotel.
Lenzkirch—Hotel Poste.
Mulheim—Hotel Kittler.
Neustadt—Hotel Poste.
Ottenhofen—Hotel Pflug.
Oberkirch—Hotel Lind.
Schluchsee—Hotel Star.
Sackingen—Hotel Schutzen.
Schonau—Hotel Sonne.
Schopfheim—Hotel Three Kings.
St. Georgen (Black Forest)—Hotel Hirsche.
St. Blasien—Hotel St. Blasien.
Todtnau—Hotel Ochsen.
Triberg (Town)—Lion Hotel.
Triberg (Cascade)—Black Forest Hotel.
Vohrenbach—Hotel Kreuz.
Villengen—Hotel Blume (Poste).
Waldkirch—Hotel Poste.
Waldshut—Hotel Kuhner.
Wehr (Werrathal)—Hotel Krone.
Wildbad.—
Wolfach—Hotel Krone.

BELGIUM, HOLLAND, THE RHINE, GERMANY, AND AUSTRIA.

Adelsberg—Grand Hotel.
Aix-la-Chapelle—Dubigk's Grand Hotel, Hotel du Dragon d'Or.
Amsterdam—Old Bible Hotel.
Antwerp—{ Hotel de la Paix. Hotel de l'Europe.
Arnhem—Grand Hotel du Soleil.
Augsburg—Hotel de Baviere.
Baden-Baden—Hotel de Hollande.
Berlin—{ Markgraf's Hotel de l'Europe. Hotel Bartickow. Topfer's Hotel.
Bingen—Hotel Victoria.
Bonn—Grand Hotel Royal.
Boppard—Hotel du Rhin.
Botzen—Hotel Kaiserkrone (Imperial Crown).

Breda—Hotel Swan.
Bremen—Hotel de l'Europe.
Brixen—Elephant Hotel.
Bruges—Hotel de Flandre.
Brussels—{ Hotel de la Poste. Hotel du Grand Miroir.
Carlsruhe—{ Hotel zum Erbprinz. Hotel Germania.
Cassel—Hotel Royal.
Coblence—Hotel du Geant.
Cologne—Hotel Hollande.
Constance—Hotel Hecht.
Creusnach—Riedel's Hotel.
Darmstadt—Hotel Traube.
Dresden—{ Grand Union Hotel. Hotel de Saxe.
Eisenach—Hotel Halben Mond.
Ems—Hotel Darmstadt.
Field of Waterloo—Museum Hotel.
Frankfort—Hotel Swan.
Freiburg (Baden)—Hotel Trescher zum Pfauen.
Ghent—Hotel de Vienne.
Gmunden—Hotel Belle Vue.
Goerlitz—Hotel Herbst.
Hamburg—Hotel Streit.
Hanover—British Hotel.
Heidelberg—Hotel de l'Europe.
Innsbruck—Hotel Tyrol.
Ischyl—Hotel Kreuz.
Kiel—Hotel Germania.
Kissingen—Hotel Victoria.
Leipsic—Hotel de Baviere.
Marburg—Hotel Ritter.
Mayence—Hotel de Hollande.
Meiningen—Hotel de Saxe.
Metz—{ Hotel de Paris. Grande Hotel de Metz.
Munich—Hotel Belle Vue.
Namur—Hotel Hollande.
Neuwied—Moravian Hotel.
Oberlahnstein—Hotel Lahneck.
Ostend—{ Stracke's Hotel d' Allemagne. Hotel de Gand et d'Albion.
Passau—Hotel Bayrischen Hof.
Prague—Hotel d'Angleterre.
Regensburg—Hotel Three Helmets.
Rendsburg—Hotel Bergman.
Riva (Lake Garda)—Hotel Soleil.
Rochefort—Hotel Biron.
Rotterdam—New Bath Hotel.
Rudolfstadt—Hotel zum Ritter.
Salzburg—Hotel Erzherzog Carl.
Schandau—Hotel Bahr.
Schwalbach—Hotel Metropole.
Schwarzburg—Hotel Weissen Hirsch.
Spa—Hotel de l'Europe.
Stettin—Hotel du Nord.
Strasburg—Hotel Maison Rouge.
Stuttgardt—Marquardt's Hotel.
The Hague—Hotel du Vieux Doelen.
Trient (Tyrol)—Hotel Trento.
Treves—Hotel le Treves.
Trieste—Hotel de la Ville.
Ueberlingen (Lake of Constance)—Hotel des Bains.
Verviers—{ Station Buffet. Hotel du Chemin de fer.
Vienna—{ Union Hotel. Special Hotel Coupons. Hotel Metropole. Special Hotel Coupons.
Weimar—Hotel zum Erbprinzen.
Wiesbaden—Grand Hotel du Rhin.
Worms—Hotel de l'Europe.
Wurzburg—Hotel Kronprinz.

SWEDEN, NORWAY, AND DENMARK.

Aarhuus—Hotel Royal.
Bergen—Hotel Bergen.
Christiania—Grand Hotel.
Copenhagen—Hotel d'Angleterre.
Gothenburg—Hotel Christiania.
Helsingborg—Hotel Molberg.
Honefos—Gladvett's Hotel.
Jonkoping—Hotel Jonkoping.
Stockholm—{ Grand Hotel. Hotel Rydberg.
Trondhjem—{ Hotel Angleterre. Hotel Victoria.

HOTELS IN ITALY.

Alassio—Hotel de Rome.
Alessandria—Hotel de l'Europe.
Ancona—Hotel della Pace.
Arona—Hotel de l'Italie.
Baveno—Hotel Belle Vue.
Bellagio—Hotel Grande Bretagne.
Bologna—Hotel Brun.
Bordighera—Hotel d'Angleterre.
Bormio—Nouveaux Bains de Bormio.
Brindisi—Hotel Oriental.

Cadenabbia (Lake of Como)—Grand Hotel Belle Vue.
Capri—Hotels du Louvre, et de Tiberio.
Caserta—Hotel Victoria.
Castellamare—Hotel Royal.
Cernobbio (Lake of Como)—Grand Hotel Villa d' Este.
Como (on Lake)—Hotel de la Reine d'Angleterre (Villa d'Este).
Corfu (Greece)—Hotel St. George.
Cornigliano—Grand Hotel Villa Rachel.
Chiavenna—Hotel Conradi.
Chiasso—Hotel Chiasso.
Domo D'Ossola—Hotel de la Ville.
Florence—{ Hotel New York. Hotel de l'Europe. Hotel de Russie. English and American Boarding House, Palazzo d'Elci, 28, Via Maggio. }
Genoa—Hotels de la Ville and Trombetta Feder.
Ischia (Casamicciola)—Hotel Belle Vue.
La Tour—Hotel de l'Ours.
Lecco—Hotel deux Tours.
Leghorn—Hotel du Nord.
Lucca—Hotel de l'Univers.
Luino—Hotel Simplon.
Mantua—Hotel de l'Ecu de France.
Menaggio—Hotel Victoria.
Milan—{ Grand Hotel de Milan. Hotel de l'Europe. Station Buffet. }
Naples—{ Hotel Royal des Etrangers. Hotel Metropole. }
Orvieto—Grand Hotel Delle Belle Arti.
Padua—Grand Hotel Fanti.
Pallanza—Grand Hotel Pallanza.
Parma—
Perugia—Hotel de Perugia.
Pisa—Hotel de Londres.
Pompeii—Hotel Diomede.
Pozzuoli—Hotel Grande Bretagne.
Rome—{ Hotel d'Allemagne. Hotel Anglo-Americain. }
Salerno—Hotel Victoria.
San Remo—Hotel Victoria.
Sienna—Grand Hotel.
Sondrio (Valtelina)—Hotel de la Poste.
Sorrento—Hotel Tramontano.
Spezia—Hotel de la Croix de Malte.
Stresa—Hotel des Isles Borromees.
† *Turin*—Hotel Trombetta and Hotel d'Angleterre.
Varenna—Hotel Royal.
Varese—Grand Hotel Varese.
† *Venice*—Hotel Victoria.
Verona—{ Hotel de Londres. Station Buffet. }

At the Hotels marked thus † Cook's Tickets may be had.

EASTERN HOTELS (SPECIAL COUPONS).

Alexandria—Hotel de l'Europe.
Cairo—Shepheard's Hotel and the New Hotel.
Suez—Suez Hotel.
Port Said—Hotel des Pays-Bas.
Jerusalem—{ Mediterranean Hotel. Hotel de l'Europe. }
Jaffa—Hardegg's Hotel Jerusalem.
Beyrout—Hotel Bellevue.
Damascus—Dimetris Hotel.
Constantinople—Hotel d'Angleterre.
Athens—Hotel des Etrangers and d'Angleterre.

TOURIST OFFICES OF THOS. COOK AND SON.

London . .	Ludgate Circus, Fleet Street (Chief Office); West-end Agency, 445, West Strand (opposite Charing Cross Station and Hotel); and Front of Midland Station, St. Pancras.
Liverpool . .	11, Ranelagh Street.
Manchester .	43, Piccadilly.
Birmingham .	Stephenson Place
Leeds . . .	1, Royal Exchange.
Bradford . .	8, Exchange, Market Street.
Sheffield . .	Change Alley Corner.
Leicester . .	Temperance Hotel, Granby Street.
Edinburgh . .	9, Princes Street.
Glasgow . .	165, Buchanan Street.
Dublin . .	45, Dame Street.
Paris . . .	15, Place du Havre.
Cologne . .	40, Domhof.
Brussels . .	22, Galerie du Roi.
Geneva . .	90, Rue du Rhone.
Rome . .	1B, Piazza di Spagna
Cairo . . .	Cook's Tourist Pavilion, Shepheard's Hotel.
Alexandria . .	Hotel de l'Europe.
Jaffa, Palestine	Hardegg's "Jerusalem Hotel."

AMERICAN OFFICES OF THOS. COOK & SON,
261, BROADWAY, NEW YORK.

With Branch Offices at Boston, Washington, Philadelphia, Chicago, New Orleans, Pittsburg, San Francisco, and Toronto.

INDEX.

TOURIST'S MEMORANDA.

Tourist's Memoranda.

Tourist's Memoranda.

Tourist's Memoranda.

Florist's Memoranda.

Tourist's Memoranda.

Tourist's Memoranda.

Ingram Content Group UK Ltd.
Milton Keynes UK
UKHW022132060323
418151UK00020B/259